OONGA

Devashish Makhija

Tulika

WHAT THE REVIEWS SAY...

"The narrative includes elements of the onomatopoeic, the impressionistic and the magical in its scathing attack on corruption, apathy and in showing the suffering of indigenous people.... This book is remarkable for building a powerful thematic structure by controlling several interacting leitmotifs. These interacting ideas bring within the novel's scope a staggering range of subtexts from hope in human wisdom to near despair at human depravity."
Citation for the Neev Literature Award

"Has the feel of a screenplay... Addresses urgent real-life problems and doesn't shy away from depicting very real horrors."
The Hindu

"*Oonga* presents itself as an 'ecological odyssey'... The charm of this novel lies in the author's narration, which is intense and multi-layered, yet sufficiently meticulous, especially in portraying geographies, people and events, and hence compelling spontaneous participation of the reader in the account.... Makhija's exposition on cultural hegemony is ingenious."
The Wire

"[Offers] unique story windows to adolescent readers who may not realize the human and environmental cost of our appetite for – and dependence on – precious metals like bauxite, whether for the production of airplanes or mobile digital devices, in the name of development and progress ... deserve[s] to be better known and read by a wider international audience – not only for [its] message and relevance, but also for [its] value as a literary creation."
Global Literature in Libraries Initiative

"[B]rings out the essence of what it means to be in Oonga's world: to straddle between pumpkins, bamboo, and grain, and rifles, blood and death."
Mid-Day

"*Oonga* is a complicated tale of a complicated existence in a place where simplicity still reigns ... very much a reflection of that dichotomy between the New India and the Old India, and why they struggle so much to speak the same language, both literally and figuratively."
Twitch

"Oonga is naughty, Oonga is lazy, Oonga is brave, Oonga is curious, Oonga is adorable, Oonga is impish ... Almost all characters are as multi-dimensional and interesting as Oonga... Highly recommended."
winnowed.blogspot.com

"Remarkably free from the good-versus-evil narrative dynamics... The gallery of characters ... reflects that non-judgmental philosophy."
Civil Society Online

"'*Oonga* resurrects Ram not as an emperor, but a forest dweller who had to fight, with an army of ill-equipped monkeys – also forest dwellers – a powerful king who abducted his wife.... As the story progresses, Oonga transforms into an idea of Ram, come despairingly alive: an angry eight year old boy, blue paint smeared all over himself, with a bow and arrow in his hands – not in the middle of a theme park or a Ram Leela field, but a battlefield."
The Big Indian Picture

"As much as *Oonga* is poetic and lyrical in parts, with the beautifully interspersed elements of magic realism, it contrasts so very starkly with the unflinching brutality, the unfiltered violence that the reader is forced to confront.... The book forces an examination of the relationship between man and nature, the interconnectedness as much as the conflict."
The Punch Magazine

"What stayed with me after reading the book is the time ... [Devashish has] taken to observe and articulate the rich cultural abundance that exists in the nook and corner of India.... The reality has been presented in its unaltered version and ... not many speak the truth out loud in such a crisp [and] clear manner."
Hercules Singh Munda, founder of tribal language learning platform Trilingo

"A fabulous cover... intriguing, instantly empathetic and makes you want to know the story! Evolving from a film, *Oonga* carries a rich visual quality into a novel written with passion, soul and sensitivity, about the difficulties of the Adivasis caught between the the Maoists and the state, a theme which needs to be understood. An unputdownable book!"
Sanjoy K. Roy, Festival Producer, Jaipur Literature Festival

Oonga

ISBN 978-81-948381-2-8

First published in India, 2020
Reprinted in 2024

Cover design by Alpana Khare

Based on the feature film Oonga *directed by Devashish Makhija, and produced by Speaking Tree Pictures Pvt. Ltd and Moo Print Pictures, 2013*

Published by
Tulika Publishers, 305 Manickam Avenue, TTK Road, Alwarpet,
Chennai 600 018, India
email reachus@tulikabooks.com *website* www.tulikabooks.com

Printed by
Sudarsan Graphics, Chennai, India

MAOIST CAMP BUSTED IN NIYAMGIRI HILLS BY CRPF

ACTIVIST JAILED FOR JOINING PROTEST BY TRIBALS 'ARMED WITH BOWS AND ARROWS'

TRIBALS KILLED BY SECURITY FORCES, CLAIM EYEWITNESSES

2 CRPF COMMANDOS KILLED IN NAXAL ENCOUNTER

BRUTAL SEXUAL ASSAULT OF ADIVASI WOMEN AS A DELIBERATE INTIMIDATION STRATEGY

Headlines such as these have rocked the country for over two decades, and continue to do so.

A familiar story plays out each time, with a typical sequence of events. Mining companies eye a mineral-rich region and resort to grab and plunder of pristine forest and agricultural land. The local population resists – in this case, the Dongria Kondhs, an adivasi tribe that considers itself protector of hills and forests. The naxalites (or Maoists) enter the fray to fight for their cause, usually to counter violence with violence. And the government, bent on 'development' that mining signifies, sends in the Central Reserve Police Force (CRPF) to quell what it sees as insurgency.

The stage is set for a conflict with no winners. And a bounteous region suddenly finds itself converted into a civil war zone.

Travelling in the tribal belts of Andhra and Odisha in 2010, this is the story that Devashish Makhija carried with him, to bring to the world first as a film and now as this novel – "without filters," as he says, "so that much needed dialogue may be had in spaces where it doesn't exist yet."

Dialogue, communication, is in fact a theme that laces through this story and ties up its plot. And being a strikingly visual teller, the author translates its schisms visibly too – diverse languages standing apart (through different fonts to indicate Kuvi, Hindi and Telugu) though written in English... A filmmaker-writer's distinctive touch in our first film-to-novel book.

~ The editors

"When the blood in your veins returns to the sea,

and the earth in your bones returns to

the ground,

perhaps then you will remember that this land

does not belong to you.

It is you who belong to this land."

~ a Native American saying

FOREWORD

Imagine a large corporation uses all its might to take away a simple adivasi's forestland for almost no compensation.

Imagine the corporation brutalises this once lush land for mining, leaving it a toxic wasteland.

Imagine they extract a whole lot of bauxite from this land.

Now imagine all the aluminium they extract from this bauxite.

Imagine this aluminium makes its way to factories to be processed into little metal parts for circuit chips...

...which are then exported to a laptop manufacturing company (because a lot of such metal for such electronic parts comes from India).

Now imagine a writer in Mumbai buys one of these laptops.

Imagine this very writer is so moved by the plight of such adivasis that he writes a story around such a situation in one such adivasi village...

...on this very laptop.

Symbolically, *that* adivasi's misery made way for *this* writer's tool of choice.

And unknowingly *this* writer is paying some unseen karmic debt by writing *that* adivasi's story.

It's perhaps how the story of *Oonga* happened.

But I can't say for sure.

~ *Devashish Makhija*

ONE

The Dongria Kondhs believe that the earth knows things before they even happen. Today too the jungle floor trembles. It speaks to the leaves through a hum in the roots of the trees. The hum makes the branches quiver. The quivering makes the leaves flap. The leaves shiver as if caught in a restless breeze. But there is no breeze. The air is quiet. The air is still. The air is listening. All at once the leaves flap. Like a thousand little tongues. Murmuring into the air that someone is about to go on a long journey. But this murmur sounds more like a hushed warning.

This jungle grew many lifetimes ago in this large bowl between these hills. Around the rim of this bowl flows a river. The far end of this river disappears into the hills. From there the sun is emerging now, its light turning the river into a ribbon of molten gold. As if to celebrate the dawn, many little bird voices explode from the murmuring treetops. The air dances now with hundreds of beating wings.

The jungle's sounds are broken by a distant patter. Thupthupthupthupthupthupthupthupthupthupthupthup it comes.

Two little running feet kick up a trail of little dust clouds. The jungle air swirls these little clouds and sucks them up into the treetops. The jungle is familiar with these feet. They belong to this jungle.

The feet splash urgently through a rivulet. The feet seem to know every little rock that they hop over. The feet race through a field of flowers. As the thupthupthupthupthup dies away, the flowers sway this way and that as if awoken by the rush. Butterflies float up to see who that is in such a hurry this early in the day.

The feet run up a steep incline and stop. They turn. Two worried, hurried eyes scan the path they've left behind. A solitary deer flashes itself and disappears. There is nothing else but the distant shimmer of the golden river, slowly turning silver now as the sun climbs into the sky.

The two feet run towards the nearest palm tree. Two hurrying hands clamber up the long cylindrical trunk. The two small hands push the long leaves apart to reveal a worried little face. Worried eyes scan everything till the horizon, and he spots them – three women, bamboo sticks across their shoulders with baskets hanging by rope down either end. They walk in single file, slowly. His little voice mutters under his breath. And as quickly, two hurrying hands clamber down the long cylindrical trunk of the tree. Two anxious feet land with a thump, and scurry back down the path they came up from, thupthupthupthupthupthupthupthupthupthup...

|||<•V•>|||

The women walk slowly. Their hips sway left to right to left to right so their shoulders stay steady. In the baskets are seeds and grains, some vegetables and sickles. The woman at the back is weighed down by a large pumpkin she carries at her hip, her arm curled around it like she might be holding a baby. The woman in the middle, her arms are free, but she seems to be carrying an extra weight too. Her tummy is swollen.

"Should we walk slower, Oongamma?" the woman behind asks her, looking at Oongamma's tummy worriedly.

Oongamma smiles, shakes her head.

"No no, Tulsa. If we go any slower Oonga might throw a coconut at us!" And they laugh.

Just then the little boy Oonga comes tearing through the trees, screeches to a stop before them, and starts jumping up and down like an exasperated monkey.

"Amma, why are you walking so slowly? I need to reach the village before they leave!"

Oongamma nods, looks guilty, and tries to walk faster, but Tulsa gently grabs her arm, gestures to slow down.

"It's okay... Didi will wait," Tulsa tells Oonga.

"No, she won't!" he squeals, and leaps for the pumpkin at her hip.

"Oonga!" Oongamma shouts, but it's too late. Oonga has made the pumpkin topple out of Tulsa's arm. He collects the heavy globe in his little arms, cradles it tight against his chest, steadies his buckling legs, barks, "Now can you please walk faster?" And he turns around and scurries back up the path he had come down, shouting "Hurry!"

Tulsa squats down to adjust the bamboo across her shoulders again. Oonga has left her in disarray. She steadies the baskets, stands up slowly, and the women look at one another, shake their heads and giggle. They start walking again, but as slowly as before.

|||<•V•>|||

Oonga scurries across the landscape – a two-legged squirrel in a little white langot wrapped around his little hips. The weight of the large pumpkin in his arms makes him tip this way and that. But he manages to stay steady, peeking above the top of the pumpkin, his sight set firmly on the path ahead.

He is in such a hurry that he does not notice that the trees have started to disappear. The ground he is running over now is a hot powdery red. The breeze here has lost its joyous swirl. It slides heavy over the rusty ground like grating sandpaper. In the distance, silhouetted by the now bright sun, stand some large, menacing, sharp-edged machines. They seem like monsters more than machines. Their large jaws reveal large metal teeth, their metal mouths frozen open as if in a hungry scream. There are a few trees left yet, but they are far apart from one another. The ground around each of them has been dug away on all sides, eaten perhaps by those metal toothed monsters. Each tree seems to be standing on its own little bloodied hill, bathed in deep red dust, holding on desperately with its long finger-like exposed roots, afraid perhaps of losing even this small piece of its home to the monsters.

But Oonga notices nothing. Except for how hot the ground has suddenly become. He scurries faster now, almost hopping over the baking earth. At the rim of this wasteland a large metal signboard stands sentinel. It reads 'INDIA ALUMINIUM INC.' As Oonga scurries past it, kicking up little clouds of red dust, the signboard vibrates with a low eerie hum.

The women stop when they spot the red wasteland. Oongamma notices smoke rising in the distance. It isn't the grey kind of smoke that rises from their wood fires when they

15] cook. This smoke is black. It rises like a thick venomous snake rearing its head into the sky, almost obscuring the sun. The women exchange a nervous look. Oongamma looks at her swollen tummy, silently wondering what kind of world she's going to be bringing her new baby into.

Suddenly, her reverie is broken by "Amma! Hurry!"

They see Oonga jumping up and down and waving at them furiously from the other end. Some distance behind him the now silver river shimmers and beckons.

There is no boat along this shore. On the far shore a solitary round basket boat bobs in the water. But where is its boatman? Oonga's searching eyes finally find him – a statue-still figure standing waist deep in the water, peering intently at something beneath it.

Oonga puts his pumpkin down, starts jumping up and down, screaming, "Boatman! Boatman!"

But the boatman can't seem to hear him. In his fists he holds two ends of a small fishing net that he has immersed in the water. He watches the water intently, waiting for a fish to swim into his net.

Oonga isn't the kind to give up. "Come on, boatman, or I'll get late!" he screams, just as Oongamma and the others arrive.

Tulsa has mischief in her eyes. She puts her load down, sighs tiredly and says, "Dalmoni you must be really hungry. Should we cook something until the boat gets here?"

Dalmoni catches on, announces, "Okay, I'll go get us some wood for a fire."

Oongamma catches on too. "And I'll cut that pumpkin open."

Oonga is horrified! "No! No! No! I'll get late!"

The women laugh. But Oonga is not amused. He turns to call the boatman, but realises it's futile. The boatman hasn't twitched a muscle ever since. He's still peering into the river, his breath held. Oonga starts looking for something on the riverbank.

The boatman has broken into a sweat. He feels a gentle splashing around his feet. His muscles grow taut. A fish! He cannot let it know that he's been waiting for it. The unsuspecting fish swirls around the boatman's statue-still legs, and is about to enter the net, when –

SPLASH!

A large pebble scares the fish away. The boatman curses. He looks up, furious, to see – on the far shore – little Oonga, about to hurl another pebble his way. Oonga stops, drops the pebble and jumps up and down waving frantically. The boatman cannot follow what Oonga is shouting. The only word that carries across the river breeze is "Em-er-gen-cy!"

Oonga watches in triumph as the boatman wades through the water towards his boat.

Oongamma whacks him gently on the head, "Why did you lie to the poor man?"

Oonga is quick to reply. "I didn't lie."

"Where is the emergency then?" asks Oongamma.

"I'm getting late. Isn't that an emergency?" Oonga struggles to lift his pumpkin again, getting ready for the ride.

When the boat hits this shore, the muttering, unhappy boatman gets out to allow the women to get in. With every passenger the reed boat sinks a little deeper. When all four have got in, with their pumpkins and baskets and bamboos and grain, the boat has sunk up to its rim. The boatman looks worried. "One of you will have to stay back," he says. "This boat can't carry all five of us."

Oonga, pulling the anchoring rope back in, says, "Don't worry, we'll tie it safe on the other side."

The boatman gapes as Oonga hands one oar to Tulsa, takes the other, and they start rowing away. The women giggle, helpless now in the face of little Oonga's determination.

Oongamma waves to the boatman, "Brother, don't worry, I'll leave your money in the boat."

As his boat reaches the other shore, the boatman looks up at the sun, and grumbles, "It'll be another hour before anyone shows up that side. That little rascal!" He glowers at Oonga, who is scrambling out with his pumpkin as Tulsa tethers the boat.

Oonga waves the boatman goodbye, before turning and scurrying away.

"Go go. I'll show you next time!" the boatman grumbles unhappily.

Oonga scurries uphill, over sloping ground that is a carpet of fallen mahua flowers, frightening the occasional squirrel, waking a few sleeping bats, hopping over a startled frog. Some way off Oonga's path, fluttering atop a long bamboo pole, is a red flag. A lone flag planted in nature's abdomen might mean nothing. But another kilometre out, another red flag seems to be fluttering with the same intensity. Another kilometre from that one, is a third red flag. They flutter in chorus, as if murmuring a silent anthem of protest. At a particular time of the day, when the sun is high in the sky, this jungle reveals many such flags, far apart, yet aware of one another, conveying their restless dissent to the breeze. And the breeze carries their murmurs down the slope to the river, attempting to reach the other side. But often failing.

Oonga scampers through a troubled herd of bleating goats, scattering them this way and that. He runs up a slope, past a large peepal tree, on the bark of which a pinwheel made of tendua leaves whirs happily as if to welcome him back. Below this pinwheel is a broken piece of black slate, nailed to the bark. Scrawled on it with chalk, in a child's hand, is the word 'Pottacheru'. But the name of this adivasi village is written in Hindi, which seems to be odd for a people who speak Kuvi – the ancient language of these jungles.

Oonga stumbles into the village shouting, "Idma! Hemla didi?!"

He drops his pumpkin clumsily outside his hut, and darts like an arrow towards a clearing at the far end of the village.

Beyond the last hut is a large banyan tree. The age of centuries hums through its roots and branches. It seems less of a tree and more of a very slow explosion of brown and green life reaching from the earth up into the sky. The banyan wears its roots and branches like elegant ropes crawling up and around its old, wise and gentle body. Hemla says that if you put your ear to its trunk, circle your arms around it, close your eyes and surrender to the banyan, you can hear it breathing. And if you listen long enough, the rhythm of your breathing will fall in time with the tree's. And then you will never be sick a day in your whole life.

A lone blackboard stands on bamboo stilts in the nightlike shade of the banyan. Next to it, leaning aimlessly against the trunk of the tree, is a small bamboo ladder. Oonga runs up to this blackboard, looks around crestfallen, mumbles,

"Idma? Hemla didi?" one last time before he goes quiet, and his rapidly beating heart starts to sink.

"They waited for you. But then the sun climbed. And they had to go," an old voice says. Oonga turns to glare at the old woman who is weaving baskets with reed. Then he drops his head, and turns away. He walks up to the blackboard, picks up a piece of chalk and slashes at the board with it. And then he slashes again. And again. And again. Leaving a criss-cross of many lines – sharp angry white scars on the once quiet black surface. And then he turns and storms off.

Oongamma is about to squat to take her basket-laden bamboo off her shoulders when Oonga's furiously stomping feet stop before her. "If you weren't so slow I would've reached in time!" he says, his eyes filling up with hot tears.

Oongamma reaches out for her little boy but he slaps her hand away and storms off. She watches him go and then looks at her pregnant belly, pats it gently, mumbling a little prayer to calm the turmoil. The prayer murmurs its way into her belly, into her unborn child, into its tiny whispering heart, and through it into her own heart, travelling through her body into the soles of her feet, which carry the murmured prayer into the earth, vibrating through its pasts, its presents and its futures, looking for those two little soles that are receding into the distance now – thupthupthupthupthup – so it can wriggle in and travel up into little Oonga's angry heart, to calm it. And bring him back home in time for lunch.

While Oongamma is cutting the pumpkin into little pieces, Madvi walks in, drops his axe and sickle, takes an empty gourd, fills it with water from the pot, and throws his head back to empty it into his thirsty throat.

"Padua is gone. Every hut has disappeared. Even the trees stand alone and afraid. Their roots don't touch one another any more," says Oongamma, fear trickling into her voice.

Madvi nods silently. Many scared words have hurried up into his throat. But he swallows hard, pushes them back down. And nods again.

"Where are the villagers? All we saw were those metal monsters that have been eating up those hills." Oongamma searches Madvi for some response.

"If we had sold our land to the Company, the trees here would be prisoner too," says Madvi, his eyes lowered, lost in a private despair.

"But those villagers also didn't want to sell. What happened?" asks Oongamma.

Madvi thinks for a moment, then pushes away the fear that always comes with thinking about these things, and shrugs.

|||<•V•>|||

Oonga stands knee-deep in a stream peering into the water. He watches a small fish swimming in circles around his feet. He bends over, slides his hands into the water gently so as not to disturb the flow, cups them around the fish and lifts it out of the water in one smooth sweep. "Where are your friends, fish?" he asks. "Did they also leave you all alone like mine did?"

As if in response, the fish thrashes about in Oonga's hands. He parts his hands, letting the fish drop back into the water, and watches the flowing water carry it away from him.

|||<•V•>|||

21] Oongamma is straining the rice when thupthupthupthup thupthupthup… Oonga appears in the doorway. She looks at him, but he doesn't look at her. He goes into the hut, emerges chewing on a bamboo stick, comes and sits on his haunches next to his mother, waiting for her to finish. The hut vibrates softly with Madvi's snoring. Oongamma watches Oonga from the corner of her eye, silently, as he chews on one end of the stick shooting out of his mouth. She seems to know what Oonga seeks. When she puts the vessel down, Oonga lifts the lid. Oongamma hands him a small bamboo bowl. Still not looking at his mother, sulky Oonga dips the bowl into the steaming rice, scoops out some, springs to his feet, and is gone.

"Aye Oonga, come back in time for lunch," calls Oongamma after him.

But there is no response.

|||<•V•>|||

Oonga pours some liquid resin into the bowl of rice, and uses a twig to mix it all into a white paste. He plants his backside into a recess between the thick roots of the peepal tree, settles against the trunk, dips the chewed, sharp-tipped end of the bamboo stick into the white paste, and with it he starts to paint white shapes on his leg. He draws tribal human shapes – triangular bodies, circular heads, sharp angular lines for serious arms and legs, wiggly lines for arms and legs that seem to be having fun.

On his left leg now are many wiggly-armed and -legged figures having fun, dancing. But on his right leg is a solitary straight armed and legged figure, sitting underneath a tree. Oonga's bowl is now empty. He puts the bamboo stick down, and looks at both his legs. First the left one. Then the right one. Why did he draw this? Why is he alone? Why did they leave without him? How can they be having fun knowing he's alone and not having fun like they are?

Furious, Oonga springs to his feet, grabs the bowl and hurls it into the bright midday sun. The sun, hungry now – since it's nearly lunchtime – seems to gobble the bowl right up.

High up on the tree, Oonga now sits on a branch, with his back against the trunk, his legs hanging down either side. He has plucked some large leaves on his way up here. He bends each leaf into a little hood, bunches four such leaf-hoods together and pins them with a thorn. He fastens this leaf-wheel onto the tip of a long twig, holds it up, away from himself, and watches the breeze slowly pick up and fill the hoods, making the wheel spin; slowly at first, then faster and faster, as Oonga gently twists and turns the pinwheel so it can catch more wind in its curves. The soft furrfurrfurrfurrfurrfurr of Oonga's pinwheel seems to lull the branches and the leaves and the tree itself into a noon-time doziness. Hypnotised by the spinning, Oonga too sinks into the branch, and his eyelids grow heavy.

|||<•V•>|||

Oongamma emerges from their hut, a large leaf in her hand bearing rice and pumpkin curry. She looks around, calls out, "Oonga? Aye Oonga! Come, eat," and she places the food on the threshold next to an empty hammock. The hammock is an old saree tied between the pillars of the hut. It sways gently in the breeze, as if missing its little occupant. Oongamma is used to Oonga disappearing at lunchtime. She looks around once more, calls "Oonga! Come!" and goes back inside.

23]

The sun is sliding slowly across to the other side of the sky when a sharp glint of faraway light attacks Oonga's sleeping eyes. He wakes with a start, almost toppling off his branch. He peers into the distance. High up on the hill a truant gleam of light teases him.

The glint of light appears and disappears as Oonga climbs higher up the hill, until he reaches the mouth of a limestone cave. Right outside the cave, at the edge of a steep cliff, with his back turned to Oonga, sits a wizened old man, his long hair matted into ropes, his thin muscles unmoving, as if carved out of the rock of this very hill, his bare skin baked a deep bronze by what might have been a century spent out in the sun. Around his neck hang hundreds of stones and beads and little bells. Every little shuffle the man makes is a soft chorus of tinkling.

Thunk… thunk… thunk… the man seems to be hammering some metal. He stops, holds a metal trinket up to inspect it by the sunlight. The trinket catches the afternoon sun sharply, throwing a blinding slice of light into Oonga's eyes. Oonga winces. But then he crawls towards the old man, the flashing trinket drawing him to it almost magically. The old man brings the metal piece down and starts hammering it again, thunk… thunk… thunk…

Before the old man is a small fire. In a shapeless old bowl on the fire some metal slowly turns molten. The old man holds the trinket with pincers and dips it in the molten metal. As he holds it there, Oonga crawls in before him on all fours and perches on a low rock facing him. The old man doesn't acknowledge the boy. There is an unspoken familiarity between them.

The old man takes the now hot metal piece and plunges it into a long stone container of water. It cools with a hissssssss. He keeps it back in its original place before himself, takes the hammer, and looks at Oonga from the corner of his eye. In Oonga's hand a large stone hovers in the air, waiting to be brought crashing down. But Oonga's hand waits. Until the old man brings his hammer down on the trinket – thunk. Oonga brings his stone down too – thunk. The old man goes thunkthunk. Oonga tries to match the timing: thunkthunk. The game is on. Trying to suppress a smile the old man carries on with his work.

Oonga tries to keep time with the rhythm of the hammering, but the mischievous old man keeps varying his thunks. And Oonga soon gives up trying. He drops his stone, crawls in closer, and asks, "Kunja? Whom is that for?"

Old Kunja pauses, holds the trinket up before Oonga's face, pretending to inspect it once again. It appears to be shaping into a bracelet. Kunja brings it down, looks deep into Oonga's eyes, and says, "For you, O Oonga, when you become a man."

Oonga isn't happy with that response. "But I am a man!" he protests.

"Not yet, Oonga, not yet," says Kunja mysteriously. "But you will be… sooner than most."

Oonga looks at Kunja suspiciously. Kunja smiles. He knows this boy will not be convinced of anything easily. He pats the earth between them, leans in close to Oonga as if about to convey a secret, and whispers, "This earth… she tells me about all that is to come."

Bemused, Oonga puts his ear to the ground. Kunja watches him, indulgent. Oonga closes his eyes, pretends to listen closely. Then he opens his eyes, looks up, having obviously heard nothing, and asks, "What else does this earth tell you, old man?"

Kunja's eyes travel now, beyond Oonga, beyond the cliff's edge, beyond the hill, beyond the jungle, beyond the sun slowly sinking into the horizon. His eyes take wing, soar above the earth like a bird watching over it, trailing its own shadow on the ground far below.

His voice soars just like his gaze, and he says, "This earth tells me that these trees, these mountains, these rivers won't be ours for too long now. We who take from the earth and give back, will be replaced by those who take and never give back. And the wheel will turn again Oonga... the wheel will turn... again."

And he gives Oonga's little pinwheel a flick with his finger. Uncannily, the wheel starts to whir at top speed.

"What does that mean?" Oonga asks.

"It means, little boy, that you are going to go on a journey. That will take you far away from here," Kunja murmurs.

"How far?" asks Oonga, suddenly interested.

"Beyond the hills. Beyond the river. Past the red eaten lands," says Kunja.

"To the city?" asks Oonga, stiffening with anticipation.

"Maybe," says Kunja, slightly wary now of being questioned like this.

"They all went. Without me," grumbles Oonga.

Kunja grows silent. He goes back to shaping the bracelet. His thunkthunkthunk begins again.

Oonga eyes the bracelet. "Why don't you give that to me now only?" he asks.

Kunja's thunking suddenly stops. He raises his head into the wind like an animal onto a scent. He turns his head, trains his ear to the breeze, and closes his eyes to concentrate. Oonga looks at him, confused.

"Do you hear that?" Kunja asks, his voice an apprehensive whisper.

Oonga stands up, tries to listen. But he's not sure which direction he should be listening in. He turns, this way, and that. He closes his eyes, and knits his brow as Kunja had done, and strains to listen. But…

"What?" Oonga asks. "I hear nothing."

"Your friends," says Kunja mysteriously, "they have returned." Oonga glares at him.

"You're crazy, old man!" he growls, and storms off, angry at being teased this way. Kunja watches him leave, his old eyes betraying a sad smile.

And as Oonga hurtles down the side of the hill, behind him the thunkthunkthunk grows softer and softer… until the silence of the treetops engulfs it.

TWO

Oonga, eyes lowered in deep sulk, is about to climb the incline into his village, when a small arrow comes flying into his chest, bounces off and falls to the ground. Oonga looks up, to see a dozen small faces grinning at him. They're all carrying small bows and arrows. Little Idma comes tearing through the group, her two stiff, tiny pigtails growing out of her head like antennae. "Where were you Oonga?!" she exclaims. "You missed so much!"

Oonga just glares at her, then at the other children, all of them in soiled yellow shirts and blue shorts or skirts. He's the only one in a langot. The fact that he's the only one in many ways is not lost on Oonga. "I came running like a deer," he growls. "Ask Oongamma. But you didn't wait for me."

Another arrow comes flying at Oonga. It too bounces off him. Oonga glares at the grinning boy who fired it. The boy puffs his chest, preens and announces, "I am Rama!" But then another arrow flies at Oonga. And another little boy raises his bow and declares, "No. I am Rama!" And all of them break into a happy scuffle firing arrows at one another, the air ringing out with so many "I am Rama"s that it makes Oonga's head spin.

He turns to walk away from his friends, unable to take this any more, but Idma trails after him. "You don't know what you missed, you donkey," she says. "It was magical!" But Oonga doesn't want to hear this. Not right now, when his heart has already sunk so low it's churning in his stomach.

Oonga heads straight for his hut. He wants to dive into his little corner and shut out all these happy voices mocking him. *If another arrow comes at me now, I'll… I'll… I'll break it into little little pieces and feed it to whoever fired it!* But a cycle bell breaks his angry trance. He tries to ignore it. But the bell is rung again. "Oonga?" a gentle voice calls out. He turns to look at Hemla, his eyes now brimming with furious tears.

"We waited for you Oonga. What happened?" she asks.

Oonga simply turns to look at Oongamma who is standing at the entrance to their hut, one weary hand resting on her pregnant tummy. Oongamma and Hemla exchange an understanding look. Oonga sucks his angry tears back in, turns and hurtles past his mother into the darkening shadows inside his hut.

|||<•V•>|||

Hemla, a transistor radio slung across one shoulder, parks her cycle by the side of Oonga's hut. The men of the village, returning from their fields, axes wedged on their shoulders, pots of toddy hanging from their hands, start to gather in the clearing in the middle of the village. Here lies a large mound of cold ash and some burnt splinters of wood. Some of the women carry firewood into this clearing. It's time for the evening bonfire.

Oongamma pours water into Hemla's hands. Hemla splashes some onto her tired face. In her hair are the same large pins the other women and men wear. She has as many tattoos and piercings as them too. But she wears her saree in the manner of city women. She has rubber chappals on her feet while all the other men and women in the village are always barefoot. Her eyes betray a knowledge of the world beyond these jungles, a knowledge she carries like a burden. Hemla is young, yet the villagers gather around her like she is everybody's teacher, not just their children's. Clearly, she is the only one here who has seen and experienced the world of the cityfolk, a world the villagers fear but hold in mysteried awe.

As the first log of wood catches fire, the men and women start to flock to the bonfire like moths to a flame. The children have all gone into their huts now. Their parents sit by the bonfire, facing Hemla, respect in their gaze but a hushed uncertainty in their murmuring voices. Hemla hasn't looked up yet. She holds the transistor to her ear, tuning it, adjusting its antenna, trying to catch the evening news, which is in Hindi, a language she understands although the others in the village don't.

Oongamma brings a large leaf laden with rice and pumpkin curry and places it before Hemla. Hemla smiles at her, puts the radio down, attacks the food hungrily. Chewing her third mouthful, she looks up at the others and sees the shadows of fear flickering on every face in that firelight. She stops chewing.

"What's wrong?" she asks.

"The Company man came," says Tama.

"Again?!" Hemla puts her handful of rice down.

"He asked us to show papers," says Dalmoni.

The mention of 'papers' brings a hush over the group.

"For what?" asks Hemla, not too pleased to hear this.

Madvi, his eyes burning like the embers in the fire before him, says, "To prove that we own this land."

Wiping her hand on her saree, Hemla grows stern, "No one but the Collector of this district has the right to ask you for papers. I hope you told him that?"

An epidemic of murmurs breaks out among the villagers. Oongamma, the colour drained from her face, says, "But we don't even have any papers."

"Where will we get papers, Didi?" Sikoka asks helplessly.

"Can they throw us out now?" asks Tulsa, her voice quivering.

"Shh, you should not be scared. This is why Padua lost their village. They got scared." Hemla tries to calm them.

"But what if they take our land from us by force?" says old Timi, her face wrinkling up like a map to a forgotten world.

"Where will we go, Didi?" Ghosa throws up his hand in despair.

"Will they take *our* fields also?" asks Madvi.

"How will we survive? This is all we have. We are nothing without our land!" Tama's voice has the frightened fluttering of the hunted.

They plunge into an uncertain silence. The bonfire seems to crackle softly with the villagers' fright.

"They can't just come and take your fields," says Hemla, her jaw setting in steely resolve. "These are just the Company's tactics to scare you, so you run away. And once you're gone, they'll come and occupy your land. It's what they always try to do."

Damboru is not convinced. "But how do we stop them if they want to take it away from us? One by one they've taken all the nearby hills," he says.

"We saw those big metal monsters in Padua today," Oongamma offers by way of proof.

"And smoke," adds Tulsa. "Thick fat smoke, like when this forest had caught fire many seasons ago. Remember that, Timi-ma?"

Old Timi nods so vigorously, her paper-thin earlobes shake. She shudders with the memory, "It was a dark black year that one. You were so little Tulsa, so little. We had prayed that this forest must never see fire and smoke like that ever again."

"But it's happened in Padua now," says Tulsa. "We could be next, no?"

"No, Tulsa, that won't happen to Pottacheru," assures Hemla, her mind racing, her heart feeling heavy for the future. But she tries not to show it to these people. These are the times when they need her to be solid, like steel.

Steel, thinks Hemla, *what an irony. Steel is exactly what that Company needs this land for. Steel to fight steel. What have we come to? Why do we need to fight all the time? When will we get the time to live? To swim in the river? To talk to a bird? To climb a tree? Is that all we will be left with? Iron and steel?*

"What should we do now, Didi?" asks Madvi.

Hemla pushes her despair back down inside and pulls out her resolve. "Tomorrow I'll go get an appointment with the Collector, and we will all go and talk to him. You will tell him all of this," she says.

Another anxious titter runs through the group.

"No no, Didi!" says Dalmoni, her hands doing a nervous dance before her face. "We don't know how to talk to a big officer."

Hemla looks Dalmoni in the eye, and says, "You want the same thing that happened to Padua to happen to you?"

Dalmoni shakes her head from side to side, slowly.

"Then you have to speak up," says Hemla, stern. "Sitting here scared like this won't solve your problems."

The villagers look at one another, unsure. The chill of the night has started to creep into their hands and feet. Hemla can sense every stomach there slowly and silently knotting up with dread.

She softens her tone. "Look, I'm here for you, but only you can fight for your own rights. Okay?"

They nod their heads, but anxiety hangs like a heavy iron lock on their tongues.

"There's a system in this country. It's there to protect us," Hemla says. "We're going to go make sure those people don't come here ever again. Okay?"

Once again everyone nods, but there is a little more certainty to their nodding this time.

Hemla picks her leaf-plate up, asks, "Have you all eaten?"

Everyone shakes their heads, still quiet.

"Come on, eat with me," Hemla says, "Your children need you to be strong. Especially the ones that are yet to be born."

And Hemla looks at Oongamma, whose quietly pursed lips now erupt in a shy smile.

THREE

Like in most adivasi villages, the walls of all the huts in this village too are covered in white drawings. Of men and women with triangular bodies, circular heads and worm-arms. These little white geometric people dance round the corner of a hut, hunt wild boar along an inside wall, climb trees on either side of a doorway, run in a caterpillar line with their bows and arrows, chasing one another along the bottom of a wall, always in geometric harmony with squiggly rivers, triangular deer, semicircular fish, straight line trees and rectangular elephants.

Unlike in most adivasi villages though, next to each of these drawings is some letter of the Hindi alphabet, scrawled in a child's hand. This village has been turned into a large pop-up alphabet book.

Amidst all these busy walls there is one that has just one small drawing of an adivasi woman. This drawing seems to have been done only recently. It looks fresher and whiter than the others. The woman's body isn't exactly triangular though. One of the triangle's three sides is a curved line. It makes her look pregnant. Round the corner from this singular drawing is that saree-hammock, in which a familiar figure lolls, faded white small people still dancing faintly on one of his legs.

From where little Oonga lies, swinging gently in his saree-hammock, he can see the dawn sun peek at him mischievously from between the tops of the faraway sal trees. It's as if the sun is trying to make sulky little Oonga smile. But that's going to be really tough today. Oonga has spent all night in this hammock, unable to sleep, thinking of Rama, and what he must look like, and how none of his friends even thought of him when they met Rama, and how he's now not going to talk to any of them for the next four seasons.

The rainy months.

The falling leaves months.

The cold months.

And the next round of hot months.

He's not going to talk to anybody. He's decided to be all by himself. *Anyway nobody cares if I am alone,* thinks Oonga. *All everyone cares about is Rama.*

Would Kunja know anything about this Rama? Should I go ask him? There's no way I'm going to ask all those donkeys or Idma or Hemla didi or even my Amma about Rama. Not until the next season of hot months has come and gone.

I won't even talk to them until then. They will beg me to play with them. I know it.

But what if they don't?

As if in response, from far away, a cycle bell rings.

Twice.

Oonga knows what this sound is. A few moments later, the cycle bell rings again. Twice. But the sound is closer now. Oonga can hear some children's voices too, bright and happy and bantering. Again the bell rings, twice. The sound is even closer now. A new voice joins the chorus of excitement. Oonga can hear their bare feet pattering on the ground as they hop and skip and bounce closer towards him. Feeling even more sulky now he turns his head away from the sounds and clenches his eyes shut. He'll pretend he's asleep. That way they might not bother with him and go away. That's what he wants them all to do right now... go away. And leave him alone.

But does he really want to be alone?

Yes! He does. Oonga wants to be all alone. But the cycle bell seems to be coming for him. It rings right outside his hut now. Twice. Oonga clenches his teeth, refuses to open his eyes. The giggling dies slowly into a hush. A suppressed chuckle escapes the silence.

Oonga is curious.

He waits for the bell to ring again.

He listens, rapt.

Why is it not ringing?

No! He cannot open his eyes.

He cannot give in to that urge.

He will not be curious.

He will ignore them all.

But he gets jabbed in the ribs by a playful finger. Startled, Oonga squeals! His eyes snap open and he sees – looming over him – a grinning, beaming Hemla. "Aye Oonga!" she says playfully. "Time for school."

But Oonga, grumpy, turns away from her, and clenches his eyes shut again. Hemla is expecting this. She turns to the line of giggling boys and girls standing single file behind her cycle, puts her finger to her mouth, gestures 'shhh!' and she starts gently swinging Oonga's saree-hammock.

Oonga looks unhappy but now he doesn't know what to do. If he opens his eyes he loses. But if he lets her carry on swinging him like this he loses too! His heart in tumult, Oonga tries to curl up into an angry little ball. But Hemla is not deterred. She swings the hammock rhythmically chanting, "Come on Oonga, time for school... Come on Oonga, time for school..." until the others take up the chant. This brings Oongamma to the doorway. She stands there watching the fun, until Hemla swings the hammock further and higher and suddenly turns it over, toppling Oonga out of it!

Oonga, smarting, his ears red, scrambles to his feet and glares at Hemla. Before he can say anything, Hemla scoops him into her arms, carries him to her cycle, and perches him on the handlebar. He wriggles and squirms. But Hemla puts her arms on the handle on either side of him, and as the children let go of the cycle carrier she starts pushing the cycle along, to the next house, to collect the next child for school, ringing the bell, twice.

Oonga puts his chin in his hands and continues scowling. Little Drika breaks the line to come and poke Oonga with a twig. Oonga glares at him. Drika raises his twig like an arrow and announces, "I am Rama!" These three little words cause a flood. A chaotic chorus of "I am Rama"s rings out in the ranks. Hemla tries to hide her giggle. Oonga reaches for the bell and rings it hard – twice – and settles down to his grumpiness again. Hemla takes his cue, turns to the others and mock-scolds them "Aye! Enough! No Rama-Rama. It's school time."

The little caravan reaches the banyan tree. Hemla parks the cycle on its stand, is about to lift Oonga off the handlebar when he wriggles out of her hands, leaps down like a monkey, and walks towards the blackboard. A long thick snake-shaped banyan root rising out of the ground, smeared with ash and circled with leaves, has been turned into an altar. One by one each of the children places a small personal offering before this altar... a single ear of corn... a fistful of rice... one coconut... a yellow flower... a banana... a small brinjal... and then they go and sit down before the blackboard. Oonga just stands there watching the others place their offerings. He is even more irritated now, since he didn't get a chance to bring anything. He didn't even want to come to school in the first place. He wonders if he should quickly make a pinwheel, when Idma, the last to place her offering, digs a small hole in the ground and plants a pinwheel she has brought. As she pats the mud down around its stalk, she smiles at Oonga. Oonga scowls at her, and then at the pinwheel, as a gentle breeze picks up and makes it spin.

"Oonga? Did you do this?" asks Hemla, pointing at the criss-cross of angry white lines all over the blackboard. All the little heads turn to Oonga, who just glares at everyone silently, and then at Hemla, and then goes and sinks to the ground at the back of the group, collecting his knees into his chest and wrapping his arms tight around them, to protect himself from the world.

Hemla wipes the board clean, and starts drawing on it.

"What are you drawing, Didi?" asks little Dasru, curious.

"I won't tell you," says Hemla, her chalk sliding busily over the blackboard. "You have to tell me."

Everyone is curious now. All of them strain their necks to get a better look at the shapes forming on the blackboard. All of them, except Oonga, who pretends to be disinterested but sneaks a peek from the corner of his eye.

"It's a river!" cries Drika.

"No," says Hemla, enjoying this little game. She starts to draw a cottony shape above the vertical lines.

"A cloud!" exclaims little Laichan.

"A river and a cloud!" announces Dasru.

"No," says Hemla, smiling mysteriously, and she adds some smaller horizontal lines, and some leaves.

"It's a tree," says Idma, miniature authority in her voice.

"Yes. It's a tree. But say it in Hindi. What's a tree in Hindi, now?" asks Hemla.

"Ped," says Idma. "Pa se Ped."

Hemla smiles at Idma, turns to the class, "Everyone together, now. What is this?"

"Pa se Ped!" The class lets out a war cry.

The enthusiasm of the children's response always fills Hemla with warmth. And happiness. And hope. She looks at them for a moment. In this moment the future of the adivasis appears secure. Secure and free. Free and empowered. In this moment it feels like she's doing the right thing.

"Pa se Ped."

What can go wrong if in this country everyone started to not just listen to each other, but understand what the other was saying? It all starts and ends with dialogue. And dialogue cannot be had if the two people trying to have it speak in different tongues. The rest of the country is never going to bother learning Kuvi. So we must learn to speak the tongue that most others will understand.

This was what Hemla believed. And in this moment her belief feels like the right kind of belief.

These little children would grow up to a more just and humane world. Sometimes she feels it in her bones. In moments like this one she also feels it in her genes. Her ancient genes.

Her two-thousand-year-old genes. The genes that know everything that has come before this, and everything that is to come. Such genes cannot be wrong. In this moment she feels like she cannot be wrong either. In this moment a tree is 'Pa se Ped'. In this moment these children are free.

And no Company is ever going to take their tree away from them.

|||<·V·>|||

Hemla turns to the blackboard and draws another tree next to the first one. Oonga doesn't look very impressed. He wonders if he should get up and go away. But then that might attract everyone's attention. Staying put right now seems to be the safer option.

In a broken cacophony of voices, the children wonder aloud, "Another tree, Didi?"

"Yes," affirms Hemla. "I'm going to tell you a story now."

The word 'story' runs through the class as fast as an outbreak of gooseflesh. And then… silent anticipation.

Oonga watches too, from the corner of one eye. His breath has held, but he hasn't realised it.

As Hemla starts the story, she continues drawing little curved shapes along each branch. "So, once there were two trees –"

"Mango trees?" pipes Idma.

"Yes," smiles Hemla, "mango trees." She continues to draw those mangoes, one for each branch, on both trees. "And what is a mango called in Hindi? I taught you this. Come on… Aa se – ?"

"Aam," proclaims Idma. Hemla turns and smiles at her proudly.

Little Idma preens, looks around at the others, who repeat, "Aam!"

Idma's happy gaze catches Oonga's unhappy glare. Idma scowls at him, turns back to the blackboard, where Hemla has finished filling both trees with mangoes.

"Every year the two trees would flower," continues Hemla, "and the flowers would turn into – ?"

"Aa se Aam!"

"Good," Hemla nods. "One day a man came to the first tree. He was very hungry. His name was – ?" And Hemla waits for someone to suggest a name.

"Oonga!" squeals Drika, pointing his twig-arrow at Oonga. Oonga lunges for Drika's twig but Drika is quick and all Oonga can grab is a fistful of air.

"Oonga," says Hemla. "The man's name was Oonga." *This is going to be fun,* she thinks.

Giggles burst through the ranks like firecrackers.

"Shh… do you want to hear the story or not?" Hemla tries to sound stern. But a small mischief still dances around her eyes.

Everyone goes quiet.

Hemla glances at Oonga before turning to the two trees again. Oonga glowers at her, his toes starting to curl.

"So when Oonga came to the first tree, another man came to the second tree. He was also very hungry. His name was – ?"

"Rama?" suggests Idma.

"Okay. Rama," says Hemla.

And – ntok! – a small pebble bounces off Idma's head.

"Aye!" she squeals, and turns to see Oonga throwing her the angriest look he can muster.

"Oonga, no!" warns Hemla. And Oonga drops his gaze to his curling toes. "Come and sit here." She calls Oonga to the front of the class. "Closer to your tree, come."

Oonga drags himself up, trudges towards Hemla and drops himself noiselessly near her feet.

"Now both Oonga and Rama saw that the trees were full of – ?" And Hemla waits.

"Mangoes!" say the kids in chorus.

"No," says Hemla.

The kids are confused. All, except one.

"Aa se Aam," says Idma.

Aha! The confusion is dispersed.

"Aa se Aam," repeats everyone.

Hemla nods. "So Rama climbed his tree and plucked one aam. It was big and juicy." With that Hemla rubs one mango out from the second tree.

"Rama was really hungry, so he quickly ate up the aam." She pretends to eat one too. "It was so juicy that the juice squirted all over his shirt. It happens to you also, no?"

All the kids, their memories of mangoes invoked, nod excitedly, little saliva bombs bursting inside their mouths.

"But before he left, he planted the seed of that mango back into the – ?"

Hemla waits for someone to fill in that blank.

"Dhar-ti," says Idma.

"Yes. Dha se Dharti," says Hemla. "Rama dug a little hole in the ground near the tree and gave the mango seed back to the – ?"

This time, a unison of voices. "Dha se Dharti!"

"But Oonga," Hemla says with a tinge of mischief, sneaking a sly look towards Oonga, "who was also hungry, went to his tree, and was about to pluck one mango, when he thought, 'So many mangoes, if I sell them in the market, I will make a lot of money.' So he plucked all the mangoes off his tree" – Hemla starts to rub out all the mangoes from the first tree – "and he took them away to sell them."

Oonga is confused now. This isn't something he would do. *Why didn't Hemla didi call the other man 'Oonga'? The one who planted the seed after he had eaten his mango? Why did they decide to call that man 'Rama'? Can Oonga never be Rama?* Oonga is very disturbed by this thought.

"Some days later," Hemla continues, "once again, Rama and Oonga were both hungry. Rama went to his tree, plucked another mango and ate it, squirting juice all over himself."

The kids giggle with glee, their own private mangoes back on their minds. Hemla rubs out a mango from Rama's tree. "After he had finished the mango, he – ?"

"Planted the seed!" chirps Bela.

"Into the Dharti!" adds Hurre.

"So it can grow into another tree!" finishes Idma, not to be outdone.

Hemla flashes a smile of triumph, turns back to the board, and where her chalk touches the black near Rama's tree, a small white sapling starts to rise out of the ground. It sprouts a small solitary leaf.

"Now, Oonga was also hungry, no?" the story continues. "So he also went to his tree."

"But Oonga had plucked all the mangoes!" exclaims Drika, with a devilish grin.

Everyone turns to snicker at Oonga. Oonga growls at them.

 "Correct," says Hemla. "But Oonga was hungry and he needed food. Since there were no mangoes left on the tree, he decided to cut the –" And she starts rubbing out the branches of Oonga's tree.

"Branches?" asks a scattered cacophony of bewildered voices.

"Yes," says Hemla, a vacant grimness bleeding into her voice. "Oonga thought, 'If I sell all this wood, I can buy food with the money'."

The kids look on in silence. Oonga is growing unhappier by the minute.

"Some more days passed," Hemla resumes. "Rama and Oonga felt hungry again. Once again Rama plucked a mango, and planted the seed." And her chalk conjures another little sapling near Rama's tree. The previous sapling sprouts two new little leaves.

"But Oonga had no mangoes to eat," says Hemla's voice of gloom.

"And no branches to sell also," adds Idma, visibly upset by what seems to be happening to this beautiful tree.

"Yes," says Hemla. "So he decided to –" and she starts to rub out the trunk of the tree, until just the stump remains.

"He cut the tree?!" Dasru's voice is a deflated whisper.

Hemla nods. "He brought a large axe and chopped the trunk down, cut it into pieces and carried it all to the market, where he sold the wood, got lots of money for it, and with the money he bought himself some food."

"But," stutters Dasru, bewildered, "mangoes are the best food."

"Didi?" asks Idma, her brows knit in worry. "Did he buy mangoes with the money? That would be so stupid, no?"

Everyone giggles again. Hemla gifts Idma an indulgent smile.

The seed she planted in these little people's minds is already bearing fruit. The sapling in Idma's mind is already reaching up towards the sky, growing stronger and livelier and curiouser with every passing lesson. *Some day,* thinks Hemla, *this little girl will carry forward this legacy. She will plant seeds of curiosity and empathy in the little minds that sit before her beneath some other tree in some other village in some other forest on some other hill. As long as that is a possibility, hope cannot die.*

"Some days later," Hemla says, "Oonga was hungry again."

"But the donkey has no tree," says Idma, annoyed. Oonga turns to dart her a glare.

"But look at Rama," says Hemla. She rubs out another mango, draws another small sapling, and makes the previous saplings grow, giving them a few more small leaves. "He not only has his tree but also –"

"Many little mango trees!" This makes Idma happy again.

"So what does this story teach us?" Hemla asks.

"That we should never cut trees?" says Bela innocently.

"It teaches us something far more important than that. It teaches us that we cannot take more than we need. Because if we do, then a day will come when – ?"

"There will be nothing left for us," says Idma, her worried wrinkles returning.

"Very good, Idma," says Hemla, and offers Idma the duster. Idma takes it, beaming, like a winner receiving her trophy. She goes up to the blackboard, climbs up the small bamboo ladder to reach the board, leans in, and starts wiping it clean.

"What do trees give us?" asks Hemla, gesturing to the imposing banyan.

And Hemla leads the chant as everyone says, "Fruits... Flowers... Clothes... Honey... Shade... Wood... Salfi..."

"And if we keep giving back to Mother Earth even a little of what we take," concludes Hemla, "she will keep giving us more and more, no?"

"Like she gave Rama!" announces Idma, hopping down from the ladder, the board wiped clean.

"Yes," says Hemla. "Rama now has mangoes for ever and ever."

"And Oonga has nothing!" quips Drika, and pokes Oonga in his ear with the twig. Oonga whips around, teeth clenched, when Hemla intervenes, "Okay, okay. Enough. Now pick up your slates and chalk. We have a new Hindi word to learn today – Ma se Maa."

Everyone fishes their slates out. Everyone except Oonga, who has not brought anything with him. Except his own devices. As Hemla turns to the blackboard to write 'Maa', Oonga looks around as if searching for something.

Drika puts his twig down to scrawl on his slate. In a flash, the twig disappears.

"Your Maa is just like the earth. Which is why we call the earth 'Dharti Maa'," says Hemla. "Your Maa gives you everything – clothes, food, toys, a massage, she even puts you to sleep. But you must also give her back something no?"

"What can we give her?" asks Hurre, perplexed.

Hemla sits down on her haunches before Hurre and says, "Some love."

And then she sees that like everyone else, Oonga too is hunched over, scrawling out the word 'Maa'. Not on a slate, but in the mud, with Drika's twig.

The class has dispersed. The sun is high. Oonga sits alone, digging the ground with his now broken twig.

"What happened, Oonga?" asks Hemla, squatting before him. He doesn't look up. Hemla leans in close, cocks her head to one side to catch Oonga's lowered gaze. Swivelling on his bum, Oonga turns away from her, starts digging a fresh hole with his twig.

"You didn't cut your tree, okay? Rama did. You planted your mango seeds. Okay? Now please stop being like this, come on," says Hemla and reaches out for Oonga's shoulder.

Oonga shrugs her hand off and springs to his feet. "I ran like a deer. But you left me behind. Now I am not Rama. Leave me alone." And he flings his twig to the ground and storms off.

Hemla watches Oonga's little figure charge towards his hut and plunge into its gaping mouth. Oonga must have hit the inside walls in anger because the hut's mud cheeks suddenly quiver and its thatched head gets all ruffled.

"Oongamma?" Hemla calls out, hitching her cycle up onto its stand. Oongamma pokes her busy head out of the hut's mouth. Hemla points into the hut's dark throat, and twiddles her eyebrows at Oongamma, as if asking how Oonga is. Oongamma makes an angry-Oonga scowl, and bursts into giggles. Hemla puts her finger on her lips, shh… They're going to play a little game now.

Raising her voice so Oonga, deep inside the bowels of the hut, can hear her, Hemla asks, "Oongamma, if you allow I'd like to take Oonga with me to the Collector. The town is not far from there. I'll show him Rama."

Oongamma fishes out her most serious look, raises her voice too, and says, "I don't think Oonga would want to go. He's in a bad mood, you know?"

But suddenly Oonga springs out of the hut! "I want to go, I want to go. We can go right away!"

Both Hemla and Oongamma melt with relief. Hemla cups her hands around Oonga's excited face. "Eat your lunch, wear your shirt, and wait by the peepal tree. I have to go to the post office. I'll come back to get you."

A sudden cloud of doubt eclipses Oonga's smile. "You're not making a fool of me, no?" he asks, unsure if this is yet another game.

Hemla holds his gaze for a long moment before she shakes her head and says, "No."

"Promise?"

"Promise."

"Near the tree?"

"Near the tree."

"You won't go without me?"

"I will not go without my Oonga. Okay?"

Oonga nods, grins. Satisfied, he turns and leaps back into the hut, a monkey on a mission.

FOUR

There are places in this forest where the sunlight cannot reach. Where the trees close their green fingers tight and hold their wooden arms out to shield the ground from sight. The wind doesn't venture into these parts. The air hangs about silently, crouched like a beast of prey, ready to pounce on any strange whisper and carry it noiselessly to the ears of the guardians of this forest.

The softest creak of Hemla's pedalling echoes off the treetops, skims off the surface of the stream, and slithers into the dark belly of the jungle. Hemla knows it. She passes through this place often, on her way to the anganwadi where some tense, troubled adivasi always awaits her help. Hemla pedals faster. Nothing scares her. Least of all this deep dark jungle. She too was born of the same earth these trees grew from. She is a part of them. And they, an extension of her. But she doesn't like delays. There is so much for her to do, in so many villages. She's always short on time. If there's one thing that annoys her a little about her brothers and sisters, it is that they have no regard for Time. The adivasis move slowly. But the cityfolk move at express speed. And it always troubles Hemla that it is this difference in speed that might become the adivasis' undoing. It's not their fault, but when the world is changing this fast what can one do but try and keep pace with it, or fear being crushed under those giant giddy wheels.

Hemla doesn't like to pressure her people to change their ways, but deep down in her heart she knows that to survive one must adapt. Even the wild beasts do it. In Hemla's book, adaptation and justice are two different things. She will not fight that creature the cityfolk call 'development', not entirely at least. Some things development brings could be empowering. But in bringing these things, the adivasis' legal rights cannot be compromised. That's where Hemla draws the line. But on some days another thought haunts her. *What rights do these trees have, if the cityfolk make all the laws? And if all these laws are of humans, by humans and for humans, what chance does a tree have? Is it fair to force a tree to make way for a road? A railway line? A building? Who fights for the trees?*

It is when this thought grows inside her like a slithering vine that Hemla feels fear. Fear for the loss of goodness. Fear for the loss of kindness. Fear for the loss of green. Fear for the loss of life itself. Fear for all the things the trees give. For all the things the trees are. She fears for them. In turn she fears for her adivasi people. And for herself.

The trees know she feels this way. And they encircle her protectively.

But in doing so, they shut the sunlight out.

And the jungle becomes dark.

As Hemla turns a sharp bend she squeezes her brakes hard! Her path is blocked by a grim teenaged boy in a dusty bottle-green uniform, a transistor radio slung across one shoulder, and a large automatic rifle across the other. From below the rust-red bandana around his forehead a large old burn mark travels down the side of his face, over his neck, and disappears into the collar of his shirt. This burn mark has excavated the flesh along one side of him. It seems to have healed, although the fury it birthed has not.

The boy reaches for Hemla's cycle with his hand to reveal that his hand is burnt too. Beneath his shirt then must be a burn that travels all the way down his side. The pain that it wrought must be unimaginable. The anger that it left behind must be unimaginable too. Hemla, though, is unperturbed. She recognises Linga. She lets him grab the handlebar from her. He takes the cycle to one side, drops it into some foliage, out of sight.

When he turns he sees Hemla hasn't moved yet. He says in a low, almost emotionless voice, "Amma wants to talk to you."

Hemla is statue-still. She doesn't like unnecessary delays. "About what now?" she asks, revealing some of her exasperation.

Linga doesn't enjoy dialogue too much. He just points the gun at her, and watches her, waiting for her to start walking.

And, taking a deep breath, she does.

Hemla walks ahead without hesitation. She knows the way. Having crossed the stream, she turns left to climb the bank, when Linga stops her with his rifle. He points in the opposite direction. At first Hemla looks puzzled. And then she understands. The jungle-lok don't stay in one place for long. They need to keep changing their coordinates. That makes it difficult to hunt them, even for the most experienced foe.

The slender forest path cuts away from the stream, and without warning cuts back towards it, where Hemla walks past a silent figure scrubbing a green uniform in the water. The figure pauses to watch Hemla pass. Her hair comes undone. It is

51] long and lush. And falls like a stream down her shoulders and back. She would have been a beautiful sight, if the large blood stain on her green uniform was not there to puncture the beauty. She goes back to her washing.

A pair of wrinkled eyes silently watches Hemla walk past. They look like the eyes of the past. So wise and cold and fearsome they look. They belong to an old woman, noiselessly peeling potatoes in the dark behind a tree.

Turning up the bank, Hemla spies a very young girl stitching a tear in another green uniform. The uniform must be her own because her legs are unclothed. Her legs are skinny but dark and muscled and strong. She snaps a thread with her teeth as she watches Hemla walk past. There is a vacant familiarity in the look they give one another, but the familiarity stays unacknowledged.

In an orderly pile below a tree are stacked several rifles like the one Linga bears. A young boy, no older than Oonga, pours oil into the barrel of one of the rifles and proceeds to clean it with a long reed stalk. His hands are too small to bear the weight of the rifle easily. So his brows are knit, his focus unwavering. He concentrates on his chore so hard it makes Hemla's heart break a little. She betrays some recognition of this boy too.

Hemla can hear a low chanting now, "1... 2... 3... 4..." and she sees about half a dozen children with heavy rifles in their little hands practising to

1 Load

2 Cock

3 Aim

and 4 Fire

their unloaded rifles. On '4' they all pull the trigger with an empty but frightening CHHUK.

Hemla knows these little ones. She remembers a time not too long ago when those little fingers used to be covered in chalk dust, not rifle grease.

A tarpaulin has been strung like a low-slung darkening sky above their heads, tethered at its four corners to tree trunks. Hemla turns to Linga. He has stopped many paces back. From where he stands now, silent, steady, like he's grown out of the ground, he glowers at Hemla. It's a glower of suspicion, of dislike. Hemla stops beneath this tarpaulin, looks around, unsure what she should do next. The "1... 2... 3... 4..." continues steadily, accompanied by the threateningly soft CLICK-CLACK-KHATAAK-CHHUK of the children's rifles.

All else is silence. Until Hemla hears a soft, painful moan. She looks around, but she can't see anyone. And then she hears a branch creak. She looks up. Above her, hung upside down by his ankles from the highest branch of this tree, is a man in camouflage print uniform. His hands have been tied behind his back. Hemla goes a little dizzy with shock. The jawaan is barely conscious. Hemla looks at the others around her. But no one there acknowledges this man's presence. He moans again. It is the moan of a dying animal, one aware of his life slipping out of him. That is when Hemla notices the blood. His pants and shirt and arms and legs are bloody. A trickle of blood crawls down the front of his upside down face. And even as Hemla watches, a thick red drop falls off his hair and onto her cheek. Hemla chokes a scream, staggers back. A hand stops her from stumbling.

Hemla turns to face Laxmi, a hunched but steely figure in the same green uniform as the others. Laxmi looks spent. It could have been because she was hunting a wild animal. Or it could have been because she was ploughing a field in the unforgiving sun. But Hemla knows it's not because of either of those things. Laxmi's exertion is why that CRPF jawaan is now bleeding to death.

Behind Hemla, the children's voices and the clacking of rifles melt noiselessly into the foliage. Hemla and Laxmi are suddenly all alone beneath the tarpaulin. All alone, save for Linga, who watches them like a guard dog from a few feet away. Laxmi smiles warmly at Hemla. The warmth of her smile doesn't belong in this place. But the warmth is genuine. Her smile crinkles up the sides of her eyes, revealing a small secret reservoir of affection.

Hemla is bursting with questions. But she knows better than to ask them. Instead, she steels herself, turns to Linga, and asks in Kuvi, "I would have come if called. There was no need to point a gun at me."

Linga glares her down before repeating that for Laxmi in Telugu.

Laxmi listens to Linga with her head lowered, then turns to Hemla, nods. "I'm sorry. It won't happen again. Sit?"

Linga repeats that to Hemla in Kuvi.

Hemla is in no mood to sit. Not in this place at least.

"Why have you called me here?" she asks, and waits for Linga to translate that into Telugu.

"Did you think about it?" asks Laxmi.

A tense moment passes between the two women as Linga repeats the query.

"What's there to think about? I told you that day itself, I do not agree with your ways."

Linga's face flushes with fury. Laxmi turns to him, waits for a translation. Grudgingly, Linga repeats what Hemla said. Laxmi is disappointed but tries not to show it.

"Hemla, you don't have time. By the time your Pottacheru kids learn to read and write, these people –" Laxmi gestures to the dying jawaan, "will have destroyed their village too. What will you do then?"

"Could you save Padua from being destroyed?"

Linga snorts, an angry animal straining at his leash. Laxmi stops him from translating this. She may not speak Hemla's tongue but she understands what just flashed in Hemla's eyes. Laxmi tried everything she could to save Padua. But an onslaught of violence can only be countered with an equal and opposite violence. Laxmi believes that. If she had enough force she would've taken on the Central Reserve Police Force, the Company, the court, everyone who sought to destroy that peaceful little village. But she didn't have enough Comrades. And Padua paid the price for it. No one wants to fight until they're forced to. But by the time they're forced to it's always too late. Laxmi has spent the last twenty years moving from forest to forest trying to explain that to the adivasis – to fight before it gets too late. But in all these twenty years she has seen very little success. They always return to her when their backs are against the wall. What these twenty exhausting years have taught her... is to wait. Bloodshed doesn't come naturally to the gentle. Laxmi recognises that in Hemla too. So she stays quiet, and listens, her heart on fire, but her face cold as ice.

"Stay away from Pottacheru," says Hemla, firm and final. "And don't ever call me here again. Please."

Hemla turns to leave, but is stopped by Linga's gun. He barks, "How dare you talk to Amma like –"

"Linga!" he's cut short by Laxmi. "Let her go."

Linga lowers his gun. But he doesn't lower his eyes.

Hemla charges out of the camp and pummels through the

foliage, almost breaking into a trot, walking as fast as her legs will carry her over this rough and tumble ground, trying to put as much distance between herself and *them*, as fast as possible. All these years she's worked so hard to find an alternative route to justice. One that does not bow at the altar of anger. One that will not have blood on its hands. She has worked with patience. She has taught her adivasi brothers and sisters to work with patience. With faith. To take the long route because it's the only way that will surely bring you home. Not today perhaps, but some day. The short cut, the angry road, the path made slippery with spilt blood can never take you home. That road can only take you to your own end. To hurry is to waste. To hate is to be hated. To kill is to bring your own death upon you. Blood can only earn you blood in return. And this Laxmi might undo everything by calling Hemla here again and again. If she gets spotted in a 'camp' how will she ever explain to the authorities that she didn't go there of her own free will? These are difficult, complicated times. Hemla is upset now, that Laxmi cannot – will not – see what Hemla is trying so hard to achieve for the adivasis. She must hurry now. She's lost an hour. The Collector is a difficult man to pin down. *And Oonga? Poor fellow. I'll be late now. I hope he doesn't think I won't come to fetch him.*

|||<•V•>|||

Linga cannot understand why his leader is so adamant on recruiting Hemla. Laxmi speaks to him like a parent would, a parent who is mother and father, as well as teacher and god, all at once. "My boy, we need every pair of hands we can get. More than anything we need that village on our side," she says.

"I'll speak to them," Linga offers.

"I know you will. And you will speak well, I trust you," says Laxmi. "But those villagers will listen only to Hemla."

"They'll listen to me too."

"They'll hear you out, boy. But they'll listen only to her. She joins us, they all join us."

"We should hang her upside down. She'll come to her senses."

"LINGA!"

Rebuked, Linga lowers his head, backs down.

"She's just like us," says Laxmi, her voice softening. "She too wants the best for those villagers. But unlike us, she's yet to see someone she loves being burnt alive, or being beaten to death with a rifle butt, or being raped so many times that they die of bleeding. The day she does, she will be left with no choice. She will come to us. Until then we must keep trying."

Linga listens, his hair bristling, but he is unconvinced. Like Hemla, Linga too knows only too well how ruthless Time can be. Unlike Hemla, though, Linga is acutely aware of how little time they all have now. He hates delays. To his mind, anyone who slows them down now deserves to be treated the same way as those jawaans. But Laxmi amma saved his life. And Laxmi amma wants to save the adivasis of Pottacheru. And so, for now, he must do what Laxmi amma wishes him to.

The hanging soldier has turned deathly silent now. Laxmi searches his upside down eyes for a flicker. A fly buzzes around his face, drawn there by the sweet smell of blood. The fly settles on his open eye. The eye doesn't flinch. Laxmi turns to Linga. "Take Sanmati with you. Find a spot where the stream won't reach. Dig him a grave by sunset."

FIVE

Oonga buttons his yellow shirt in such a hurry that he puts all the wrong buttons in all the wrong buttonholes. But he doesn't care. Left to himself he would have gone to the city in his langot. But Hemla didi insisted he wear his uniform. Everyone in the city wore it apparently.

Why would they? It's so uncomfortable. Why don't they wear langots instead?

The right side of Oonga's shirt-front is now higher than the left. The right collar touches his ear, while the left collar struggles to rise above his collarbone. He hangs his red gamchha around his neck and is about to dash out of the hut when Oongamma grabs him by the wrist, spins him around, and shoves a morsel of rice and curry into his mouth. Oonga protests, but his mouth is now full, and he can only make grumbling sounds as he struggles to swallow the food. "Chew. Slowly. Didi won't leave without you," says Oongamma, preparing another morsel with her free hand, not letting go of Oonga's wrist with the other.

Oonga gulps the rice down, and protests, "You got me late the last time. Didi left without me. I'm not hungry. Let me go!"

"No. You don't eat, you don't go," says Oongamma, her mind made up, and shoves another morsel into Oonga's protesting mouth.

Oonga realises he can't fight this the normal way. So he settles down on his haunches, and starts to chew obediently. Oongamma smiles, starts to prepare another mouthful, when she notices his awkwardly buttoned shirt, "Oonga, what have you done?"

"I'm hungry, give," he points at the next morsel. This distracts Oongamma. She smiles, lets go of Oonga's wrist to lift the leaf-plate off the floor, glad that he's suddenly hungry. But in that split second, Oonga leaps to his feet and bolts out the doorway.

"OONGA! Come back here! Finish your food!" yells Oongamma, but she knows it's pointless now. Her irrepressible son has hoodwinked her yet again.

Oonga scurries to the peepal tree and scampers up its side like a squirrel. He stops at a low branch, wonders if he should settle down here. But then he changes his mind and climbs higher, to the highest branch that will bear his weight. From here he has a clear, uninterrupted view of the horizon. He'll be the first to spot Hemla didi and her cycle. The only creature that might spot her before him will be the eagle. So he looks up into the sky above the treetop and tells the eagle to let him know if she spots Hemla didi.

The only eagle circling the treetop must have heard little Oonga's plea, because she breaks her circling and soars higher and higher till she dissolves into the midday sun.

59]

The hot black road glistens in the blinding white sun, its tar melting in some places. Hemla cycles carefully, watching out for the sticky spots. If her cycle tyre hits a single one of them she'll have to walk back to Oonga. By the time she reached him on foot the sun would have set. And she can't afford to break her favourite little man's heart all over again. One part of her is angry. At the contractor who was given charge of making this stretch of road. She knows him to be a corrupt man. Like most of his kind. If the tar had been of good quality this road wouldn't be in this state. In fact when this road was kuchcha it was a lot sturdier. The locals know how to make pathways that last them years. But these contractors, they get sent in by those money-guzzlers, and decide that anything kuchcha needs to be made pukka, no matter how useful or not it may turn out to be. *How can I ever convince the adivasis that they must be open to the idea of development, if this is what they get in the name of it?* thinks Hemla, a cloud of worry starting to descend upon her all over again.

So lost in her own worrisome thoughts is she that Hemla does not notice a dusty jeep lying in wait off the side of the road. It sits there – a hunting beast made of cold metal – as still as the hot thick air in these parts, as if waiting for its prey to amble by unsuspectingly.

This is the last stretch of pukka road before Hemla needs to turn off into the jungle pathway. She can see the jungle trees up ahead. The shade they promise is inviting. The kuchcha pathways of the forest may be bumpy but the softness of the dirt and the cool of the shade and the absence of noise more than make up for the bumpy ride.

In her eagerness to dive into the forest once again, Hemla

starts to pedal faster. She doesn't notice the high-pitched rumble of the jeep as it drives past her and slows down. And just as she's about to pass it again, it swerves sharply into her path. Hemla screeches to a halt, hops off her seat. She's not sure why but she's unwilling to engage with whoever might emerge from that jeep. Today she must get to Oonga at any cost. She holds her handlebar and walks briskly with her cycle, hurrying towards the trees. As the jeep shudders and dies, it coughs out two men. Their uniforms have the same camouflage print as the CRPF soldier Hemla saw just a little while ago. She tries her best to walk past their enquiring gaze, but the older of the two strides up behind her, grabs her cycle carrier, and she's forced to stop. The younger one hurries over to block her path.

Pradip pulls the carrier clamp open and slides out a package. Covered in postage stamps, this parcel has clearly travelled a long way to reach Hemla. Pradip reads her name on it, "Hemla Mandingi." Hemla is quiet, her face shuttered. "That's you, right?" Pradip asks, in Hindi.

"Yes, why?" asks Hemla, starting to get very uncomfortable.

"Take that radio off you and get in the jeep," Pradip says, and reaches to grab Hemla's elbow.

Hemla shrugs his hand off, demands to know, "Why? What have I done?"

Pradip is in no mood to chat. "Ask the sahib when you meet him," he snarls, and tries to pull her transistor radio off her shoulder.

Hemla jerks her arm away, almost stumbling. "Show me a warrant first," she shouts defiantly.

Pradip looks at her, incredulous, scoffs, grabs her elbow hard, rips the radio off its strap, tosses it to the ground, and tugs her towards the jeep.

Sushil has been holding onto the cycle by the handlebar all this while. He looks a little perturbed by all of this. He watches Pradip jostle with Hemla and shove her into the back of the jeep. Sushil quickly wheels the cycle off the road and allows it to clatter into a ditch by the side. He clambers into the back of the jeep as Pradip starts the engine in the front.

As he drives, Pradip adjusts the rear-view mirror to catch Hemla's reflection in it. He tilts it away from her face to her chest. Hemla notices this. She's been in similar situations before. In areas plagued with conflict it's the women that have the toughest time. She adjusts her saree to cover her sides, and throws Pradip her most furious glare. She knows her glare will make no difference to a man of his sort, but she glares him down anyway, to let him know that she is not just a regular adivasi, she knows her rights, and she knows where to go to get them. The real battle, Hemla believes, is between minds, not between hands or feet or guns or arrows. And if the mind can be trained to be strong, the mind can prevail. At times like these she prays she can help deliver to all those little adivasi children a world free of glares such as the one she's being forced to give Pradip right now.

Sushil has been struggling to point his rifle at Hemla. The jeep is cramped for space, and the rifle is long. Unsure of how exactly he should negotiate with this situation, he asks his senior, "Sir, is it necessary to point this gun at her?"

Pradip scowls, "It's not necessary... "

Relieved, Sushil starts to bring the rifle down, when Pradip barks, "But it is an ORDER!" Startled, Sushil snaps the rifle back up again! So sharply that it knocks Hemla on the chin.

"So-sorry!" stutters Sushil.

"Where did they train you, Milktooth?" growls Pradip. "Or did they even train you at all?"

The rifle wavers before Hemla's face, swaying with the rocking of the rickety jeep. "HOLD IT TIGHT!" Pradip barks, glowering at Sushil in the rear-view mirror. Sushil stiffens, holds his breath, tries to keep the rifle rock steady. But it's pointing at Hemla's ear now. She reaches out for the tip of the barrel, slowly pushes it into her own face, steadies it, and looks into Sushil's confused eyes, making him look away.

"How long will all this take?" Hemla asks Pradip, getting restless. "I need to be somewhere. I don't want to be late."

"It's already too late, amma," hisses Pradip, as he swerves the jeep off the road and onto a dirt track leading to a large gate that reads – 'Birsa Munda Ashram School'.

Hemla recognises this place. What she doesn't recognise is the rigorous wall of piled sandbags and barbed wire fencing coiled tight around this school as if it's deathly scared of something. Something that might come raging at it from the dark insides of that forest it faces.

In each of the four corners behind the school wall are tall wooden watchtowers. Hemla can see CRPF jawaans in each one, ducked behind sandbags, just their helmets and their rifles visible, pointed towards the forest.

There was a time when adivasi children from all the eight villages in the region came to this school. There was a time when they would hang paper flags all around the school where the barbed wire now runs. There was a time when all you could hear from inside those walls were happy songs and a chorus of voices chanting the alphabet. Hemla strains to hear something now, anything. But all she's greeted with is a fearsome silence. A deep, hollow silence, like at the bottom of a coal mine. The kind of silence that hangs off the edge of fear. She sees that fear in the faces they pass as the jeep is waved in through the large makeshift corrugated steel gates. The CRPF jawaans look mistrustful. Of her. Of one another. Of the air they breathe. Of the very reason they are even here. They all seem like they'd rather be somewhere else right now.

This troubles Hemla.

On one side are her people who don't want to fight. But are being forced to.

On the other side… it is the same.

|||<•V•>|||

"He was eeeeeeevilll!" says Drika, menacingly.

"He was huuuuuge!" says Dasru, awestruck.

"He had tennnnn heads!" says Hurre, nodding her head dramatically from side to side.

"DON'T TELL ME!" screams Oonga from high up in the tree. "I want to see it for myself."

But they don't stop.

"There were flying monkeys," says Bela, and leaps in the air.

"And trees of fire!" exclaims Laichan, just as a bird's egg comes soaring through the air and smashes on his head.

Oonga stands up on his branch – a furious monkey, another egg in his hand, ready to bomb anyone who dares utter another word now.

Squealing, the children scatter.

All except Idma.

It's too late to leave for the town," she calls out to Oonga. "Hemla didi won't be coming."

"She will come," says Oonga defiantly. "She promised."

The scattered boys and girls start to flock around the tree again, chanting "Hemla didi won't be coming… Hemla didi won't be coming…"

Up in the tree, exasperated Oonga claps his hands over his ears to shut their voices out. But he can still hear their annoying chant. To drown it out he presses down on his ears even harder, crouches into a ball, tucks his head between his knees and starts mumbling to himself, "Nanananananananananana…"

Idma looks concerned. Not much for Oonga. But for Hemla didi. It's not like her to make a promise and not keep it.

|||<•V•>|||

Strung diagonally across the classroom are two clotheslines. Along them have been hung chuddies, baniyaans, socks, gamchhas, handkerchiefs, napkins and what look like washed and inverted used condoms. As a result, an unwelcome humidity hangs heavy inside here. The blackboard behind the teacher's desk bears many concentric circles drawn with chalk. Scattered over these circles are several small holes with cracks radiating out from each of them. Most of these holes are clustered around the small innermost circle. This must be where Manoranjan indulges himself in the occasional target practice. Chalk dust has settled on all the little desks and chairs and windowsills like warm snow. The windows have been sealed shut from the outside. The unmelting permanence of this snow casts an eerie whiteness on the insides of this room. Hemla takes it all in grimly. This room and others like it were, till recently, full of the hope that only young voices carry.

Hope.

What she notices most of all now is the utter absence of it.

Manoranjan, in his baniyaan and his soldier pants, is squatted on the teacher's desk, flipping intently through the slim books that have emerged from Hemla's parcel. His elbow rests on the rim of an empty plastic bucket, emptied very recently of its contents, which now hang along the clotheslines above. Hemla has been made to sit on a small student's chair before Manoranjan. She shuffles awkwardly, trying to find the most comfortable position by which to occupy it, and failing. This must be a way to keep someone like her on edge, to make them sit on a seat this small. She has a bad feeling about all of this. A bad feeling that slithers slowly up the back of her throat. She clears her throat, swallows hard, to push it back down, but it is persistent in its slow climb. And it makes her want to throw up.

The flipping pages in Manoranjan's hands blow some chalk dust off his hair and eyebrows and moustache. Which is when Hemla notices that the Commanding Officer of this CRPF unit isn't as old as she thought he was. All the time spent inside this room has made Manoranjan look aged, but he isn't. It's just the chalk powder. Which makes Hemla wonder what else isn't what it seems in this place.

That's when Pradip interrupts her thoughts. He slides noiselessly behind her chair, rests one hand on its back, his fingers uncomfortably close to Hemla's shoulder, and he stares shamelessly down the front of her blouse. The bad feeling climbing up inside Hemla threatens to explode angrily out of her mouth then, but she takes a very deep breath, and adjusts her saree once again to veil her chest.

Standing ramrod tense next to Manoranjan, Sushil has noticed this. He looks away, unsure what he should do about it. He's always startled by Pradip's brutal manner. Is this what will happen to him too, once he's spent as many years in service? He hopes not. What Sushil fears most at times like this is his service rifle.

Manoranjan thwacks yet another book onto the table, throwing up a cloud of chalk dust. Sushil feels a sneeze coming on but grabs his nostrils shut, forcing it to implode. If he knows Manoranjan well enough, even a badly timed sneeze can cause an unpredictably terrifying reaction.

Manoranjan looks up from the twelfth book of the lot, slightly puzzled by what he's found. They're all books of the Hindi alphabet. He has spent the last ten minutes trying to find some hidden code in the images and words, somehow convinced these books are not what they seem, that they must be communicating something far more dangerous than an official language of India. He is also convinced that an adivasi in these parts has no business with this language, since they've never spoken it, and don't ever intend to. If they did, they wouldn't be waging this war against the state. He looks at Hemla, searching her face for evidence to prove his theory right. Finding none, he finally speaks, louder than someone like him ought to.

"You're adivasi?" he bellows, knowing fully well that she is. Hemla looks at him, slightly unsure of what her response should be. He doesn't wait for any. "And you teach children?" Another pointless question. Followed by, "Have you taken permission to teach them?"

"Permission?!" Hemla doesn't quite get what that means. "Why do I need permission? I've trained in teaching."

Manoranjan peers queerly at Hemla's mouth as she speaks. A strange silence follows.

Manoranjan waits.

Hemla looks around, confused.

Pradip glares at Sushil. It's a signal.

Sushil, nervous, steps in close, stretches his short frame up to Manoranjan's right ear, and stutters, loudly, "SH-SHE'S TAKEN TRAINING IN TEACHING SAHIB! N-no per-permission… " Sushil tapers off, unsure of quite what to repeat and how.

"But we had information that you work with that tribal NGO. We never found you in their office though. We had to hunt you down in the jungle," says Manoranjan, searching Hemla's face for clues. "You teach these children inside the jungle?"

Hemla stares him down. "Where else can I teach them? There's no school left in this place."

This puts Sushil in a tight spot. He coughs nervously, then relays, "SH-SHE'S SAYING THERE ARE NO SCHOOLS LEFT HERE, SAHIB! Wh-where else can she g-go?"

Manoranjan scowls. "Why? Where did all the schools go?"

Hemla looks at Manoranjan incredulously. She can't believe the question. Neither can Pradip or Sushil. But no one challenges the CO. Hemla is increasingly unnerved by Manoranjan. It's starting to seem more like a game now than an interrogation. She steels herself, and says the obvious, "You've made your camps in each one of them." And she points at the socks drying above her head.

Sushil is wondering how he's going to rephrase that so it doesn't get him a kick in his rear, when Manoranjan slides his behind off the desk and lands noiselessly on his feet. Sushil lets out a small sigh of relief. It looks like he won't have to relay this after all.

For all the cheap liquor flab on Manoranjan he moves as lithely as a wildcat. He stands before Hemla, and he cuts to the chase, "You sure you *teach*? Or do you *train*?"

"What do you mean?" asks Hemla, perturbed by the question.

Manoranjan waits, frozen into a statue. It's Sushil's cue. He trots up to Manoranjan, repeats, "WHAT – WHAT DID YOU MEAN, SAHIB? SH-SHE DIDN'T UNDERSTAND."

Manoranjan's voice drops to a low threatening rumble, "Do you train these children to be naxalites?"

"What?!" Hemla wasn't expecting this. Not after all the care she has taken all these years to distance herself from precisely this.

Sushil, jittery as hell, oversteps, "SH-SHE COULDN'T HEAR YOU, SAHIB!"

Pradip gestures to him to calm down.

But the damage is done.

Manoranjan cocks his head to one side, turns one ear to Hemla, asks, "You're hard of hearing?"

Pradip chuckles. He enjoys it when his boss messes around this way. It's like watching a wild animal play with its food. Pradip jumps into the game. He leans close into Hemla's ear from behind and murmurs dangerously, "Do you teach kids or train little naxalites? Don't fuck with us now. Or we'll have to fuck with you."

"No. No, I don't. We're not naxalites. We have nothing to do with naxalites. I teach them Hindi," implores Hemla.

"SH-SHE TEACHES THEM HINDI, SAHIB, HINDI!" repeats Sushil immediately.

"Hindi?!" Manoranjan is not quite convinced. "But you people speak adivasi, not Hindi!"

Hemla is exasperated. This must be explained once and for all.

She enunciates, like one would to a moron, "We *are* adivasi, sir. We don't *speak* adivasi. It's like saying you speak Indian. We speak Kuvi. Which you don't understand. So I teach adivasi kids Hindi so that when they grow up they can speak with you, like I am doing right now."

Manoranjan stares at Hemla, waiting for Sushil. Sushil swallows hard. That's a lot she just said. How is he to relay all of it? What if Manoranjan loses his cool? "IT'S THE OF-OFFICIAL LANGUAGE, NO, SAHIB? EV-EVERYONE'S LANGUAGE?" screams Sushil, avoiding Hemla's confused gaze.

Manoranjan shifts gears. "Then why did you take them to Lohabad?"

"To show them the play," Hemla says.

"THE P-PLAY, SAHIB. TO SHOW THEM THE PLAY!"

"What play?"

"Sitaharan."

"Why do you mutter? SPEAK LOUDLY!" Manoranjan barks.

"SAHIB, SI-SITAHARAN!" Sushil pipes in.

"I got ears, dimwit!" Manoranjan snarls at him. Confused, Sushil stumbles back.

"What's the abduction of Sita got to do with teaching?"

"I teach Hindi," Hemla explains. "It was a Hindi play."

Manoranjan leans his ear into her mouth, points at it.

Hemla, not sure what she's supposed to do, looks to Sushil for help. On impulse, Sushil hops in, "THE PLAY WAS IN HI-HINDI, SAHIB!"

Manoranjan thrusts an angry finger into Hemla's face. He's now over the edge. Pradip steps away from the chair, as if to get a clearer view of the action.

Manoranjan growls, "I know how much Hindi you teach your kids. Now, for the last time, why did you take them to Lohabad?"

Sushil steps forward. Manoranjan raises his hand, stops him from coming any closer. Then he leans into Hemla's face, turns his ear to her mouth, gestures to speak up, "And tell – me – the – truth."

Hemla's heart is racing now. She senses there might be no way out of this. But she knows nothing else but the truth. It's what she's spent her life by. Nothing and no one can change a truth. "Look," she says, and sees Sushil fearfully gesture that she raise her volume. "LOOK," she yells into Manoranjan's ear, "I ONLY TOOK THEM TO WATCH THE PLAY. I TEACH THEM IN THE VILLAGE WHAT I USED TO TEACH THEM IN THIS SCHOOL BEFORE. WE ARE NOT NAXALITES. NEVER HAVE BEEN. NEVER WILL BE." Her rising volume brings back some of her confidence now. "NOW KINDLY HURRY UP WITH YOUR QUESTIONING," she says with an air of irritated finality. "I HAVE TO BE SOMEWHERE AND I'M ALREADY VERY LATE!"

Manoranjan, surprised, backs away, sizes her up for a moment, then turns to Sushil, and orders him, "Slap her!"

Sushil is caught off guard. He looks to Pradip, who simply smirks. Sushil steps up to Hemla, his eyes betraying an apology. He carefully raises his hand… and pushes her face!

Before Hemla can react, Manoranjan kicks Sushil, hard! His kick sends Sushil careening into the desks and chairs, landing in a messy bruised tumble.

"Slap, I said!" grunts Manoranjan. "Ever got one?" And he charges at Sushil to show him. Pradip lunges for Manoranjan, holds him by the shoulders, "Sahib, sahib, let it go, he'll learn."

"They pick these little fucks out of primary school, stick a rifle in their soft hands and throw them in my lap. What the fuck do I look like? I don't have breasts for them to suckle from,"

71] Manoranjan rages at Sushil. "Aye? Do you see breasts on me, haan?" And he gropes his own chest. "Do you?!"

Pradip stifles a snigger, steps away. Sushil is smarting. He hasn't noticed a bloom of blood growing on his temple where a desk's chipped edge got him. The higher his pressure rises the thicker the gush of blood swells.

Manoranjan points at Hemla like she might be a practice target, not a person at all. "Let's try this again," he says to Sushil. "Slap her!"

Tears spring into Sushil's eyes without warning. To ensure no one sees them he leaps forward and lands Hemla a hard slap! Hemla topples off her chair, scrambles back up in shock and screams, "WHAT DO YOU THINK –" But Manoranjan rams his hand into her chest, pins her down to the ground, leans into her face, roars, "Where – did – you – take – those – kids?!"

Hemla is finally scared. "I told you sir, I'm not lying," she pleads. "I only took them to watch a play. I swear –"

From far behind them, Sushil, despite the stinging, repeats without emotion, "SHE TOOK THEM FOR THE PLAY, SAHIB, THAT'S IT."

Pradip glares at him, as if asking him, "What do you think you're doing, you fool?"

But Sushil doesn't care any more. Bleeding he can take. Tears he can't.

Manoranjan's been here before. To his mind every adivasi is a naxalite until they prove themselves otherwise. But even the frailest of them never admit it. He pulls away from Hemla, his eyes taking on a glassy, distant coldness. He nods at Pradip, who grabs Hemla, flips her face down on the floor, presses down on her back with one knee, fishes out a thick rope, pulls her hands behind her and starts to tie them tight.

"Sir! You have to believe me, sir," Hemla implores, trying to be heard even though Pradip's weight is pressing the breath painfully out of her. Sushil just gapes, horrified. He expected this to get bad, yes, but not this bad. "SIR! PLEASE... BELIEVE ME –" Hemla tries to reach out to Manoranjan, who pulls a sock off the clothesline, tosses it to Pradip who grabs Hemla's forehead, pulls it back, shoves the sock into her mouth, and starts to tie rope around it.

Hemla's eyes scream for help. They beseech them to believe her, to understand her, to understand that she's not a naxalite, that she never could be, that she still believes in this country, and its laws, and its justice, and the greater common good, that she wants peace, not brutality, that this – what they're doing to her right now – is exactly what the problem is, that even now she is prepared to have a dialogue with them, if they untie her and hear her out. She is not their foe, she is probably the only friend they have in this jungle. To please *please* not do this, because after all these years of trying to make the adivasis believe that her way is the only way forward, this – this behaviour – could prove her wrong.

It's not her body Hemla feels getting crushed under the weight of Pradip's hostility now.

It's her soul.

|||<•V•>|||

In the distance Oonga can hear Damboru starting to play his drum. As his rhythm slowly picks up, Oonga hears Somaru's drumsticks join in. Then all the little bells on all those feet start jangling, one by one, out of sync at first, but slowly flowing into the rhythm like little bubbling streams converging into a rumbling river. Until the thumping of all those feet, the beating of every drum, the tinkle of every anklet, the clap of every hand, the ulululululululu of every tongue, the ayiayiayiayiayiayiayi from every throat harmonises into the daily bonfire dhimsa dance.

The sun set a while back. And took the wind with it. Oonga looks at the leaf-pinwheel in his hand. It just sits there, lifeless. Everything is dark and still and joyless up here in the tree where Oonga has been perched all morning, all afternoon, all evening, until now. *But what do the villagers care,* he thinks. *They will still dance, and be happy and drink salfi and do the ulululululululu, not bothered if I am unhappy or angry or sleepy or hungry or if I am even here any more.* With that, Oonga snaps the lifeless pinwheel in two and flings it into the darkness, as his eyes sting with the threat of tears.

A small hand picks up the wrecked pinwheel, calls out, "Aye Oonga, you still up there?" And she thumps the ground with her feet, thrice, her anklet sending jangles up into the tree.

Oonga looks down at Idma, sulks, "What do you care?"

"Come down, donkey, come dance with us," she says and jangles her anklets some more.

"I'll only come down once I've become Rama," Oonga announces.

"But what if the play has gone from the city?" Idma plants a seed of doubt in the shifting soil of Oonga's mind. "You know how those plays keep travelling from place to place?" she says. "Who knows where it might go off to?"

Oonga had never thought of that! His brain does confused flipflops now.

Should he climb down?

Should he stay put here?

What if Idma is saying this only to get him to give up and go home?

But…

What if Idma's right?

What if he can never be Rama?

"You're lying," Oonga says, not sure why he's saying it, but feeling like he must challenge this theory Idma has presented.

"You really are a donkey," Idma says and jangles away, back to the faraway dancing flicker of the bonfire.

Oonga sinks into the branch, trying to hide his worried face in the safe shadows of the large leaves. He doesn't know what to do now. He thinks if he waits here till morning he might know what to do. This high up from the ground good ideas must strike smart boys like him much faster, since he's so much closer to the sky, where all good ideas come from. That thought brings him some solace. And with solace comes sleep. The deep, tired, high-up-in-a-tree kind of sleep.

Darkness is stacked up tight around the CRPF camp like pitch-black coal. Two large sharp knives of light spring out of searchlights high up on the watchtowers, slicing the coal night this way and that every once in a while. The jawaans hope that these knives of light will keep the jungle shadows from harming them. But deep down in the lowest corner of their frightened hearts, the jawaans also know that if the jungle shadows want to harm them, the sharpest of knives won't be enough protection. Not in this place.

Hemla can't tell what she feels more of right now – pain or exhaustion. She tried to fight the ropes for the first hour.

The only thing she managed to extract was blood. From her wrists, her cheeks, her ankles, from every place on her where the rope met her skin.

Pradip knew how to tie people. It's what he had done for the better part of his fifteen years as a Central Reserve Police Force jawaan. On most days he hated this job. He saved up all the frustrations it brought him in a rusty little box in a dark, fetid corner of his soul. It was on days like this one, when he got a chance to unleash his frustrations, that he would reach into that rusty little box with a frightening glee. At first this glee used to startle him. As the years passed, and his postings took him from one bloody hellhole to another, he learned to question his glee less and less. Until he began to look forward to such days. Days on which he would be sent out hunting like a bloodhound, to bring back a Hemla or two for 'interrogation'. Everyone knew what 'interrogation' entailed in such places. And Pradip was a particularly experienced 'interrogator'.

Hemla's cheeks are streaked with tears. These tears are hot. They have sprung not from her eyes, but from her tearing heart. They are not tears of fear or pain or anger. These are the worst kind of tears. These are tears of sorrow. A sorrow that is now opening up inside Hemla's stomach like a bottomless abyss. She does not know how she can ever repair this wound. It's the kind that she will take with her to her grave. On his way out, Pradip had left the door to the classroom ajar. It rattles now, as Manoranjan waddles in. In a very business-like manner he turns, shuts the door, latches it from inside, and starts to undo the belt around his pants.

Sushil sits in a corner of the school assembly hall. The other jawaans are gathered in huddles, eating their last meal of the day. The small mound of rice and watery dal grows cold and lumpy on Sushil's plate. He's hungry, but he can't bring himself to eat tonight. Hemla's eyes haunt him still. That look she gave him from the floor where she lay as he turned to shut the classroom door behind him. He shut it tight, latched and locked it too, and handed the key to Manoranjan sahib. But Hemla's eyes – they wouldn't stay inside.

They followed him out.

And have stayed with him ever since.

He sees her look at him even now. Her eyes don't plead for help or pity. Her eyes are bewildered. Like the eyes of that deer his Bapu had made him hunt when he was only thirteen.

Sushil remembers that moment when he stood twenty paces from that unsuspecting deer, his bow taut, his arrow aimed. Another split moment and the deer would've been their lunch. But then that gentle creature had turned and looked... straight into Sushil's eyes. Sushil had frozen then. And the deer had bolted. Sushil never forgot that look. Hemla's eyes were that deer's. The bewilderment was the same. Just like the deer, Hemla too couldn't understand why. Why someone would want to hurt her.

Sushil hears that same muffled scream again. It's a howl more than a scream – a howl from deep within the earth, the mud and the stones muffling its pierce.

First it was her eyes.

Now it's her scream.

Sushil clenches his eyes shut.

"If you're not going to eat that, can I?"

Sushil unclenches his eyes, looks up to see Pradip, tucking his shirt into his pants, eyeing Sushil's plate of food. Sushil holds his plate up for Pradip, who takes it, turns and walks away, eating noisily.

|||<·V·>|||

A bamboo ladder noiselessly leans its shoulder against the peepal tree. Two careful feet climb up the ladder, their many little bells muffled by the chirping of crickets. Oonga is too high up for the ladder to reach, so Oongamma steps onto a branch, reaches up with her hands, and tilts her sleeping son till he topples into her arms.

The bonfire is a glowing pile of dying embers. Oongamma carries Oonga past it to their hut, where she gently spills him into his hammock, tucking his legs and arms in. She stands there for a moment, looking at her son. *So peaceful he looks when he's asleep,* she thinks. *No one would believe what a little wild beast he can be when he's awake.* She touches her swollen tummy and wonders if this one inside her will be as much of a handful as the one in the hammock.

|||<·V·>|||

The keychain is a tribal puppet monkey. The irony is not lost on Sushil. That the key to the only motorcycle in this CRPF camp should be strung to a souvenir from the world of the adivasi.

"Go on two wheels. You'll get there and back faster," instructs Manoranjan, as Pradip plays with the miniature puppet in his hand. "Get going before the cock crows. Check every maidaan and roadside theatre in the city. This bitch is a tough one. We won't get the truth off her tongue."

"WHAT IF WE FIND SITAHARAN PLAYING SOMEWHERE?" asks Sushil, as usual, loudly.

Manoranjan looks at him stony faced, "You tell me?"

Sushil isn't expecting that. He looks from Manoranjan to Pradip and back to the CO, stutters, "We-we le-let the teacher go?!"

Manoranjan looks on, expressionless. In his nervousness Sushil forgets the most important thing. He repeats, loudly, "WE LET THE TEACHER GO?!"

Manoranjan keeps looking at Sushil, slightly incredulous, turns to Pradip, tells him to "Keep a sharp eye on this fellow" and then he turns and waddles away into the darkness.

Pradip looks at the sky. "We've got less than four hours," he yawns. "Wake me up before the sun. I can't leave without taking a good dump. And a good dump takes time. Okay?"

Sushil nods.

"And Milktooth, for god's sake take that bloody rifle off your shoulder," Pradip sneers. "Look at the sky. You see the sun? No, right? You know why? Because it's not there! You're *not* on duty. And can you please stop behaving like you've seen a ghost? You're starting to unnerve me."

Sushil hasn't realised his rifle has been hanging from his shoulder all day now. He never knows what to do with it. He watches Pradip walk away unaffected, unbuttoning his shirt. Sushil feels all kinds of things right now. Anger. Confusion. Frustration. Fear. For himself. For Hemla. For Pradip. For everyone. What scares him most though is that he doesn't feel afraid *of* anything. He can't remember the last time he felt afraid *of* something.

And that scares him.

Ever since he held this rifle two days into his training he was made to feel indestructible. This rifle sometimes makes him feel urges. The urge to shoot anyone who upsets him. Anyone who belittles him. Anyone who angers him.

He could've shot Manoranjan sahib today.

And that is what scares him. This rifle makes him become what he is not. He's afraid it might make him kill someone someday. But what makes his gut go stone cold is what if – what if that someone he kills… is innocent?

That thought makes the rifle feel very, very heavy.

He slips it off his shoulder quickly now, unwilling to have its company any longer. Relieved of the weight, his shoulder suddenly starts to ache. He remembers this ache. He had it for days after he had shouldered his Bapu's corpse, carrying it for miles to the only crematorium in their zilla.

He wishes now that he hadn't taken this job. But his mother and sisters need the money. Jobs are hard to find. And it seems as if sons of farmers make good soldiers in this war.

Unable to motivate himself to walk to his assigned classroom and peel his uniform off, Sushil sinks to the ground right there, in the compound. And he lies down on his back so he can look at the sky. For many sleepless nights after Bapu died, the sky used to give Sushil consolation. This sky is deeper and darker and starrier than the one back home. Sushil watches it quietly, grateful that it's here to give him company. Because, he knows, he won't be getting much sleep tonight.

SIX

A small shadow creeps thief-like through the darkness of the hut. He climbs cautiously over two large sleeping bodies before stopping near a small one. The only shaft of moonlight in this hut catches an eagle feather as it emerges at the end of the small shadow's arm. The feather tip hovers over a small sleeping face for a few moments before precariously entering its ear. Idma grimaces in her sleep, swats the feather away, and goes still again. But the feather is incorrigible. It hovers over Idma's sleeping face, looking for a way to poke its tip into… her nose. Idma twitches, her nose wrinkling up as if summoning a sneeze, her eyes snap open, and she almost squeals, when the shadow's hand claps her mouth shut! And it whispers, "Shh! Come with me."

"Oonga! Are you crazy?" Idma is horrified by his idea. They sit crouched by the dying glow of the bonfire. Oonga's eyes have embers too, but they're the kind that have only just been set alight. "You know how far it is? And you don't even have money," Idma whispers loudly.

"I don't care, I have to see Rama." Oonga doesn't have time to argue.

"Hemla didi said she'll take you, she will. Now go back to

 sleep," Idma scolds him like an adult and gets up to go back to her hut.

Oonga grabs her hand, pulls her back down, his eyes dancing with an excited fire. "What if Rama goes away to another town? You only said he might. Hemla didi never came. It might get too late. I'm going on my own."

"I'm going on my own!" Idma mocks Oonga. "Lohabad is further away than anywhere you've ever been."

"I have gone to the market on my own. And the market is far."

"You donkey, it is much much much further away from the market. You will get lost."

"How far can it be. If you could go there, I can go too."

"You can't."

"Ah, understood! You don't remember the way! Tchah!"

"Of course I remember the way!" Idma snaps.

"Liar." Oonga lets go of her hand. He knows Idma only too well. "You don't remember anything."

"Yes I do," insists Idma, thumping the ground with her little foot. "First we cross the river and reach Nagamma..."

Oonga pretends to be disinterested. "Aye, that much even I know."

"Shut up. From there we turn away from the forest."

"This way?" Oonga points.

Idma looks in that direction, then in the other, then she turns around this way and that, slightly confused, but isn't one to give up or give in.

"Wait, I'll show you." She grabs his hand and leads him towards their banyan tree.

 Oonga lowers his head so Idma won't notice his sly triumphant grin.

In the darkness Idma gropes the ground around the blackboard for some chalk. She finds a big enough piece, adjusts the little bamboo ladder against the tree trunk, slowly starts climbing it, rung by careful rung. It's hard to see in this darkness, and it doesn't help that she's still half sleepy. *That wretched boy*, she thinks. *I'll draw him a map and then he can just go jump in the river!*

As she squints to make out the white line she's trying to draw on the board, magically, a dull golden glow spreads across the blackboard like a miniature sunrise. She turns to see a lantern come alive in Oonga's upstretched hand. He steps in close to let the flickering light from the lantern wash away the darkness, and pokes his face in from under Idma's arm to watch her draw him his map to Rama.

Idma is a natural before the blackboard. She draws with a teacher-like flourish, instructing Oonga as she draws each landmark in tribal shapes.

She draws an inverted triangle atop many horizontal squiggly worm-lines, commanding Oonga, "First take the boat across the river... don't swim, okay? Or you will drown!" Oonga is offended by Idma's complete disregard for his intelligence. He scowls but stays quiet. He'll let her feel superior this time. It's the only way she's going to give him what he wants right now.

Next, Idma draws a triangle with a circle-head and straight-line arms and a solitary straight-line leg. "Then you come to Nagamma," she says with an air of much importance, as if this is something Oonga may have forgotten.

"I know, I know," Oonga grumbles.

"But," as if to tell Oonga that she's in charge at this moment, Idma says, "that is just the first part. We did not go straight from here." She starts to draw a big triangle and breaks it up with horizontal lines. "We took the other road across the fields, till we saw these tall-tall men made of shining metal, with six-six hands. They were this huge!" She stops drawing and stretches up with her other hand to show how huge they were.

"Men made of metal?! Don't lie."

"No. Really. Then we kept going till we came to a big pinwheel up on a hill." And Idma draws a pinwheel with triangular blades. She follows that with, "Then we came to a huge bidi. It was growing out of the ground, and was made of stone. So much smoke was coming out of it that all of us kept coughing."

"How can a bidi be so huge?" Oonga is not sure now if Idma really remembers the way or if she's making some of this up.

"When Hemla didi takes you, you will see," Idma brushes him off. "Everything on the way to the city is huge. In fact the closer you get to Lohabad, everything just keeps getting huger and huger."

"Okay okay. Then?" Oonga is getting restless. Why haven't they come to Rama yet?!

"Once you enter Lohabad you will come to a huge wheel," and she draws a circle with many little triangles along its circumference. "It is standing in the middle in the air going round and round and round."

"Why?" asks Oonga. All this sounds so strange, how can it even be real?

"See? I told you. You cannot even imagine it. Below this wheel, very near by, you will find Rama." And she draws a stick human figure with a bow and arrow.

Oonga gapes. "Rama!"

Idma drops the stub of chalk, dusts her hands dramatically, and starts to climb down the ladder. "You see? It's very very very far away. Firstly, you'll never manage to get there on your own. And secondly, you need money to see Rama, which you don't have." She nudges him aside, and starts walking back to her hut. "Now go to sleep."

But Oonga stands transfixed, his lantern still aloft, hanging from one end of his arm which is frozen stiff with wonder. His eyes travel from the first drawing to the second to the third to the fourth… until they settle on Rama. He can't believe he now knows how to get to him. *But wait!* His reverie suddenly broken, he looks around for Idma. How is he going to remember all this?! He wants to ask Idma if she'll come with him. It'll be so much easier. She never forgets anything. And he never fears anything. Together they can get to Rama easily.

But she'd never come.

And even if she did she'd drive him crazy with her scoldings and her instructions and her whining. No! He's better off going alone. He just needs to find a way to remember all these things she has drawn.

He stands there for many long moments, studying the figures on the blackboard, murmuring to himself, repeating their names over and over again, trying to commit them to memory.

Huge metal men.

Huge pinwheel.

Huge bidi.

Huge wheel.

Huge problem.

His brows knit in worry. He brings the lantern down, sits it down on the ground, before squatting himself down before it, his head dropping into his hands for a quick, deep think. Which is when his eyes fall on a faded white figure dancing on his left leg.

Idea!

The flame in the lantern does an eager little jig, before Oonga blows it out. Plunged in darkness little Oonga is a little shadow again.

|||<•V•>|||

Little shadow Oonga creeps into his little hut on tiptoe and crouches behind a sleeping figure. Oonga's hand reaches for this figure's hip. The end of the saree at this hip is knotted into a small bundle. Oonga seems to know what this bundle holds, because he lifts it very carefully into the air and tries to unknot it. It is dark, so Oonga's little fingers have to feel their way through this tricky knot. Just as the knot starts to give way, the figure stirs, her swollen stomach turning over before her face does. Oonga can't drop the little bundle. It might come undone. So he crouches into the smallest version of himself, his hands held up in the air, frozen, like branches, the little bundle dangling precariously from his twig fingers. Oonga holds his breath until he hears Oongamma's soft snoring return. He uncrouches slowly, and his fingers start working the knot again.

When the knot is finally undone, Oonga cradles the open bundle in his palm. The coins in there catch a small sparkle of moonlight. Oonga doesn't know if this will be enough but he'll have to make do. Gingerly he picks up each coin and slides it soundlessly into his pocket. He can't grab them all at once in his fist. What if they make a clatter? Oonga is nervous now, and his fingers grow cold and sweaty. The last coin slips, and rattles to the floor. Oonga quickly claps his hand over it. But Oongamma's snoring breaks. In a flash Oonga lies down, pretending to sleep. But his eyes are open, watching his mother, as she groans, and turns over again, away from him.

For a moment Oonga wonders when Oongamma will take that other child out from her tummy. Why is it in there in the first place? It's been months. It must have grown big enough to be taken out now and sent to school. He thinks perhaps by the time he becomes Rama his brother or sister will have been plucked out of Oongamma's belly. He'll tell the little one all about Rama. But for that he'll first have to get to Rama. And for that he needs to get out of here before the cocks start crowing their heads off.

Oonga crawls out of the hut on all fours like a cautious cat. The moment he crosses the threshold he straightens up and bolts.

The sky awakes, its dark blue horizon cracking open in a silver yawn. Oonga has been waiting, hidden amidst the tall grass below a mahua tree. He has been waiting for this first wink of dawn. He picks some of the fallen mahua flowers, fills his pocket with them, mops his face with his gamchha, ties it round his waist, pulls up his knickers, looks back at his village one last time, and thupthupthupthupthupthupthup his feet kick up little clouds of dust as he scurries through the trees, towards that familiar distant golden rope that twinkles at him invitingly.

“Take me to the other side,” Oonga tells the boatman, who’s busy scraping the scales off some fish with a large knife. He doesn’t look up, mumbles, “Not now. Come later.”

But Oonga can’t come later. Oonga has to cross right now. “Please. It’s an emergency.”

The boatman has heard this before!

He looks up from his half-cleaned fish, peers into Oonga’s face. Oonga looks at him innocently. The boatman grumbles, “You’re that fellow! Left me stranded on the other side all morning. I couldn’t catch a single fish until now. You scared them nice and proper with your pebbles. You scoundrel! No boat ride for you.”

“Please, boatman, please. I have to reach the other side or I’ll be in trouble,” Oonga implores, shaking his hands and head frantically.

“You ARE trouble, you scoundrel. You want to get to the other side, swim,” and he pulls his stash of fish closer to himself, afraid this boy might steal one.

Oonga goes quiet. He knows he can’t convince this chap the normal way.

The boatman continues muttering angrily to himself, cursing Oonga for making him go without a good meal for a whole day by scaring the fish away. He curses Oonga, and Oonga’s ancestors and each and every one of Oonga’s future generations. He is so angry now that he starts scraping his fish furiously. So furiously that the head breaks off! He curses himself, reaches for it, when he notices the boat’s mooring rope slither past him like a silent snake.

"AYE!" he screams, drops everything, and lunges for the rope, trying to grab it with his hands. But his hands are slippery with fish, and the rope keeps slithering out of them, until he scrambles on all fours behind the running rope and grabs it between his teeth.

He stands up slowly, his teeth clenched down tight on the rope, to see Oonga in the basket boat, tugging at the other end of the rope to free the boat.

The boatman must be saying many angry things to Oonga but Oonga hears only a low incomprehensible grumbling. The rope is thick and it muffles the boatman's words. He stands there, furious, confused, unsure if he should let go of the rope to yell at Oonga, because if he does, the little rogue might pull it away in a jiffy. Oonga though knows the position of power he has wrested from the boatman. He smiles his sweetest innocent smile, lets go of the rope, joins his hands, and makes the humblest request in the history of humble requests, "Please, brother boatman, please take me to the other side?"

The boatman glares at him, sizing him up carefully. He twists the rope around his slippery hands until he's sure it can't slip out, parts his teeth, releases the rope, frees his aching jaw, and asks, "What exactly is this emergency now?"

"Rama," says Oonga.

"Rama?! What is rama?"

"If I don't get to him in time he'll leave and go to some other town."

"I don't understand."

"Boatman, you'll never understand. Pleeeeeease, lets go-o-o-o-o-o-o!"

The boatman can't figure this boy out, but something tells him this boy is not lying. He keeps his eyes trained on Oonga as he unhitches the mooring, rubs his hands dry on the ground, takes his oar, and grudgingly steps into the boat.

As the boat hits the other shore, Oonga fishes a closed fistful out his pocket, holds it up for the boatman. The boatman steadies his oar, holds his hand out for his payment. Oonga uncloses his fist, and the boatman's palm fills up with… mahua flowers! Before the boatman can gather his wits, Oonga has leapt out of the boat like a frog and sprung into the forest.

"You rascal! Wait till you come back. I'll feed you to the fish!" the boatman rants, hopelessly aware that he'll be able to do no such thing!

|||<•V•>|||

Oonga runs through the forest, the wind picking up from behind him as if to welcome him and speed him up. Every tree that he runs past starts to flap its leaves, until a thousand jungle tongues go ulululululululululululululu all at once. But when Oonga reaches a hot little clearing, the wind dies. And the jungle voices fall silent.

There must have been some trees here until recently because their gnarled roots remain, writhing in and out of the ground as if trying to burst free to go look for the trees they once belonged to. In the middle of this clearing a two-legged metal signboard stands silently. It reads 'INDIA ALUMINIUM INC'. As Oonga scurries past it, kicking up those familiar little clouds of dust, the signboard vibrates with a low eerie hum. This signboard knows something, something that the jungle wants to warn Oonga about. But Oonga is in a hurry. He hears nothing except for a small hypnotic voice inside him that keeps chanting "Rama" in time with the beat of his heart. And he sees nothing except for the horizon towards which he scurries, his little legs pumping furiously.

SEVEN

In the quietest corner of what used to be the school library, in the cosy darkness beneath a large desk, Pradip, one hand tucked inside his pants, snores loudly. His snores echo off the underside of the desk making the tiny library vibrate. Gandhiji, his photo frame trembling, smiles helplessly from the wall. But Netaji next to him doesn't look as forgiving.

Every time Sushil comes to wake Pradip he feels like he's stepping inside a dholak that is being beaten, without rhythm, from the outside. This time Sushil has decided to try something different. Politely calling out "Pradip sir" doesn't seem to be working too well. He readies himself, takes a deep breath, positions his hand a foot above the desk, and 1… 2… 3…

SLAM!

Pradip jumps up with a start, knocking his head against the underside of the desk. He rubs his head sleepily, and scowls. He mumbles, snorts, sneezes, scratches his privates, looks around, sees sunlight flooding the room, panics, scrambles out of his corner, grabs Sushil by the collar and hisses, "Why didn't you wake me earlier? It's way past dawn!"

Sushil looks at him tiredly. He is prepared for this. "I've been trying to wake you for the last hour, sir."

Pradip knows this must be true. He knows what a lout he can be when it comes to sleeping. It's the one thing he hasn't got enough of in fifteen long years. "Is Manoranjan up?" he asks.

Sushil nods, "I saw him head straight to the toilets outside. He's still in there."

Pradip tries to digest that information for a moment. His stomach growls in protest. He takes a deep breath, curses his stomach for needing to empty itself every morning, grabs Sushil's arm, "Let's leave quickly."

But he stops as soon as he's started, looking at Sushil's arm, and then the rest of him, in horror, "Why the fuck are you in uniform?!"

The query confuses Sushil. "Ar-aren't we going on duty, sir?"

Pradip takes a deep breath, exhales, explains, "Do you know that the naxalites in these parts have better aim than us?"

Confused, Sushil shakes his head.

"They do. Do you know why?"

Sushil shakes his head again.

"Because they practise their shooting skills on moving targets." Pradip continues, "Do you know what they make those moving targets wear?"

Still confused, Sushil shakes his head again.

Pradip looks at Sushil's uniform. Sushil follows his gaze.

Then why do they call this print 'camouflage'? Sushil wants to ask, but doesn't.

93] Pradip drives the motorbike out of the camp, up the dirt track and onto the road. Sushil, in a faded kitschy pink shirt sits behind him. "Is this blouse all you had?" Pradip grumbles, getting no response. "Remind me to buy you a shirt one day." He slows down the bike, and stops it by the side.

"Why are we stopping, sir? We just left," Sushil is starting to worry about being on the road with this unpredictable hooligan.

"You're going to drive," Pradip says, getting off, and waiting for Sushil to slide down the seat to the front.

"Er, why, sir?"

"Are you sleepy?"

Sushil shakes his head.

"Did you take your morning dump?"

Sushil nods.

"That's why. I've got both shit and sleep inside me still. And I'm sure you can think of better ways to die than being ridden off the road by a sleepy shithead you don't like too much."

Sushil stutters, "Arre no-no sir, I –" But Pradip shuts him up, gestures that it's okay… *Let's not kid one another, let's not die in the process either, come on slide up, start up, we're late.*

|||<•V•>|||

The earth has turned a hot red. The metal monsters have eaten through a lot more of the land than when Oonga was here last. The distant hill now bears a large gaping hole in its side, as if some big beast descended from the sky one day and took a huge bite out of it. The few trees that once stood here have disappeared too. It's as if the earth is being permanently disconnected from the sky.

The static red rustiness is broken by a dull yellow truck crawling away, towards the horizon. The truck is heaped with rocks – bits and pieces of the hurting hill. On its behind, visible even from this distance, is a painted raakshas, his bloodied tongue stuck out in permanent contempt of this world. Beneath his frightening scowl are the words 'Keep safe distance'. But Oonga, as always, doesn't notice a thing. He's got too much on his mind.

He scampers past another two-legged metal signboard. Above the 'I' in the middle of the 'ALUMINIUM' in 'INDIA ALUMINIUM INC.' is a large eye. Wide open. Unblinking. All seeing. The eye is etched deep into the metal. It is black but the swirling red dust of this place has settled in its grooves and makes it look like it is sleepless, reddened with wakeful staring at this world that it seeks to claim. The red dust shifts now, making the eye appear as if it watches Oonga patter past. The eye will be here when Oonga returns. As if to make that fact known to this land, the metal board vibrates once more with its eerie hum. It makes Oonga's skin crawl, so he runs even faster, trying to put as much distance between the board and himself.

|||<•V•>|||

The fields are waking, their blankets of mist sliding off them slowly. The paddy twists in its bed to see who this is in such a hurry this morning. The wet earth mutters into the roots of the rice – "It's that hurry-hurry boy again – Oonga."

The fields stretch and tighten their skin so that the little boy they secretly adore can go thupthupthupthupthupthup across their stomachs to wherever it is he needs to get to in such a hurry.

Oonga's furiously pattering feet slow down when he sights his friend the scarecrow. Her pumpkin face has a smile carved into it. Oonga remembers how last season Idma, Bela, Laichan and he came all the way out here to make this scarecrow smile. The farmer who owned her wasn't sure if the smile was a good idea.

"She might have to be scary to the crows, but she can still smile for us, no?" Oonga had argued. The farmer hadn't been entirely convinced, but allowed it. Unknown to him the children even gave her a name!

Nagamma still has her smile. But now she even has a gamchha tied around her pumpkin head like a scarf.

Oonga greets Nagamma and wonders aloud which way he's supposed to turn now. Nagamma's wooden arm points him to the west. Oonga thanks her, says he'll see her later, and takes the dirt path going left through the fields.

The sun is up now. And Oonga is sweating. There is so much running to be done today. He can't get tired already. He wonders if he should slow down until he reaches some shade again. No! No, he can't! If he slows down he might not make it to Lohabad in time. *What if Rama goes away?!* That thought brings the wind back into his feet and he starts running again. Until he turns off the dirt track onto a much wider kuchcha road, and runs into… an idea!

Some way ahead a Commander jeep stands. The luggage carrier atop it is heaped with bags and cartons. One of the windows is rolled down. Inside, a pudgy man in a beige safari suit and cheap shades eats a banana. He tosses the peel out where it lands on a small heap of crushed paper, torn biscuit packets, and empty plastic mineral water bottles. This seems to be the only small pile of litter in the entire landscape. But this man – busy talking on his cellphone – doesn't seem to notice or care. Oonga doesn't notice either. His eyes follow another – a sallow creature – who is walking away from this car, looking this way and that restlessly as if searching for the right spot.

Oonga thinks the man inside with the small dark windows over his eyes looks like an overfed rabbit. And this restless underfed fellow scavenging about looks like a rat. Oonga squirrels into the underbrush after the Rat.

The Rat exhales in relief as a yellow rope of piss shoots out of him onto the bark of the tree. He's been holding this in for over an hour now. Thank god his boss found a spot of network and they could stop for him to make all his goddamned phone calls. Or he'd still be driving right now with a tank full of piss. It's pointless pressure like this that makes men want to kill one another in these godforsaken places. He'd have to drive at 80 or over to get them out of naxalite country before dark today. He refuses to be caught in this place with his pants down.

That's precisely when Rat gets the start of his life. A small head pokes out from the other side of his pissing tree, and asks him in a language he doesn't fully understand, "Are you going that way?" The little tribal boy points in the other direction.

Rat could swear he was tribal by the way he almost popped out of the tree itself! And he could tell what he was asking because Rat has been driving around these tribal areas for years now. He doesn't speak Kuvi, but he sort of knows what's being said when he's spoken to in that tongue. It helps him survive this place. Most times he pretends he doesn't know the language and then eavesdrops slyly when unsuspecting tribals get chatty around him. He's learnt a lot about the politics of the jungle this way. But he keeps it all to himself. Unlike his piss, which he likes to relieve himself of sooner rather than later.

But this little jungle mongrel, he wants a lift. Rat shakes his head at Oonga, and points in the other direction, away from this wilderness, towards the city, where he wants to be desperately right now, and find himself a desi theka for a stiff drink. He could've sworn the little tyke smiled then as if that's what he had wanted to know. But then why did he point in the other direction?

Oonga pops his head back behind the tree. Rat pushes his remaining piss out quickly, zips up and walks around the tree, but the boy... has vanished. Rat blinks hard to make sure he's seeing right. Did he imagine this fellow? How can someone appear and disappear like that? He has heard legends of these jungle people. But this is unreal!

Rat hurries out of the bushes to the waiting jeep, where Rabbit is on the phone still, his head bowed in sycophantic devotion to someone on the other end of the line. Rat waits outside the driver's door, watching for a signal from inside. These sahibs of the Company are the trickiest customers. They will throw drivers like him out of their own cars when they need to conduct secret business over their phones. The more secret their business, chances are the more illegal it might be. He watches this sahib through the rolled up window. He can't hear what he's saying. But he can tell whom he's talking to. It must be someone above him in the food chain. *The moment I open that door to sit in my seat, sahib's humility will fly out his window,* Rat thinks. Must be all that tobacco these traders chew. It makes their tongues slippery. Rat knows to never trust words that drop off a slippery tongue. Such words owe allegiance to nothing, least of all to the tongue they slide off.

As Rabbit brings the phone down from his ear his head instantly unbows itself. He's hiding something behind those shades. Rat is sure of that. A conceit. A deceit. Something.

Something unhappy. But Rat isn't allowed to think about it. Rabbit suddenly gestures to him. And Rat dives in obediently and starts up the jeep.

As the jeep picks up speed the cartons and bags in the carrier rattle about. The roads in these parts are bumpy. And Rat is trying to get the needle of the speedometer to slide past 80. *This is going to be a pain in the ass*, Rat thinks, *both literally and figuratively.*

In the back seat, Rabbit is lost in thought, chewing what might be his twentieth packet of paan masala today. *This job is stressful*, he thinks. *Why can't anyone see what I keep trying to make them see? Some of them see it, but always too late.* With that he rolls the window down and spits out a large red glob. Rat grimaces, but doesn't let his displeasure show. He knows some of that is now splattered across the side of his car. He's tired of cleaning this man's spit.

Rat is right. A few streaks of dirty red have scarred the words printed on the side of the jeep. The words are 'India', 'Aluminium' and 'Inc.'. Above the 'I' in the middle of 'Aluminium' is that same Eye. Rabbit's spit seems to have missed the Eye, which stares ominously at the passing countryside, as if claiming all that it can possibly see.

But, unseen to this Eye, atop the jeep, from amidst those cartons, a small head emerges, slowly, cautiously. Two wary eyes peek out over the square shoulder of a suitcase. Satisfied that he is invisible up here, Oonga straightens up, jostles with his inanimate co-passengers to make some space for himself, settles his tiny bottom into a groove in the carrier, and throws his head back to gobble up the breeze!

The cartons around him must belong to the Company too because each one of them has the Eye printed on its sides. These Eyes have seen Oonga, and they watch him now without blinking, as he stares enthralled at the world whizzing by. He has never experienced this before – this speed, this wind, this height from which he can peek into the upper branches of passing trees without having to climb them.

Oonga loses himself to this world speeding past. He must ask Hemla didi to get them a motorgaadi like this one. No, wait! He won't ask Hemla didi for anything. She makes promises she cannot keep. If it weren't for her lies he wouldn't have had to go off on his own to find Rama. Which brings Oonga's racing mind back to why he's up here on top of a motorgaadi in the first place.

He slips the shirt sleeve up his left arm to reveal... his secret map! All the tribal figures Idma drew he copied off the blackboard, and painted onto his arm! The first white drawing high up near his shoulder is of the boat. Where his bicep begins is the second landmark – Nagamma. And now Oonga peers intently at his little bicep muscle, where the third figure sits – the triangular metal man. *No,* Oonga reminds himself, *the HUGE triangular metal man.* And he looks up at the landscape speeding by, his eyes searching. The wind and the speed and the ride have lost their thrill now. Oonga is on his mission again. He has to spot the huge metal men. This motorgaadi is moving so fast he might miss them if he even so much as blinks. So Oonga flares his eyes and steadies himself, scanning the scenery for the only thing he now seeks of it.

|||<·V·>|||

Pottacheru doesn't seem to be missing Oonga. Not yet.

Oongamma awoke to an empty hammock. But that wasn't unusual. Oonga is a creature of his own devices. Oongamma's learnt not to get in his way. Until of course it's time to eat or have a bath, both of which Oonga is highly allergic to.

Madvi got off his chaataai this morning and promptly climbed up the nearest sal tree again. He has motkas hitched to the top of each such tree around the village, to collect the heady sap seeping out of those cheeky cuts he makes in the bark. The salfi he extracts from the sap is everyone's biggest joy. The villagers look forward to getting tipsy on Madvi's salfi and dancing the dhimsa. That makes them forget their fear for a while – the fear of losing their fields, their village and their trees. A few gourdfuls of salfi can make it go away. Until the next morning at least.

Since Hemla's not appeared this morning either, the children celebrate their holiday by playing with their goats. Hurre though is drawing a mango tree – just like the one Hemla didi drew yesterday – on her hut wall.

No one seems to be worried about Hemla. She disappears often. It takes so long to get from one place to another in these parts that things often take longer than you think they would. And Hemla didi goes to such frightening far-off places. The post office. The Collector's office. The police thana. The town court. The town hospital. The very sight of those buildings drives dread into the adivasis. Those buildings are so tall. And there are so many people in them. And they speak in so many alien tongues. One must be superhuman to be able to deal with all of that and not get hurt. To the villagers, Hemla didi is superhuman. But superhuman or not, such things take time. So there's no telling when she might return from any such jaunt.

But there is one little person in this village who is restless with concern.

The first thing Idma did when she opened her eyes this

morning was look for Oonga. The second thing she did was go wipe the blackboard clean. Something tells her that Oonga the donkey is actually a monkey. And monkeys like him are hard to contain. She wonders if she should tell Oongamma what happened last night.

She stands outside Oonga's hut watching Oongamma sweep the hut floor. Oongamma spots Idma, comes out to speak to her, but Idma bolts like a deer.

She doesn't want to raise an alarm. What if it's a false alarm? What if that donkey has simply gone up to Kunja's cave? Or climbed up some tree? She doesn't know what to do. She wishes Hemla didi was here now. She always knows what to do.

But if Hemla didi were here now Oonga wouldn't have gone.

But what if Oonga hasn't gone?

He's quite the drama king. He says all these fancy things but never does any of it. But if he hasn't gone then why isn't he here?

I should've stopped him, thinks Idma. *I shouldn't have drawn that stupid map.*

Idma looks around at all the villagers going about their day. Her heart is filled with so much confusion that her head starts to spin. She decides to wait. She'll wait till the sun is right atop her head.

But what will she do once it is?

Wait till it topples off her head?!

Idma's head starts to spin so much that she lies down and closes her eyes.

EIGHT

Sushil has to ride much slower than he would like to. Pradip has fallen asleep on his back. Sushil is amazed by how Pradip hasn't slipped off the moving bike yet. Must be all those years on the move. Sushil has heard it teaches you to sleep in every conceivable position in every conceivable place for whatever conceivable duration. He has heard legends of soldiers on the battlefront taking power naps right there in the trenches in between rounds of shelling. What else can one do? A sleepy mind takes all the wrong decisions. And a sleepy driver can kill his passengers. Sushil is glad Pradip forced him to ride. These roads are a nightmare. Sushil wonders if Pradip is having a nightmare too because he dribbles and snorts on Sushil's shoulder every once in a while.

Sushil is also grateful that Pradip's ever-moving mouth is shut. It gives him a chance to watch the world they ride past. The paddy fields. The farmers. The adivasi men and women walking by the side of the road in single file, baskets on their heads, bamboos across their shoulders with baskets hung from each end. All those pumpkins, gourds, goats and poultry. It all reminds Sushil of his own life back in his village, when Bapu was still a farmer. He'd walk with Bapu for days to get to the market in town to sell their excess produce. He misses all that walking. Riding a bike is not the same.

A motor never gives a true feeling of how far one has travelled. He remembers his first train ride. In the time it used to take him to walk to the village post office and back, the train had carried them into another state!

So lost in his thoughts is Sushil that he doesn't notice the pothole.

WHUMP!

And Pradip nearly topples off, waking just in time to land on his hands and not his head. He sleepily scrambles to his feet, muttering drowsy curses, as Sushil climbs off, slowly pulls the front wheel out of the little ditch, and starts to push the bike along.

This stretch of road seems to have been personally targeted for a pounding by the rains. Its skin is bruised and blistered all over. The scars have dried in the summer heat, but they're still deep. Nobody seems to have visited this stretch of road to treat it.

"Greedy fucking bastards," Pradip spits. "Half the money for this road must have gone into the cars each of them bought back home."

"Isn't there some way to hold them accountable?" Sushil asks, knowing he's just made a mistake asking a question that naïve.

"Milktooth? Did you really ask me that just now? You know where we are? There are spots in these jungles that are not even on any sarkaari map. Who do you think comes to survey these roads once the contractors have built them? My father? Your father? Gandhiji?"

Sushil continues pushing the bike silently, manoeuvering it around craters of all shapes and sizes. Another few feet and they'll be clear and they can ride again.

And hopefully Pradip will go back to sleep then.

But Pradip has other ideas. "I'm going to quit the force next year and become a private contractor. I know of places that don't have roads. Places that those dimwits in the Collector's office don't even know exist. Wherever this great nation decides to shove its cock and birth some 'development', there's a lot of money to be made. You just need to get there before the nation's cock gets there, you know?"

Sushil has pulled the bike clear, and is getting ready to straddle it once more. He can't help asking, "But why quit next year? Why not today?"

Pradip looks at him grumpily. No reply to that question would be good enough. As he climbs onto the back seat, he does what he's always done when he doesn't have the answer – he throws a googly. "I enjoy the interrogations too much," he says, and taps Sushil's shoulder to start up and get them out of here.

Bit by unsure bit, the speedometer swings sceptically past 70. The windows rattle like loose teeth in a never-ending shiver. But the wind is hot and scratchy here. It doesn't like having to graze over the dead skin road. Oonga's eyes are starting to burn. But still he stares unblinking, searching both sides for his huge metal men. The dreary rumbling is suddenly punctured by a yodel! Oonga gets so startled he almost leaps off the roof.

Down below, Rabbit's drowsy phone is ringing with a Kishore Kumar song. Crackled back to life, Rabbit taps Rat on the shoulder. Rat nods, relaxes his foot on the accelerator as Rabbit takes the call, silencing the yodel.

"Agarwal saab," Rabbit says obediently, summoning his inner sycophant again. He listens warily before replying, "Agarwal saab, those Pottacheru villagers aren't like the others. I don't know who's putting these things in their heads but they were asking too many questions. Which is why I put Plan B in motion this time. I didn't have time to check with you. There's also no blasted network, no, in these jungles?" And he goes quiet again, his brow knitting tight as he listens.

"Sir, don't worry. All these rules have been made by the government only. All we are doing is using them when we need to. I'm on it. You relax."

Rat has been trying very hard to not sneak a peek at Rabbit in the rear-view mirror. He looks now as Rabbit tucks the phone into his safari suit pocket, plucks out a pouch of paan masala and empties some into his mouth. Rat's not sure if Rabbit can see him watching. His eyes are well hidden by those shades. But even as Rabbit puts the pouch back into his pocket and begins chewing slowly, his face doesn't turn away. This unsettles Rat. He could be looking at him, but then again he might not be. This makes the hair bristle on Rat's neck, and he turns his attention back to the road, his foot slowly pressing down on the creaking accelerator once again.

Just as the jeep starts to pick up speed again Oonga spots him – the huge metal man, his six arms held out fixedly, approaching them from the right. Long ropes seem to be growing out of his head and floating away. He's exactly like Idma had described. Oonga grins in relief, and points at his new friend, like the captain of a ship would, silently instructing his vessel to now turn and sail towards Him.

But right then the jeep hits a Y-junction, and swerves left. Oonga watches his metal man quickly recede from the tip of his pointing finger. Oonga is aghast!

"No! No! Not this way! That way!" Oonga squeals, pointing feverishly at Him. But He is disappearing as quickly as He had appeared. And the droning wind drowns Oonga's voice. Desperate, he thumps the roof of the jeep, "STOP! STOP! You're going the wrong way! STOP!"

But Oonga's hands are small. The thumps they make on the rusting metal are even smaller. Between the rattling of the unhinged windows and the shuddering of an unhappy suspension, Oonga's pleas go unheard.

Oonga turns to see his metal friend disappear from view.

His eyes filling up with desperate tears, Oonga squeezes forward through the cartons and suitcases to the front of the jeep's roof, clutches the carrier like a bird would with its claws, and drops his head over the front to peek in through the windscreen.

Rat squeals in shock. How could a small upside down face be peering at him like this?! His foot attacks the brake. But the brakes are elderly. And the jeep stutters and clacks like a really old woman tumbling down a hill, until it finally stops with a stomach-turning lurch.

The impact tosses Oonga off the roof. He topples down the windscreen, rolls over the bonnet, and lands spreadeagled before the jeep.

"What the hell?!" Rat springs out of his seat, but before he can lunge after Oonga, the sprightly little squirrel has scampered away.

Rat just stands and watches Oonga scurry away into a speck. He could have sworn this was that same little tribal boy, the ghost from that tree. The thought sends a small chill crackling down his spine.

He pulls himself onto the bonnet, inspects the roof, shoving the cartons aside, afraid he might find something he'd rather not.

"Who was that?" Rabbit asks from below. "What was he doing up there? How long was he there? You know him?"

Rat just looks down at his master foolishly, and shakes his head. With the jeep standing deathly silent now, Rat can suddenly hear the wind. It sounds like the murmur of many unhappy voices. Voices that seem to be passing hushed warnings to one another. An endless chain of Chinese whispers. Rat can't shake the chill out of his spine. He hurries off the bonnet, scampers into his seat, turns on the engine, and kicks the accelerator like one would whip a horse. The jeep lunges forward with a grunt and starts to rapidly pick up speed.

Rabbit takes his shades off. His eyes dart about suspiciously. The jeep starts to feel like a prison now. What was that fellow doing on top of the car? How long had he been there? Could he be what the CRPF commander had warned him about? Even little kids in these jungles were not to be trusted. How had they not known he was there? What was up with this driver now? Should he tell him to stop?

But there is nowhere to go to even if they do stop. They'll have to keep moving.

But now Rabbit doesn't trust Rat.

And Rat is too spooked to care.

|||<·V·>|||

Oonga runs, his feet hardly feeling the ground beneath them. He doesn't turn to see that he's not being chased. So intent is he on running faster that his eyes have nearly shut in concentration. The world before him is a jiggling blur.

He runs and runs and runs until the blur is punctured by the far-off metal man, his six arms beckoning Oonga closer.

Oonga slows down now, allowing his eyes to open wider. His breath is scraggly now, his chest rising and falling like a stormy sea wave. He gobbles in breaths, turns to see that he has no one on his tail. The jeep has disappeared into the horizon behind him. But on the horizon before him – perplexity!

The long ropes floating out of his metal man's head seem to be floating into another metal man's head behind him! And behind that one, there is another. And another. And another. An endless military row of gigantic metal men stand tall and unmoving, trailing one another into infinity. *So many?* thinks Oonga. *Why didn't Idma tell me there would be so many?!*

Oonga looks at the map on his arm. He decides to walk in stride with the metal men until he finds the huge pinwheel. Would one of the metal men be holding this giant pinwheel? Who makes these men? What do they do? And why aren't there any trees in this place?

Hills have been sliced through the middle here to let endless electric lines run through them. Oonga walks over hot stony paths, his gamchha wrapped round his head. There is something about this land that does not make sense to him. The metal man is hot to the touch. Oonga walks through his humongous legs, looking up at the criss-cross mesh of metal tapering towards the top.

"Where can I find your giant pinwheel, O giant metal man?" asks Oonga. The metal man is silent. A low constant crackle buzzes through the air. It's coming from the ropes that run from one metal-man-tower to the next. Oonga follows the crackle, curious, his heart filling up again with the thrill of discovery. His feet crackle to life too, and he starts running again, from metal man to metal man to metal man, looping through the portals of their giant legs, being led by their collective crackling hum into infinity, unaware that the land he is running over is recording each patter of each footstep to carry it back over road and river and forest and stream to where his Amma's heartbeat now changes to accommodate the worrying rhythm of his unannounced departure.

|||<•V•>|||

Oongamma sits by the leaf-plate of rice and curry she had placed outside their doorway some time ago. In a slightly nervous voice she calls out again, "OONGA?!" She doesn't want to worry. She doesn't want her unbirthed little one to worry. So she tells herself a little lie – that Oonga is just being difficult, and he will come. He always comes. Because he always gets hungry around now. She jangles her bangles to her tummy, mutters a little rhyme to her baby, and gets up to go inside.

|||<•V•>|||

Hemla's face is swollen with bruises. She is upright now, tied tight to the small chair she has been forced into. Her captive hands seem to have lost their fight. Blood has caked on her wrists. Her fingers are turning white. As a cruel joke her feet have been bound by bits ripped off her torn saree. On a small desk before her lies a plate of cold rice. It has been placed close enough for her to be able to lean over and use her mouth, like a dog would. She watches tiredly now as a fly sits on her food and starts to taste it with impunity. The only thing she is thankful for is the darkness in this classroom. So that no one can see her battered naked body.

She had never imagined that the thought of this classroom filled with curious children could horrify her. But it does. If even one of them sees her like this now, they would never be able to unsee this sight for the rest of their lives. *Could this be the feeling that turns adivasis like Laxmi and Linga into monsters?* thinks Hemla. *If I get out alive from here will I turn into a monster too? No! No! I cannot think like that. To have such thoughts is to destroy everything, everything! I must breathe. I must stay calm. I must think of... of... trees.*

And slowly the pain and her exhaustion and starvation creep over her body and make it slacken. The thought of trees calms Hemla's mind. It even makes her consider eating. So she pulls her heavy eyelids open and watches the fly hover hungrily about her rice.

Oonga's stomach makes a low rumble. He wonders if he should look for something to eat. But just then he runs out of metal men! He has walked past the last one. He looks this way and that. Right before him is a hill. The thought of having to climb makes him want to curl up and go to sleep right there. But then the wind changes direction and carries to him a slow whirring sound. It seems to be coming from the top of the hill. Oonga takes the gamchha off his head and ties it tight around his tummy.

Food can wait.

Rama cannot.

The climb is dusty. The wind here is different from the wind in Oonga's world. It swirls in raggedy fits and starts as if in protest against something trying to make it submit to its will. The wind here sounds unhappy. It groans to Oonga, blowing some dust into his eyes, hoping he will listen, since he seems like one from the land of those who listen to the wind. But Oonga simply shakes the dust from his eyes, peeling them open again to find the source of this raggediness…

The giant pinwheel!

He stands atop the hill and lets his gaze freefall down the other side – littered with giant pinwheels turning slowly as if being commandeered by some invisible higher force. If Oonga would listen, the wind would tell him that it doesn't control these pinwheels, men do. The kind of men that would like to control earth, water and fire as well. *And not just control, enslave us. Like they will you.*

But Oonga now has just one thought on his mind. He needs to get to the next milestone on Idma's map – the giant bidi! There appears to be a road at the bottom of this hill, where the last of these giant pinwheel-windmills stands. Perhaps it will take him there? Oonga almost expects the wind to tell him. But the wind – disappointed in Oonga – has died.

NINE

The little red flags hang limp, taking a break perhaps from eternally murmuring missives of heartache to one another.

The leaves in the jungle are still too.

Kunja's ears bristle. Such windlessness is foreboding. Kunja would have liked to be able to tell Oonga that although his journey is predestined he must reconsider it. But to interfere with the preordainment of his destiny would be to guarantee his doom. It is at times such as this one that Kunja regrets being born with the 'gift'. He didn't ask to be 'spoken' to. He was born into it. The nights are the hardest. That is when he is alone before his fire, and the four elements converge before him in secret alliance, and tell him things that he sometimes doesn't know what to do with.

He knows the boy is hungry. And the wind refuses to help him any more. So Kunja sucks in a breath, places his palm on the earth, and closes his eyes, sending a gentle tremor through it like the low grumble of a starving empty stomach.

The road is tarred, yet dusty. Oonga's bare feet can weather anything nature throws at them, but this road – it's not natural. Oonga scalds his feet in just a few steps. He walks on the dusty side of the road now, braving the sharp pebbles, frustrated at having to slow down so he doesn't cut his feet. He needs a ride now. A motorgaadi. A boat. A cycle. Anything. He wishes Hemla didi had brought him. He would be perched like a bird on the carrier of her cycle now as they happily rolled and bumped along this road together.

Hemla didi.

Cheater.

Maker of false promises.

She even turned me into the man who chops his mango tree! thinks Oonga suddenly, upset by the memory. *I'm better off walking alone!*

Some way up, the earth starts to become cooler beneath Oonga's feet. This can only mean one thing – and Oonga spots them – trees! A cluster of them. He rushes to them. His eyes search their branches. He spots the one he seeks – a mango tree!

Oonga stands on the highest branch of the tree, on his toes, stretching his arm as far as he can without tumbling off the branch, but he still can't reach the only ripe mango in sight. So he does what only a monkey would. He grabs a high branch with one hand, and one… two… three… he *swings* himself to the mango… and back!

He misses.

He readies himself, tightens his grip on the branch above, and one… two… three… he swings… his other hand grabs the mango… and –

Thup! He lands on his branch with monkey precision.

 He's good at this. He knows trees better than the others back in school.

There's no way he would have chopped his tree down!

Oonga is about to perch himself on the branch to eat his trophy, when from far away he hears an approaching smoky rumble. He looks to the horizon behind. Sure enough, a speeding jeep appears to be rattling towards him.

Oonga scrambles to his feet, hops from branch to branch as fast as he can, slips off the bark, lands in a tumble, scampers over the pebbles towards the road just as the jeep whizzes past like a gigantic arrow. Oonga leaps onto the road, squeals, jumps up and down waving his arms frantically at the disappearing jeep, growls, howls, calls out to them to *Stop! Come back! Oonga needs a ride!*

But no one seems to hear him.

He sucks the mango dry of every last fibre, some of the juice having trickled onto his shirt. He tears the skin off the seed, then looks around. He circles the tree, patting the ground with his feet as if searching for some hidden hollow. He finds a spot, drops down on his knees, and starts digging the dusty earth with his hands. Having scooped out a big enough bowl of earth, he drops the mango seed into it, and starts filling it up again, thinking aloud, "Hemla didi, see? I planted the seed. I am also Rama. You don't know anything!"

When Oonga has hit the road again, there seems to have sprung from his hand a pinwheel, freshly made from mango leaves. He turns it around this way and that hoping to catch some breeze. But the wind doesn't seem like it wants to play.

Oonga walks faster, hoping the pinwheel will pick up a spin, but it doesn't. He breaks into a trot. The sun is now sliding into the roof of the sky. And this road seems to go on forever. What if he doesn't reach Lohabad today?

Almost as if in response he hears a distant horn, peep-peep-pi-pi-peep! Oonga whips around just in time to see the horizon spit out a tiny speck growing larger as it rockets towards him. Oonga squints to make out what it is.

It's a motorcycle.

Two men on it.

Oonga spreadeagles himself in the middle of the road, stretching his arms to both sides as wide as he can, the pinwheel still in his fist. This motorcycle is not going anywhere without taking him. The rider seems to have noticed Oonga and swerves a little to his right to avoid a collision. Vigilant, determined, Oonga moves a little to his left too, to *ensure* a collision. Confused the rider swerves to his left. Oonga, his arms held out taut, his legs spread wide, inches back to his right. His focus is unwavering. As the bike approaches Oonga, the rider relents, slows down, and brakes a few feet from the boy.

"You want to get killed, boy?" asks Sushil, perplexed.

Oonga hops onto the front wheel, grabs the handlebar with his free hand, beseeches, "Please please please take me to Lohabad?"

Pradip, still grumpy, tries to reach out to Oonga to swat him away like a mosquito, "Hutt! Get off!"

But Oonga is undeterred. "Lohabad! Please! Lohabad!"

Sushil seems to get what the boy wants but before he can say anything Pradip tumbles off the bike, grabs Oonga by the scruff of his neck, forcefully plucks him off the front wheel, tosses him to the side, and tumbles back onto the bike, "Lets go, quick."

Uncertain, Sushil tries to rev up but the engine coughs, sputters and dies.

This is the chance Oonga needs! As Sushil kicks to start up the bike again, Oonga leaps onto the carrier, sticks his pinwheel between his teeth, and wraps his arms and legs around the carrier... tight!

Pradip turns to face the scamp, snaps, "Aye! Little fucker! Get the fuck off!"

But Oonga's pluck seems to have won Sushil over. "Sir, looks like he wants a lift. It's no big deal. He's the size of a rabbit. And the city's not far."

Pradip glares at Sushil, then turns to Oonga, sizes him up, slides off his seat, stands before the boy, gestures to him to "Aaa," open his mouth. Oonga, suspicious, frees one hand to pluck the pinwheel from between his teeth, and goes "Aaa."

Sushil looks on, puzzled, as Pradip peers into Oonga's gaping mouth, then frisks him from his shoulders down to his crotch. Through it all Oonga doesn't let go of the carrier. His knuckles are turning white with the strain of his grip.

Done with the security check, Pradip nods to the boy. Oonga grins, "Dharti-maa will bless you with a lifetime's supply of mangoes!"

Pradip pretends to whack Oonga, growls, "You keep that mouth of yours shut until we reach Lohabad, okay?" and gestures with his finger on his lips.

Oonga, confused, nods.

Pradip lifts Oonga off the carrier and deposits him on the fuel tank before Sushil. Sushil protests, "Arre, sir? Keep him on the seat, no? How will I see the road with him up here?"

"You wanted him. You keep him," grumbles Pradip. "He's the size of a rabbit, no? Now move it."

As Sushil adjusts Oonga before him, almost regretting this, Oonga grins at him and pokes his pinwheel into a crevice in the handlebar. As they move, the pinwheel starts to spin, and Oonga points to it, looks towards Sushil, is about to say something, when he notices Pradip glaring at him from behind. He shuts up, turns to face the road, and closes his eyes, letting the hot, dusty breeze attack his skin.

Sushil adjusts the left rear-view mirror to catch Pradip leaned over, peering at the boy. "Aren't you a little too paranoid, sir? He's just a little kid," he says, raising his voice over the whipping of the breeze.

"You still haven't figured why Manoranjan doesn't trust that teacher?" asks Pradip, slightly bemused by his subordinate's naiveté.

"All she did was take some kids to a play, sir. She didn't deserve to be treated that way."

"Aha. Milktooth, you wouldn't have spoken to me this way yesterday. What changed?" Pradip smirks. He's enjoying this already.

"It was too much," Sushil clenches his teeth.

"Last night was your first lesson in growing a pair, Milktooth. In a job like the one you've chosen you don't let your heart meddle with your head."

By now, Oonga has turned the right rear-view mirror towards himself and is making faces into it, when Sushil, irritated, whacks Oonga's hand, and adjusts the mirror back to where he needs it. Oonga still tries to sneak a glimpse of himself in the mirror slyly.

Pradip has noticed this. He leans in close to Sushil's ear,

planting his bristly chin on Sushil's left shoulder. "You must have heard of Javed? The jawaan you've replaced?"

Sushil nods.

"He was Manoranjan's right hand. I was his left, until Javed disappeared." Pradip has lowered his voice to a drone of doom.

"H-he di-disappeared?!"

"Yes," drones Pradip, mimicking Sushil. "H-he di-disappeared. No one told you this? Sons-of-rusty-guns! They leave all this dirty work to me. Not that I complain. Breaking bad news is my second favourite gig in this job, after –"

Sushil just looks at Pradip in the rear-view dumbly.

"Go on. I told you what I enjoy the most about this job," Pradip grins.

"Interrogations." Sushil grows sombre.

"Yeah! But don't distract me now. Javed. This was just two weeks ago. Manoranjan, Javed and six other jawaans were returning from the market in a Commander. It got really late so they took the kuchcha road through the jungle. Before you ask me why – the main road – the pukka one – passed too close to a village that we had combed just a couple of nights before that. It would have been foolish to drive past that village in the dark, no?'

"Why?"

"Why? Really, boy? No one tell you about combing ops when they handed you your camouflages?"

"I – no – uh, yes, it's just a search and investigation, no?"

Pradip smiles a helpless smile. *Hey Rama, all this innocence. Wish I still had some of mine. I might have been able to sleep better at night.*

"A combing operation, son, is where we slam a village, burn a few huts, rape some of their women, take all their grain, their cocks and hens and goats, and basically make these tribals piss in their little langots. So that even if there isn't a naxalite in the village, they will never dare to let one in, ever."

Sushil feels the urge to stop the bike, get off it, and walk all the way back to his village and never return, but instead he finds himself helplessly saying, "Are we allowed to do that?" knowing fully well the response he is now going to get.

"I'll ignore that," mumbles Pradip, and fishes out a small packet of paan masala, rips it open, and empties it into his mouth, tossing the empty packet onto the unlittered landscape. He will now need all the help he can get to relieve this newborn cadet of the crushing weight of his conscience.

"So they took the jungle path. The driver was in a hurry to get the fuck off that path and out of the jungle before the sun set. Anyway inside the jungle the sun doesn't need to set for it to grow dark. Those fucking trees are Comrades too. They make it impossible to see. He had the headlights on. Plus these rusty Commanders make enough noise to wake up a dead horse. All that rattling and rumbling. The government might as well give us coffins to travel around in. That jeep was a sitting duck. Everyone's heart was thudding in their fucking ears. When suddenly, eeeeeenn! – the driver slammed the brakes."

And *screech!* Sushil slams his brakes too. So engrossed was he in Pradip's story that he didn't notice this thick herd of cows in the middle of the narrow road. Oonga hops off in a heartbeat, gestures to Sushil that he will take care of this. And he dives into the herd, making clicking sounds with his tongue, patting the cows on their slow-moving behinds, trying to coax them to make way.

In a tone that Sushil could swear was intended to creep him out, Pradip continues, "Everyone froze. Right there, bang in the middle of the jeep's path was a little kid," and Pradip points to Oonga. "A little adivasi kid. The driver leaned out of his window – he was nervous now – he said to the little kid, 'What are you doing in the middle of the road, kid? I could've killed you!' That's when his eyes fell on a basket lying near the kid's feet. It was filled with mahua flowers. They fall off the trees only in the evening, you know?"

Sushil nods, nervous now, gently pushing the bike forward with his feet, through the slowly dispersing herd of cows. They seem reluctant to leave the shade that the trees on either side of the road offer here.

"The driver took the jeep forward inch by inch, hoping the little kid would step aside. But the kid's eyes were on the ground. He was watching the remaining fallen mahua flowers get crushed under the jeep's wheels."

Pradip pauses to spit his paan masala. He knows the impact the pause has on his audience of one. Sushil is staring at Oonga who seems to be whispering something in the last obstinate cow's ear. Oonga catches Sushil looking at him. He calls out, "I'm telling her I'll bring her sweets from Lohabad if she lets us pass!" and he grins. Sushil doesn't understand a word this tribal boy says. But Oonga's mysterious grin runs a cold finger down Sushil's spine. Pradip catches this, pokes Sushil in the ribs, gestures to keep moving. Sushil, hesitant, slowly starts pushing the bike forward again.

"The jeep also moved ahead like this only, slowly," continues Pradip. "When it was two feet from the boy, he stepped aside and allowed the jeep to pass him."

The bike is two feet behind Oonga now, who is bent over, collecting something off the ground.

"The jeep must have gone thirty feet before... BHUMM!"

Sushil gets a start!

Pradip drops his voice to a menacing murmur again, "That's where Manoranjan sahib lost his eardrums. And that's why his blood starts to boil at the mere mention of little adivasi kids. If you ask me I don't think his blood boils as much as it fucking curdles. He's shit scared of little kids like this one here."

And, again, Pradip points to Oonga, who has straightened up and is feeding the pigheaded cow something from the palm of his hand, to get her to step aside.

"But, sir…" Sushil's having trouble adding up the pieces. "How's this the kid's fault?"

"I knew you'd play the defence lawyer again. We all start there when we get our first postings. Then two years in, we all switch sides to prosecutor," Pradip sniggers. *God, how he loves taking a new cadet's emotional virginity!*

"It was a remote bomb blast," he says. "The kind of BHUMM that happens when a button is pressed. The fun part? For it to activate the bomb, this button cannot be more than twenty feet from the bomb."

The last cow has made way. Oonga gestures for Sushil to bring the bike through. Sushil can't decide if he wants to leave this little boy behind or take him along.

"Manoranjan sahib said he was the first to regain consciousness. He saw that little son-of-a-mahua standing right there, staring at them."

Oonga holds his cupped hands up to Pradip and Sushil. In them are some small fragrant flowers. Pradip nonchalantly takes one, as if he was expecting this all along. He pops it in his mouth, and chewing, says, "Mahua. Try one."

Sushil shakes his head, spooked beyond words.

As Oonga clambers back onto the fuel tank, ducking under Sushil's arm, Pradip finishes with a frightening flourish, "Then, even as Manoranjan lay there, covered in blood, watching… that little boy picked up his basket, and slithered away as silently as a snake."

Pradip leans over, digs his fingers into Oonga's cupped hand, plucks another flower from it, and pops it casually into his mouth. Oonga grabs the handlebar and gives it a shake. "Come on! Lets go-o-o-o! We're getting late!"

Sushil kicks the bike awake, and revs it up slowly. He really doesn't want to be here right now. He definitely doesn't want to be steering this bike to where he doesn't want to go right now. He wants to stop under the next big tree, curl up and sink into the soft, moist earth, to never awake into a uniform again. But he knows low-lifes like him aren't allowed to make decisions. The most they are allowed is questions. Like the one that bubbles up inside him and bursts out of his mouth before he can reconsider it –

"Sir? What happened to Javed?"

"Lo!" Pradip slaps his forehead. "In all that drama I forgot about Javed. Miraculously no one died. It was a low intensity blast. As if they intended only to wound and maim. Everyone was covered in blood. You must have seen a set of uniforms drying on that clothesline behind the school library. They dry, they get washed again, and are hung out to dry again. And again. Those blood stains are still not coming off. When all the jawaans finally came to their senses and did a head count, Javed was missing."

"Missing?! How?"

Oonga, suddenly agitated, starts hitting the handlebar now. The bike wobbles. Sushil, rattled, tries to steady it, about to scream at him when he sees Oonga pointing at something in horror – an armless corpse of a tree lying cut by the roadside. Sushil can't help think that the tree looks like it's been murdered. They ride past several such trees – old, big, healthy trees – chopped down in a hurried massacre. Oonga is distraught. He wants to say something, but Pradip's glowering eyes shut him up.

"They checked each and every tree near the site. Sometimes when villagers die inside jungles they turn into ghosts that hang upside down from trees," Pradip says menacingly… and then guffaws, enjoying the evident discomfort he is causing Sushil.

"Javed was a villager only, no? From Chattisgarh. His heart also bled for the adivasis in the beginning. A few long sleepless nights with no food in his belly, and he fell in line," Pradip smirks. Then drops his voice again, and whispers into Sushil's ear, "Like you will too."

"But back to Javed. How much I enjoy distractions!" he sniggers. "They didn't find a single trace of Javed. His gun, his shoes, his cap, everything disappeared with him. That's why we picked up that teacher as soon as we got wind of her."

The graveyard of chopped trees now gives way to viciously dug-up land. Digger trucks stand silently on either side of the road. A valley of fields on either side has been ruptured to make way for something.

Perhaps another road.

Perhaps a railway line.

Perhaps a factory.

Perhaps a canal.

Whichever of those it might be, it will most surely be called 'development', thinks Sushil. *What else can justify the loss of those mighty, benevolent trees?*

I must keep such thoughts to myself, Sushil checks himself. *Too easily such thinking can be misunderstood in these parts as rebellion. And I've been sent here to counter exactly that.*

"So much silent simmering inside you, Milktooth," Pradip punctures Sushil's reverie, staring into his face reflected in the rear-view. "If I didn't know better I might have suspected you to be an informer!" He laughs full and loud, his joggling belly shaking the bike, and Sushil's patience with it.

"What if the teacher turns out to be innocent?" Sushil asks, beyond caring what Pradip might think of him now.

"Innocent?!" asks Pradip, incredulous, as if this question had absolutely no right to be asked. "Innocent? Son, in places like this no one is ever innocent. When bullets fly – bang bang bang – you're either on Our side… or Theirs."

TEN

Red.

It must be the colour of irony.

It's the colour of the rebellion against the tearing up of the earth.

But it's also the colour of the earth when she is torn apart by force to get at what she carries in her womb.

Oonga watches the landscape turn redder and redder as their bike rolls unhappily towards the horizon. A rusty red dust covers the few isolated trees left standing on their solitary mounds. The earth has been eaten away around those mounds, exposing her bleeding red bowels.

The road they are on is half made. The right side – the return side – is still being constructed. It's as if the city wants everyone to come to it, but is averse to letting anyone return.

There are scores of adivasis along the right side of this almost-road. They wear the same langots and sarees as Oonga's people back in Pottacheru. Excited at catching a glimpse of familiarity after the frighteningly alien journey until now, he calls out to them. But is met with stony eyes.

There are no baskets or bamboos or pumpkins here. Instead, these adivasis are carrying large stones on their heads, metal trays of gravel in their arms. Hot tins of melted tar hang from their hands. If you looked closely you could catch the immeasurable weight of despair placed permanently on their shoulders. It is this that is making them stoop.

A truck heaped with rocks creaks and groans off the road up ahead. On its angrily rattling rump is a bloody-tongued contemptuous raakshas. The raakshas licks his way painfully across the remains of what might have once been fertile fields. It might be this act that reddened his tongue. Or it might be his tongue that scraped this land till it bled.

It's hard to tell which.

Pradip starts to cough violently. Oonga adjusts the right rear-view mirror like he had seen Sushil do on the left, and watches Pradip's reflection tie a hanky around his nose. Then looks up from this to see... his giant bidi!

Before his heart leaps out of his chest in joy now, he brings up his arm and holds the map against the passing landscape, comparing the bidi drawn on the inside of his elbow with the humongous one vomiting thick dark smoke into the reddening sky.

Idma, you genius! thinks Oonga, and imagines lifting Idma onto his shoulders and dancing the dhimsa!

Sushil has been noticing the tribal boy doing his curious little private things. He doesn't know what to make of him. *But we're closer to the city of iron and steel now,* he thinks. *Though I wonder what a boy like him needs to do in that city all alone? Something about all this does not add up. Perhaps there's something to Manoranjan sahib's fears, after all?*

Pradip taps his shoulder. "Take us off this road towards that canal there."

As usual Sushil is about to ask why, when Pradip says, "And don't ask why. You'll see."

Sushil shuts his mouth.

Oonga, though, protests. He wants to ask why they're straying from their path, when Pradip glares at him in the rear-view and puts his finger to his handkerchiefed mouth – "And you keep your mouth shut, tyke, or I'll toss you into the red mud pond. You'll find enough of your clan buried beneath it."

Oonga doesn't get a word of that, but the look in Pradip's eyes silences him. Oonga remembers drunk Somaru when he went on a rampage once with his axe, wanting to kill someone who had sold his cow to a shop in the city to be eaten. "The adivasis don't milk or eat their cows!" Somaru had screamed. And his eyes had the same cold and angry look Pradip's have.

Oonga wonders if he should just hop off and run to the city from here. But who knows how far the city is. This motorcycle is the surest way to get to Rama in time.

So Oonga keeps his mouth knotted shut like the small bundle of money at the tip of Oongamma's saree.

It's not hard to do, though, since the air stinks of rotting corpses. The air stings the eyes. And every breath burns the insides of the nose. Oonga coughs. Sushil has slowed down now, unable to manoeuver the bike with one hand, since his other arm is wrapped tight around his nose and mouth.

Pradip orders, "See that stream? Stop there."

Stream? Sushil wants to say. *What stream? A stream has water we drink from. This place is a filthy river of acid.*

Large corroding metal pipes enter the stream from all sides, pouring acrid waste into it. The stream's surface is a reddish-grey foaming layer of scum.

"How long do we have to be here?" asks Sushil, restless.

"As long as it takes me to take a shit," Pradip barks. "All that braking and bumping – my stomach is about to burst now!

You might want to tie a hanky around your nose too. If the toxic air here doesn't kill you my farts definitely will."

|||<•V•>|||

A familiar two-legged signboard stands sentinel over this land too. Above the words 'INDIA ALUMINIUM INC.' the familiar large unblinking Eye seems to have grown a dark circle beneath it. It might be the chemicals in the air that oxidised it, or it might be exhaustion from staring at so much ruin for so long. Sushil is unnerved by it. He is squatted facing the Eye, and the stream of waste that flows thick and listless behind it. Pradip is squatted with his back to Sushil's, facing the other way, at the factory – a behemoth metallic octopus, its many pipe-arms radiating in many directions, taking all the effluents away from its belly, and into the lap of the land.

Pradip's and Sushil's pants are down below their knees.

"What if someone catches us, sir?"

"If an entire factory can shit here all day every day for years, how will four piddly human turds make any difference to them?" Pradip lights a bidi, offers Sushil one. "Two drags and whatever it is you're struggling to push out will tumble out on its own. Try it."

"N-no thank you sir, it must be because I didn't even eat last night."

"You don't eat. You don't drink. You don't smoke. You don't fuck. How did they let a naxalite like you into the force?"

|||<•V•>|||

Oonga has been waiting restlessly near the bike. He can't

understand why these silly shirt-pant folk don't wake up with the sun and do all these necessary things at their necessary times. These two must be from the city. He remembers Hemla didi telling them about how there's light in the cities even at night. And how some people do day things at night and sleep during the day. Oonga didn't understand it then. And he sure as hell doesn't understand it now.

It's also this horrible place. He doesn't like it one bit. The few remaining trees look like their tree-souls have left them. The land looks like a wound. Horrible smelling gassy swirls rise out of the ground in the distance. Grimacing at the stink, he hops on the hot red ground towards the edge of the stream and peeks in. A bloated dead frog covered in blisters floats past. Followed by another.

Oonga turns to the two men in the distance, still squatted, doing their 'business'. He wants to shout to urge them to hurry, but he remembers Pradip's look and decides to wait. He looks up at the sun. The sun doesn't look friendly. It could burn this world with its angry heat.

|||<•V•>|||

"We should have brought some water from the stream," says Sushil, suddenly realising he doesn't know how to clean up now.

"Yes, why not. Burn your ass with that acid so you never need to shit again. You can't be a naxalite. No. If you were, the first thing you'd have noticed is what's being dumped in that stream."

"But doesn't this stream empty into the river?"

"Yes. So?"

"We use the water from the same river near the camp?"

Pradip reaches into his pocket, pulls out an old folded up newspaper. He tears the sheet in two, hands Sushil one half, "Here. Wipe your ass with some news."

Sushil looks at the sheet. It's a full-page advertisement –

INDIA ALUMINIUM INC.

Spreading happiness to every corner of the nation.

Pradip turns, notices Sushil reading his sheet.

"Don't," he says.

"Sorry, sir?"

"Don't think," says Pradip, standing up and pulling his pants up. "Everything gets fucked inside your head when you think. Your ass is all that matters, boy. Clean it. Cover it. Save it. In that order."

And he waddles away, zipping up. "And hurry, I'm hungry now."

It's so easy to tell that you're approaching a town, thinks Sushil, the bike now cruising at a consistent speed. The green and red gives way to brown and grey. The sides of the road – in fact the sides of everything – are lined with plastic garbage. The closer you get, the more the garbage. And the noise. The hum of the breeze is scared of the city. It falls away with the green and the red. It is replaced by engines, and clanging, and horns, and distant TV and radio voices.

If you're travelling at night, the twinkling starts to disappear from the sky, and starts dotting the earth instead. The lights only increase the closer you get to the city. The eyes start to hurt. And all scents and fragrances die. The only smells that you pick up any more are those of diesel and cement and rubber on tar.

Sushil remembers the first time he had gone to the city with his Bapu, to meet the Collector. All the men had gone in a group to plead with him. They did not want to sell their land to the government for the railway lines.

Sushil was the only child on that trip. His Bapu wanted him to see what a city looked like. What Sushil remembers most sharply about that first experience of the city is the noise. The cacophony there can cause a village ear to explode. Quite like Manoranjan sahib's in that bomb blast.

Sushil drops that scalding thought as soon as he picks it up, afraid Pradip might hear it. Thankfully the old lout has dozed off. Thank god they'd found a dhaba soon. Or Pradip would've been growling into Sushil's ear for many more kilometres than Sushil could handle. He can feel his left shoulder wet with Pradip's dribble now. He's afraid of having to brake suddenly. Not because he's afraid Pradip might fall and hurt himself, or even die. But because he's afraid of having to hear him speak any more. *Every word this fellow utters seems to be with the sole intent to mess with me,* thinks Sushil. His eyes fall on the freely spinning pinwheel stuck on the handlebar. The whirring of those leaves brings him some solace. It tells him that the breeze is still with them. It hasn't left their side. Perhaps it is with them still because of this boy? This boy who would rather climb a tree to pluck fruit than eat bread and tea that he offered to buy him.

Sushil tries to get the boy's attention by adjusting the rear-view. But Oonga is anxious. His eyes are red from not blinking. He does not know when the huge wheel will suddenly appear on the horizon. They are moving so fast he's afraid if he blinks he might miss it, like he had almost missed the metal man.

There's so much to see in this world. It's unlike any world he has ever seen. It baffles him though… These tall homes with people standing in windows many feet above the ground… Iron girders sticking out of the earth in large gaping holes… Roads criss-crossing above their heads… So many big cars and jeeps and trucks roaring past them angrily. Why is everyone in such a hurry?

A signboard floats past – 'Lohabad'. It's in Hindi. Oonga cranes his neck around to be able to read it, but it goes past too quickly, and Oonga is a slow reader. Idma would've read that in a flash.

Oonga turns to Sushil, points, asks, "What was written there?"

Sushil says, "Shh. You'll wake him up. You want to pee?"

Oonga looks befuddled. He's not sure if he got a reply to his query.

Sushil is equally befuddled. He's not sure either.

This must be what that teacher meant, about us not being able to speak to each other, thinks Sushil. All such thoughts bring back memories of his farmer Bapu. And it makes Sushil's heart ache a little. He does not like that. He joined the force to forget this ache, not to be reminded of it every day.

The landscape gets busier. Sushil slows down carefully near a highway cigarette shop to ask for directions, in a hushed murmur, to keep Pradip from waking.

Oonga wants to ask the shopkeeper something too, but wonders if he shouldn't. The city looks frightening. Perhaps he should have listened to Idma and waited for Hemla didi to bring him here instead. Everything is so fast and loud and angry and screaming. How will he ever find Rama?

By the time they zig-zag across half of Lohabad looking for their destination, the sun has started skidding out of the forehead of the sky. But it watches down on these three, not taking its singular wide-hot eye off them for a moment. The sun knows something that neither the boy nor the men know – that their destinies are to zig-zag across one another's again. It is not a coincidence that they are riding the same set of wheels with the same purpose today.

The bike slows down, surer of its route now than before, but waylaid by a traffic jam. Sushil honks, waking Pradip, who watches sleepily as Oonga turns, gestures to not worry, he'll take care of this. Oonga leaps off the bike and dives into the snarl, patting cars on their rumps, urging them to move aside and let them pass. Metal doesn't relent quite like cowskin. Despite all of Oonga's tongue-clicking and hurr-hurr and whacking the cars and bikes harder as he squeezes forward, all he gets in return is a string of expletives barked at him in languages he can'tunderstand. *The city is weird,* he thinks, as he stands there in the middle of a hundred honking, impatient vehicles. *I can tell what a cow's moo means, even a bird's chirp. I can tell if they're angry, hungry, happy or playful. But these metal beasts, they all make the same sound, all the time. How is one supposed to understand them? How will they ever understand me?!*

Just then the signal must have switched because all of a sudden the entire flood of metal beasts begins to honk and inch forward. Oonga, panicked, runs in the opposite direction, earning some more curses from the bikes and cars he runs into. Until he reaches his bike and scrambles onto his seat.

Sushil just doesn't know what to think of this crazy little creature any more. He changes gears, when the bike jerks, sputters, and dies.

Pradip snarls, "Weren't you supposed to fill her up before we entered the city?"

Sushil wants to snarl back, say, "Oh I'm sorry, I was too caught up riding AND navigating. Perhaps YOU could have remembered!" But he finds himself silently muttering, "Sorry."

Sushil drags the lifeless, starving bike to the side as Pradip waves aside the furious traffic behind them to give them way.

Oonga, puzzled, stays perched on the fuel tank, his map-arm up and ready, wondering when the giant wheel will present itself.

They turn a corner for a petrol pump – and Oonga squeals!

In the distance, from between two clusters of grey, dilapidated buildings, like a spinning, multicoloured sun rising, appears a giant ferris wheel, turning. Even from here Oonga can hear high-pitched warbling screams. He was expecting to be delighted by the sight. But like all the other landmarks on this map ever since he passed Nagamma, they have first filled him with dread before anything else.

Oonga's sudden fluttering annoys Pradip. "Enough of your eee-ooo-aaa, you little mongrel. Where the fuck do you need to go?" he barks.

Oonga points at the giant wheel, and then at his pinwheel stuck up front, and grins. "I never knew they made these so big in the city!"

He leaps off the bike, waves bye-bye, and tears towards the giant wheel.

"Aye! You left your wheel!" shouts Sushil.

"Let him go. Why are you calling him back? Let's scoot before he changes his mind and reappears!" Pradip grabs the bike handle from Sushil and starts pulling the bike with renewed vigour now.

Sushil can't help himself. He lets loose a sly smile. That little boy has managed what no one ever can – irritate Pradip, the most irritating man in all of the Central Reserve Police Force.

ELEVEN

Oongamma, having been to each and every one of Oonga's favourite spots in the forest, now waddles from door to door, her heavy tummy starting to ache with all this walking. "Did you see Oonga anywhere?" she asks old Timi, whose eyes are knit in concentration as she grinds grain with an ancient pestle in an ancient mortar held snug between her bony, equally ancient legs.

She shakes her head in response, her papery earlobes flapping sadly.

Oongamma takes a deep, worried breath, walks to the next door, and repeats her question, convinced now that this is not how she is going to find her boy this time.

Near the peepal tree sits Idma, her forehead bunched in many little folds of worry. She can't make up her mind. If she tells anyone *now* about the map she drew for Oonga last night, they'll scold her for not telling them this first thing this morning. But if she waits until tomorrow morning, they'll scold her for not telling them today! *What should she do*???!!!

Oongamma has spotted her. Too drained to walk all the way to the peepal, she calls out, "Aye! Idma!"

Idma gasps, startled. There's no running away from this!

"When did you last see Oonga?"

"Uh... La-last ni-night," stutters Idma.

Oongamma looks like she might pass out with anxiety. Idma opens her mouth to say more but Oongamma is already walking away, swaying tiredly on her feet, cradling her enlarged tummy, the combined weight of two souls suddenly too much for her body to bear.

Well at least I didn't lie, thinks Idma. *I'll just wait here until that fool returns. If Hemla didi comes before he does, I'll catch her before she enters the village, and tell her everything.* This plan brings little Idma some comfort, and she sinks herself deeper into the roots of the tree so that no one can see her unless she wishes them to.

|||<•V•>|||

The sun is sinking to where Kunja won't be able to speak to it now. He will not be able to tell how Oonga is any more, until dawn. Kunja was expecting this. But he didn't know it would make him feel this way. He has never allowed his heart to get in the way of these cosmic murmurations. But this Oonga, Kunja sees a shining light in this boy's eyes – and that light makes him fear for the boy, more than he has ever feared for any living thing.

This world made by humans is greedy for light such as this one. It scares people – to see such purity inside another who looks just like them. They try to snuff it out. Kunja fears for Oonga because he knows that the boy does not feel fear. And the light within him will keep him from recognising deceit. And it is deceit that might destroy Oonga. Whose deceit? Kunja does not know. But he curses the Voices for telling him all of this.

He will not be sleeping tonight.

He must watch over the boy.

And so Kunja sets about collecting the things he will need to start the *white* kind of fire. The kind of fire that makes up the sun.

|||<•∨•>|||

The giant wheel is right there – straight as the crow flies – but then Oonga is forced to turn this way and that way when endless walls and these tall-as-trees homes keep appearing in his way. And now – after dodging hundreds of cars and motorcycles and running through all kinds of stinking lanes and clambering over walls and big ugly metal boxes of garbage – Oonga seems to have lost sight of his giant wheel. He could have used the sun to figure which direction to go in, but the sun seems to be leaving for the day too. *What to do?*

Oonga looks around for a tree – any tree – some tree – one tree – that he could climb till the top and spot his giant wheel from. But this city does... not... have... a... single... tree! Oonga is horrified. Everywhere he looks are cars and walls and these frighteningly tall homes that look like they might topple any moment now. He doesn't know how to climb these big scary things. *I'm sure I could have spotted the giant wheel from up on top of any of them,* he thinks.

But then he spots a very tall metal pole right in the centre of where all the roads meet from all four sides. Where this metal pole juts into the sky is a blinking light, which – even as Oonga watches – switches from green to red. And all the cars seem to obey it, and stop. *Perhaps the people here worship this metal tree? Like we worship the banyan? Then they might not mind if I climb it,* thinks Oonga, relieved.

The traffic signal post is hot and slippery. Oonga had made a dash straight for it, startling a few cars and bikes into screeching and bumping into the dividers. He has been climbing it for a couple of minutes now but isn't even halfway up its dull silver body. *My village trees are so happy to have me in their branches, but this one doesn't like being climbed.* He tries reasoning with it. "O city tree, please let me up just this once. I only need to find my giant wheel. And then I will slide down and be gone, forever. I promise. Please?"

Oonga is so engrossed in his quest he hasn't noticed the curious, noisy crowd gathering fast and furiously below, waiting for the traffic policeman to come.

Panting, sweating, Oonga reaches the top, perches carefully on the traffic lights and looks around, and... There it is! – the giant wheel, starting to sparkle with lights coming on one by one, beckoning Oonga with its slow, hypnotic spinning. That taller-than-tall towering stack of homes had obscured it from view. Oonga tries to memorise the direction in which he now needs to fly like an arrow. Then he sucks in a deep breath, and lets himself slide at top speed down the slippery city-tree! He lands with a signature thupp! – just as the traffic havaldaar arrives, whacking his lathi on the ground to disperse the crowd. But Oonga is fast as a deer and wily as a rabbit. His eyes dart about for an opening in the throng. He has done this a thousand times before when playing break-the-circle with his friends back in the village. He is the local champion. No human circle has ever been invented that can hold Oonga inside it. When the havaldaar parts the crowd, Oonga darts through the opening, before the havaldaar can say, "What the –"

Oonga runs... across the road... leaping over potholes... splashing through gutters... fishtailing around turns... keeping his mind focused on the direction he needs to be flying in... until...

He arrives, panting, before a large archway coloured in every bright colour he could never have imagined, and lit with enough bulbs to make it permanently morning in Pottacheru!

This is the city funfair. The huge archway reads 'Lohabad Annual Mela'. At the far end of the field, suspended in mid-air, just like Idma had described it, slowly spins – the giant wheel. There are people sitting in buckets all along the rim of the wheel, being taken up into the air and brought screaming down.

On some other day Oonga might have wondered about that. But right now, having finally reached here, he looks at the map on his arm – and right where his pulse should be, is the final drawing – a small white triangular man holding a miniature bow and arrow in his stick arms. Idma said he would be right here.

A trail of soap bubbles floats past Oonga. He looks at them curiously. He has never seen anything like them before. He tries to touch one, it pops, and disappears. He follows them, spellbound, their occasional popping a sequence of silently whispered city secrets. He catches a glimpse of his face reflected on one, until it too bursts noiselessly. The trail of bubbles ruptures into nothing, one by one, until just one small bubble still floats past a stream of people whose faces Oonga cannot see. His eyes are transfixed on this almost invisible floating ball. He follows it obediently until it too goes 'pop', and leaves Oonga frozen, gaping, awestruck, at what he has been led to –

High above him on bamboo stilts, in large screaming words, a garishly painted poster announces –

SITAHARAN
the taking of Sita
in dance, music and colour.

Below that are ten angry red-faced heads on a single human body. The ten pairs of eyes glare down at Oonga disapprovingly. Oonga doesn't like being looked at this way, so his eyes leave the ten-headed-one, skim over a beautiful woman in a saree who reminds him of Hemla didi – only this woman's skin is too pink to be real – and then his jaw drops an inch and he murmurs, "Ra-ma!"

In the centre of this poster stands a lithe, muscular archer with a garland of white flowers around his neck, the kindness of the ocean in his eyes, with skin as blue as the late morning sky.

"Rama," Oonga repeats, a lump bobbing up into his throat. He cannot believe he has finally made it here. And is standing face to face with the blue warrior king.

A huddle of long-tailed monkeys leap and hop in a circle around Rama. *There are all my monkey friends from Pottacheru, dancing around ME,* thinks Oonga, and sniggers to himself.

Oonga sees a gateway below this poster now. Beyond it is a passage, but it is dark. At the far end of this passage is an electric blue glow. Oonga knows this is Rama beckoning him in. Oonga starts to walk towards it, mesmerised, oblivious to the tightly shut collapsible gate that separates him from Rama. He is nearly upon the gate when serendipitously it is pulled open!

But before Oonga can take a step in, the blue light is eclipsed by dozens and dozens of people, pouring out in an endless river of excited chattering. Oonga gets shoved and jostled, the only one in this exodus trying to go *in*. But he is determined. He slashes about with his arms, pushing and elbowing his way in, past the endless flood of knees and waists and shoes. His feet get trampled on. Handbag after thhaili after handbag slaps into his face. He gets carried backwards more than once. But then fights his way back onto his feet and forges forward. He is a warrior. A blue warrior. He is Rama. And no one can stop Rama from going where Rama wants to go. No one. As the last of the crowd exits, the gate SLAMS shut right in Oonga's face!

"Aye!" shouts Oonga. "I want to go in. I'm here to see Rama!"

A very, very grouchy looking man has now started turning a key into a lock on the gate. He looks at Oonga disinterestedly as he shuts him out.

Oonga knows there's no easy way to do this. These city people are all so unhappy looking. So he turns on his warrior mode. And attacks the gate, trying to pull its bars open to squeeze his skinny self in.

"Hey!" growls Grouchy. "What the hell you doing? It's over."

"I want to –" and Oonga checks himself. No one here will ever understand him, so he says the one word this Grouch will get, "Rama!" and Oonga points inside at the blue – wait, where did the blue glow go? It's all dark inside now!

Oonga panics. *What if Rama is going away?!*

Grouchy gesticulates emphatically. "Today… finished… done…" And he pockets his keys and shuffles off inside, dragging his feet disinterestedly. Until the darkness of the passageway swallows him up.

Oonga's heart is now a thudding, breaking mess.

"Aye! I have come from very very far. Very far. I have come to see Rama. See – ?" He holds up the map on his arm as evidence. "I had to pass all this to get here. Please! Open this! Let me in! I've brought money also! Come on!"

But Oonga is talking to darkness.

He bangs the gate. Then grabs it with both hands and gives it a desperate shake. He bangs it again and again. "Please! Rama! Let me see Rama! Don't go away! I have to see him!"

Oonga wonders if he should... No! There is no other option. He will have to get in somehow. He managed to get this far. He can't let a gate stop him.

So he sucks in a deep breath and tries to squeeze himself through one of the slim gaps in the gate. He gets an arm in... a shoulder... a foot... even one leg... but he's not as tiny as he thought he was. His chest just won't squeeze in no matter how much breath Oonga pushes out of his lungs.

He withdraws from the gap, his shoulder and knees grazed and bleeding now.

But that can't stop him. He looks around. No openings. He looks up. The top of the gate is a foot from the poster. That looks like an opening a little mouse like him can sneak in through. He leaps onto the gate and starts climbing it. The rusty gate rattles with his climbing. Oonga doesn't care. He'll explain himself once he's in. But a loud WHACK! makes Oonga SQUEAL! and topple and tumble in a bruised heap onto the dusty ground. His fingers are stinging. In fact they're starting to swell. He looks up, angry tears refusing to spill out of his eyes. Grouchy glares at him from inside, a long danda in one hand, and a plastic glass of cheap liquor in the other.

"What the hell you trying to do, kid?"

"Rama!"

"He's gone to sleep."

Oonga now holds his hands up to indicate – *Wait… I'll act this out for you.*

And he gestures – *From very very far…*

And then he pretends to run, and keeps running – *I have come… here.*

And he points to the poster and stands like Rama, taking aim with an imaginary bow and arrow – *To see him.*

And then Oonga drops on his hurting knees, joins his palms in prayer – *I beg you to let me in.*

Grouchy looks bored, belches, puts his stick down and gestures carefully – *Come… tomorrow…* He points at the sky – *Daytime.* Then tired of this charade, he empties his glass, growls, "Now fuck off or I'll –" and he picks up the danda again and pretends to charge at Oonga.

To underline the point he's trying to make, he WHACKS the gate with it, hard. The gate rattles.

Oonga takes a step back, confused.

This is not how Rama was supposed to have welcomed him.

TWELVE

This is the time of the evening when Madvi climbs down from his sal tree to make himself his bucket of salfi. Unless he gets a little drunk he has trouble dealing with the world. And the world has been getting harder and harder to deal with ever since Padua disappeared. Today Oongamma didn't allow him to even climb up onto his tree. He's spent all afternoon shaking each and every sal tree in the vicinity, hoping his sulking little Oonga will drop like a coconut out of one of them. Then he can deposit him in his wife's lap and finally climb his tree.

But no such luck.

Oonga, thinks Madvi, *is going to turn out like his mother, not his father.* He is a mind made up of its own little devices. And is unafraid. Both of which Madvi is not. *How did a drunkard's son turn out a woman?* wonders Madvi. *I wish I'd had a mother like my wife. I might have turned out different.*

This thought makes him feel helpless again, and he aches to climb his tree and bring down the pot of sap for his evening drink. With ten gourdfuls of salfi inside him he might start to feel a little less helpless again.

The onset of dusk has made the tall grass impervious to the eye. Madvi sits on his haunches now, fishes out his flints, and starts to strike them. With the third strike a spark springs at the coconut fibre coiled around the end of his stick and sets it ablaze. He stands up again, thrusts this torch into the darkening belly of the sky, and looks at the endless fields of tall grass before him. This might take all night. *You troublesome monkey,* thinks Madvi. *Wait till I get my hands on you.*

But that's easier said than done.

Madvi takes a long, tired breath, plunges into the tall grass, and starts calling out once again, "Oonga?... Aye Oonga?"

The village is swarming with children and women peeking around corners, climbing onto roofs, tunneling through the large community haystack, calling out in a chaotic cacophony of voices, "Oonga...? Oonga?"

But getting no response.

All these desperate voices don't quite carry across the valley and up the hills tonight. The wind continues to be still as death. But a white fire licks the deepening darkness of the clifftop now, till the black of the rocky earth starts to crackle to life in flashes of silver. This tongue of fire coaxes a murmur out of the sullen wind. And then it exhales a long smoky finger into the sky, cajoling the air for the specks of water it keeps hidden in its folds. Kunja watches the fire do this. Reflected in his eyes, this fire is a two-way mirror. He lets its flickers gaze into his soul, so that in return the fire will let him see what he wants of it right now.

Oonga sits crouched by the gate, uncertain of what he should do now. The sky is dark. So it must be night. But the lights of the mela have made it so bright down here that no one would know it's night unless one looks up at the sky to double-check. The lights scare Oonga. They are not natural. Oonga feels worried for these cityfolk. But more than that, right now he feels worried for himself. Where does he wait for Rama? How long does he wait for Rama? Does he even wait for Rama at all? He looks up at his hero in the poster. Rama still smiles that gentle, considerate smile. *But then why can't he see how worried I am?* thinks Oonga. *And how hungry I am?*

From the shadows across the field someone seems to have spotted this little tribal boy. A tall wiry figure – in clothes that smell of yesterday's garbage, and ropes of hair matted with dirt that hang like tentacles about his bony shoulders – watches Oonga curiously.

Oonga gets up, his stomach grumbling. He needs to find something to eat. But in a land with no trees how is one supposed to do that? He walks towards the frightening lights, slowly, sticking tight to the shadows between tents, unwilling to expose himself. *These lights look so angry,* he thinks. *Just like all the city people.*

The man from the shadows watches Oonga crawl like a mouse through the gutters. He seems to know what a mouse like this might want from the look in Oonga's eyes as he scans the stalls. Food. Scared little mice in this city are always looking for food, but too frightened to hop out into the light and take it for themselves. The man from the shadows knows this, because he used to be one too. Until he grew into what he is now.

The fire shows Kunja all this, through the eyes of the man from the shadows who watches Oonga. Those eyes now become Kunja's eyes. Those naked sinewy feet become Kunja's naked sinewy feet. And Kunja trails Oonga now, always from a distance, never interfering, quiet but rapt, sniffing the air for danger like a stray dog would, hoping that little Oonga finds himself some food before the night gets too cold to bear.

|||<·∨·>|||

There is a desperate banging on the gate again. This time its hinges start to rattle too. Grouchy snarls from inside, "Again?! You crazy little piece of shit! Vamoose! Or I'll thrash you till you turn blue like Rama!"

Grouchy is about to take another sip of his cheap alcohol, when… banging again!

Grouchy snorts, drains his glass, pulls himself out of his cot, takes his danda, whacks it on the ground to announce himself, and howls, "You asked for it now! Wait! Wait right there." And he fumbles with the keys trying to find the one for the lock on the gate so he can let himself out and unleash himself on that annoying little viper.

Swaying drunk on his feet, Grouchy stumbles to the gate, and freezes. There's no little boy there. Instead, two grown men. Grouchy sighs. He was so looking forward to thrashing the boy. "It's over today. Come tomorrow."

"Sir?" calls out Sushil. "We need to ask you something."

"Tomorrow, man. Can't you see the lock on that gate?"

"We'll only take a minute."

"To – mo – ro!" Grouchy turns to stumble back in, pauses, turns, "And do – not – bang – on – that – gate – again!"

"Please, sir... " It's Pradip this time, the epitome of civility. "Please, we need some help. And don't know whom to ask. Please?"

Grouchy, grumbling, puts his danda down, and staggers to the gate. "Make it quick."

The moment he reaches the gate, Pradip's hand darts through the gap, grabs the scruff of Grouchy's neck, and SMASHES his face into the gate. Grouchy squeals. Pradip brings his mouth close to Grouchy's ear, and drops his voice to a menacing drone. "I don't take orders, I fucking give them."

Grouchy tries to apologise but only a whimper escapes his mouth.

That's enough bad breath to make Pradip grimace. "What piss have you been drinking?!"

"So-sorry, s-sir!" Grouchy mumbles. "I'll quit!"

"I'm not your mother, shitbreath." Pradip pulls Grouchy's face away from the grill, holds for a moment, and then SMASHES his face into the gate again!

Sushil gasps. He steps away, not wanting to be part of any violence tonight.

"Did some adivasis come to watch this Sitaharan yesterday?" Pradip asks.

"Ad-adivasis?" stutters Grouchy, as if he's never heard the word.

"A teacher and some kids. Tribals."

"Oh! Ye-yes. I gave them the la-last few seats in front. Di-did I do something wrong?"

"Yes. You did. We'll have to shut this show down."

"I-I'm so-sorry sir. I'll never do that ag-again. Please don't shu-shu-shut th-"

Pradip releases his neck, pretends to shush him like a mother would her little one, "Sh... sh... shut it now. I'm kidding."

And he slaps him, hard, sending Grouchy tumbling into the passageway, where he scrambles to his feet, and scurries into the darkness like a nervous cockroach.

Pradip turns to Sushil, watches Sushil glaring at him. "Are you judging me, Milktooth?" smirks Pradip. "You left me with no choice, no? You were too polite. We're police. Not polite. Polite, police; police, polite – these are opposites." And he starts to walk away, searching for something. "Learn to get results, kid," he calls back to Sushil, "or learn to get out of my way. One of the two."

Sushil takes a deep breath, trots up behind Pradip. "So the teacher did bring the kids to the play. Should we report that to Manoranjan sahib?"

"Yes sir," nods Pradip, fishing out a little diary and flipping its pages looking for a number as he walks up to a pay phone kept on a table outside a stall. Sushil did not expect Pradip to agree. He braces himself for another surprise from this most unpredictable beast he has had the misfortune of being sent out on this mission with.

Pradip starts jabbing the buttons on the phone, reading the number from the diary.

"Sir?" Sushil wants to know what's cooking in Pradip's mind when Pradip fishes out a twenty rupee note, points at a food stall in the distance, and gestures for Sushil to go get them something to eat. Sushil is unwilling to leave. Pradip glares at him for a second as the line starts to ring on the other end.

And then he takes a threatening step towards Sushil, shoves the note in his pocket and growls, "GO."

The growl is blood-curdling. Sushil lowers his eyes, obediently turns to leave, having been swiftly shown his place in this scheme of things.

When Sushil returns with a paper plate heaped with oily poori-bhaaji, his eyes search Pradip's face for a clue.

All the years Pradip has spent watching over his shoulder, dodging bullets, has made him reptilian.

Pradip trained himself to not blink much. All deaths by bullet occur when a man blinks.

He grew a thick skin. So that he'd be impermeable to sentiment.

He also grew a layer of oil over that skin. So that he could take the heat. As well as the cold. And most importantly, so he could slip free when caught.

The defining feature of the reptile, Pradip believes, is the face. It is expressionless. You cannot tell if a reptile is angry or impatient or tired or hungry or irritable. The look in its eyes is the same for them all.

Sushil searches for something – even a tiny flicker – that might reveal to him what Pradip just said over the phone, or what he intends, or both.

But the reptile grabs the plate from Sushil's hands, shoves a morsel into his mouth, and in between the noisy slaps of his tongue he tells him, "Sahib says we must investigate this Sitaharan, see what it's really about."

"But the next show is tomorrow! And –"

"And so we get drunk, get laid, get rest. It's been months since I got any of the above."

And Pradip starts waddling away, still eating sloppily. Sushil reluctantly follows, feeling more unsure now than ever before. Of everything. Of this trip. Of this conversation. Of being a soldier in a war that doesn't feel like one. Of this fork-tongued lizard he cannot ever overrule. Of this lizard's unpredictable propensity for violence.

When they reach their bike Pradip holds his hand out for the keys. Sushil silently hands them over. Pradip straddles the bike and frowns. Oonga's pinwheel is still stuck near the rear-view, motionless, having lost its will to spin without the boy. Pradip plucks it out and tosses it away. Sushil watches, lowering his eyes helplessly again. When the bike has thrummed to life, Sushil straddles the back seat slowly, careful to keep a few inches between Pradip and himself, and asks "Where to now, sir?"

"Duty," says Pradip, his mouth still full. "We've been asked to investigate a Sitaharan, and that is exactly what we will do," and he sniggers, bits of bhaaji spraying from his mouth.

THIRTEEN

Oonga's eyes and ears hurt. They hurt so badly that his head spins. And with that his stomach spins. His head and his stomach feel like they're spinning in opposite directions. And so Oonga can't seem to be able to walk straight. He doesn't want to be here. Here, where everything spins. The giant wheel spins downward from high up in the sky. Oonga goes closer to it, hoping he will find something to eat there. Idma had told him there were all kinds of spicy and sweet things to eat right below the giant wheel. But the people sitting in those buckets all along the rim of the wheel are screaming. They scream as they fly up into the sky with the wheel, and then they scream as they come crashing down from the sky. But they still don't let go of the wheel. Oonga goes closer to see if there is food in those buckets all along the wheel. And if the people in those buckets are eating. But how can one eat when one's stomach is spinning?! Oonga notices that the closer he goes the bigger the buckets appear, and they crash down towards him in a blur – *GRRHUPPGRRHUPPGRRHUPPGRRHUPP...!!*

Oonga crouches, throws his hands over his head, worried all those people will rain down on him. Their faces are hard to make out with all these glaring lights. Lights that make angry patterns like Oonga's slashing of chalk on the blackboard. Lights that flick from blue to green to red to yellow to white to blue to green to red to yellow to white without tiring. And in the middle of the mela where the lights are so purple and in such a hurry, Oonga sees strange looking animals dance.

A giant mouse. A small bear. An upright lion. Even a monster-sized black and white bird. And they all dance on two legs like humans. At first, this scares Oonga. But then he sees a huge duck take off his head and there is a man inside it! The man-duck drinks a black liquid from a bottle. *The drink looks like the oil that Ma puts on my head once a week*, thinks Oonga, worried that he might never find something to eat in this crazy place. Which is when his eyes fall on a coconut tree!

Only, this tree is also purple in colour. And many small hot yellow lights snake up and down and around this tree. Oonga squints now to see if there are any coconuts up in its branches. The lights are so blinding that he can't make out. He looks this way and that, and finally peels himself from the barely-shadows and steps out into the dazzling lights to go up to this tree – the only one he has seen up until now in this city. Scared, his heart beating loudly inside his ears, Oonga grasps the tree trunk with both hands, *one... two... three...* and he heaves himself onto the trunk – and YOWLS!

SSSSZZZZZ!

The wiring gives him a crisp shock!

Oonga tumbles onto his back. A uniformed man approaches him now. Oonga scrambles to his feet and prepares himself. He'll have to explain that he wants the coconuts up there, and they should allow him to climb, please. These city people and their rules!

Before the man can even open his mouth, Oonga starts acting out what he intends to do – *I... am hungry... I will climb...*

to get coconuts... break them open... drink them... eat them... but I have to climb... And then like he had done before, he joins his hands in plea. *Please allow me...*

The man doesn't quite get that. He gestures to Oonga – *Go on, scamp, scoot.*

Oonga doesn't lose heart. He steps closer to the tree, points up to its top – *Coconut... coconut... please?*

The man gently shoves Oonga to get a move on. Oonga resists, and without warning lunges for the tree to clamber up quickly again. But the uniformed man grabs at Oonga's legs, and THUMPs him down on his bum.

He lifts Oonga with both hands and carries the shocked boy away. He tosses him like garbage near the fence, taking care to gesticulate as he says, "Don't go climbing things now, okay? Or next time I'll have to toss you outside."

The man walks back to his security guard chair, muttering to himself, "So much for a job in the big city. Protecting fake plastic trees from crazy boys who want to climb them!"

|||<•V•>|||

In between picking up empty plastic bottles off the littered ground, a pair of attentive eyes has been watching all of this. His sack full now, the wiry man squats on his haunches, fishes out a matchbox, strikes a match, and holds it up to his face.

Across the fence from him, Oonga notices the flash of this small flame. *Fire? Here?* he wonders, peering into the darkness to make out the figure that lit it.

The wiry man blows the match out, letting the deep shadows gobble him up again.

Oonga wonders if he should go towards the fire – or away

from it? Perhaps the fire will show him the way to some food? Or perhaps he imagined the fire? What use is fire where there is all this blinding light? Confused, scared, Oonga pushes himself off the ground and walks away from the fire, the stinking shadows, the blinding lights, the deafening noise, the screaming, the spinning, the angry faces, the fake animals, the fake plastic trees, the dizziness, the vomity throbbing in the base of his stomach, the drumming of his frightened heartbeat deep inside his head. The further he walks from all of this the calmer his rapid, raspy breathing gets. And his startled heart starts to unstartle itself and slowly finds its Oonga-rhythm again.

The eyes follow him though, never letting him out of their sight.

Drunk, Pradip misses the glass this time, spilling some of the cheap liquor on Sushil. Sushil leaps out of his chair and starts to dab at the stain with his hanky worriedly. Pradip chuckles, “The smell of orange juice never got a man laid. The smell of booze always did. This might be your lucky night, kid,” and concentrates as he pours himself his fifth large peg, careful not to spill any more outside the glass.

Sushil sits down again, unhappy, shifting his chair another foot away from Pradip. He hates everything about this desi bar. The fetid stench of hooch. The squalid stink of a hundred men huddled in a place meant for thirty. The smoke. It carries the smell of hundreds of rancid dying lungs. And he’s being compelled to allow it entry into his own. What is he even doing here, draped around a glass of sour orange juice, eating stale peanuts when he should be in a cheap dhaba eating some dal and roti and worrying about where to sleep tonight.

He wonders if he should gather some pluck, down his juice, and tell Pradip that he's leaving, and that he'll see him in the morning at the mela. Hell, no, he'll see him back at the camp in the jungle. Better still, he'll see him in some other lifetime. Or not at all, since he's going to go straight back and give up this uniform, and take the first boat out of this godforsaken land, go back to his village and till whatever land is left to till, or just dig himself a small grave and lie down in it till he falls asleep from the acute hunger he is feeling right now. When Pradip derails his train of thought with the one question that Sushil did not ever want to be asked...

"What does your Bapu do?"

It's like this wretched reptile can read minds.

Sushil wants to tell Pradip that his farmer Bapu has been dead two years, that their fields were taken years ago by the government to build railway tracks, so he took a job with the railways, switching tracks, and got crushed by a train one day while crossing the tracks drunk on cheap hooch. But Sushil doesn't feel much like talking about Bapu or farming or death, so he simply says, "Government job... sir."

"O you fortunate son," Pradip exclaims dramatically, drains his glass, reaches for the bottle again. "My old man was a farmer."

This wretched reptile can definitely not read minds after all.

"The Company came for our land," Pradip continues. "They needed it for their factory. But of course," and he scoffs at himself, "what else does a Company do with land? They wouldn't build a school there now, would they?"

And he watches Sushil, waiting for a response. Sushil's not sure he wants to hear the rest of this story. He was so ready to walk away. But Pradip, the snake that he is, is slowly pulling the plug now on all of Sushil's plans. And Sushil, like all good victims of predatory reptiles everywhere, sinks an inch into his chair, allowing the snake to wrap around him and take him on a journey of no return.

"While the other farmers made a killing," the snake continues, "my old man decided to get himself killed. He refused to sell. But he didn't stop there, mind you. He went up to the Company officer, said, 'Officer sahib, you keep saying you're doing all this for development. But then how come I don't feel too developed by it?' "

Pradip wants to laugh now, but can't bring himself to. This is unusual. Sushil watches him raptly now. He misread this. This isn't a snake trying to plump his prey for a kill. This is Pradip's soul slowly drifting up to the surface. From some deep abyss inside of him. This must not happen very often.

Sushil leans forward, he wants to hear all of this. He wants to know that this man is as broken as he himself feels these days. And in that shared brokenness perhaps they might be able to find a way out of here?

"So a few days later the police came. They said they'd received a complaint. We had never seen a policeman at our door before. So smart they looked in their uniforms. Bapu asked the inspector sahib, 'Complaint? For what?' Bapu was an innocent fucking fool... just like you. Sometimes you remind me of him. Which is why I feel like whacking you with a danda. But I feel sorry for you also."

Sushil just gapes now. All this time. And he just didn't know Pradip at all.

"You know what the inspector said? 'You're a threat,' he said. 'A threat to the Company officer sahib's life.' Bapu's eyes went wide and round like yours are right now! 'Threat?! Me?!' he asked. So shocked he was that he might have collapsed right there if I hadn't propped him up from behind. The constable had been turning our hut inside out all this time. Like we do on our combing operations? Exactly like that. I'm sure he pocketed my marbles. I never found them after that day. But he came to the inspector then with our sickle. You know what a sickle is?"

"The curved knife we cut the crop with," **says Sushil, rueing the fact that it hasn't struck Pradip that at this table right now are seated two sons-of-farmers, not one.**

"Yes. That curved knife we cut the crop with. The inspector wrapped our sickle carefully in a hanky, and ordered the constable to arrest Bapu. 'What did I do?!' wailed Bapu, like a little child. 'You have a murder weapon concealed in your house, kaka, and you're asking, what did I do?' the constable said as he tied Bapu's hands."

Pradip drops his gaze for a moment as if in silent acknowledgement of a private despair, and then he looks up again, takes a big gulp of his spirit, continues, "Not only did we lose all our land but thanks to the old dimwit we didn't make a single rupee off it either. You know how old I was then?"

Sushil, unwilling to interrupt, shakes his head ever so slightly.

"Twelve. I was twelve. And at twelve it hit me that a man as big and healthy and strong and brave as my father could also turn into a slobbering, fucked-up mess when face to face with someone in uniform. The Uniform was everything. What the Uniform said, we had to follow. Where the Uniform took us, we had to go. That's when I decided I wanted to get into one as soon as possible. I wasn't going to waste my entire life tilling a field morning to night, only to have it taken away in a heartbeat."

Suddenly this place becomes too hard for Sushil to breathe in.

But Pradip isn't done. "Anyway, the only thing that was to grow on all our lands now… was cars." **And he sniggers, fumbles for the bottle to pour another, but the bottle is now**

empty. Pradip frowns, raises his hand to be counted, looks around, but can't seem to get anyone's attention. "See?" he tells Sushil. "We don't matter. No one will acknowledge my hand until I make a noise." He brings his hand down and starts banging the table with the empty bottle. Sure enough, a bored waiter appears, silently takes the empty bottle to go bring a replacement.

"If I were in uniform now, he'd be standing next to me, filling my glass for me," Pradip says, knocking the table with his forefinger. "I realised that at twelve, boy. That a uniform ensured no one could ever snatch anything from me ever again. If there was any snatching to be done, it would be me doing it, you know?"

Sushil just looks, forgetting to breathe, hordes of thoughts going to war inside his heart and mind right now. Pradip's new bottle arrives, is unscrewed and thumped disinterestedly on their table. Pradip looks at the waiter leave, smiles helplessly to himself, then pours his... seventh? Eighth? Ninth? How does it matter any more.

"Why did you join the force?" he asks Sushil, hoping for a story in return for his.

Sushil is caught offguard, "Job... sir?"

"That's my boy!" grins Pradip. "First sensible thing you've said in two weeks. Job. Job. That's all there is, boy. Job. If you were a farmer now would you be getting paid by the fifth of every month? No. You'd be getting cheated by middlemen and transporters and loan sharks and the monsoons. You'd be getting gangbanged by your destiny. The job is the insurance against that."

And he raises his glass. "A toast to that, my man. One little sip, come on. You just grew up in my eyes."

Sushil shakes his head ever so slightly again, his mind still stuck elsewhere.

"Sir? What happened to your Bapu?"

Pradip smirks. "Same. Job. They made him a watchman at that car factory. Win-win. He gets to stay on his fucking land till he dies. And he gets a salary for that too. The fucker finally got developed!" and Pradip starts laughing.

"Wait, wait, the best part? He's also in uniform! Just like me! Imagine?" And Pradip's belly starts to joggle again as his laughter takes over his whole being.

"You didn't expect this story to end like this, no?" he asks Sushil, enjoying thoroughly the look of stunned shock on his pale face. "I'm in uniform. He's in uniform. You're in uniform. We're all in uniform." Pradip starts chanting, still laughing so hard that tears start to tease out of his eyes.

Sushil just keeps looking at him, unable to laugh or cry, wondering if tonight he should have a glass of hooch too. From the looks of it, it seems to make all this bearable.

And who knows, he might even finally laugh?

FOURTEEN

Oongamma cradles her aching heavy stomach with both hands now as she keeps climbing. The path here is steep. In the pitch darkness it is also treacherous. But Oongamma has climbed this cliff many times before. It's where they always go when they seek answers to questions that even Hemla cannot answer.

Oongamma pauses to take a long breath. It suddenly hits her that she has been panting, her insides twisting in exhaustion now. And one long breath doesn't seem sufficient. *It's hard enough,* she thinks, *to remember to breathe for herself when she is so worried – to remember that for every breath that leaves her, another has to be drawn in to replace it, each time, over and over. But to have to do it for another person simultaneously is much harder.* Her little one has been quiet though. *Perhaps she's out of breath as well.*

She.

Oongamma knows it.

There have been no kicks inside her womb. Only gentle turning.

And when she tires herself out with worry like this she feels no palpitations in her tummy. This infant is already wise. And resilient. And understanding.

And nurturing of her own mother.

Like the jungle. Who nurtures and watches over her Mother Earth.

Oongamma shuts her eyes for a few moments, in silent communion with the unborn little woman inside her, taking some strength, and giving some back.

It is so dark tonight that when Oongamma opens her eyes again she cannot tell if they're open or still shut. She wants her son to come back home. He needs nurturing. All boys do. Boys never really grow into men. In some ways they stay boys all their lives. She cradles her stomach, sucks in a deeper-than-deep breath and starts climbing again.

|||<•V•>|||

The white fire swells a little, its many little fiery tongues flick the thick darkness nervously. Kunja doesn't need to turn around to know that he has company. "Your boy has gone very far away," he says, assured by the fire that the mother has a strong heart and does not need to be shielded from the truth.

Oongamma's legs crumple beneath her. The weight of that knowledge in that moment is a bit much for her. She thumps down to the ground, gently so as not to startle her second child. That she broke her first child's heart has already had enough consequence today.

Kunja waits for her breathing to slow down, fall in time with the tiny breathing of the unruffled being inside her, and then he says the words Oongamma came all this way to hear. "He is safe."

Oongamma's eyes finally well up. "Where has he gone?"

Kunja is silent. Through the fire he smells the oily smoke of the city. Through the fire he hears its deafening noises. Through the fire he sees...

...Metal clanging against metal. Hot oil sputtering in large vessels. Vegetables frying. Noodles being tossed in pans. Bhaaji being smashed on tavas. Onions being chopped. Corn being popped. Candy floss whirring into small garish pink clouds. Coloured syrups being poured on ice. Ice cream being scooped into plastic cups. All in a hurry. Packets being torn open. Chips being crunched. Bread being chewed. Gravy slurped. Juices sucked. By faces. Fat faces. Oily faces. Chewing faces. Sucking faces. Licking faces. Chomping faces. Caked-with-make-up faces. Sucking-in-air-to-calm-the-spice faces. Blowing-on-hot-food-to-cool-it faces. The-ice-was-so-cold-it-shocked-the-tooth faces. And money. Rates on boards. Prices on menu cards. Boxes of money being opened and filled and shut and opened and filled and shut. Notes rustling. Coins jangling. Money for food. Food for money. Made quickly. Bought quickly. Eaten quickly. Heaped plates. Too much to eat. Too hot to swallow. Too spicy to bear. Half-eaten food being tossed away. Dogs and cats and rats and flies and cockroaches. Swarming all over the leftovers.

And standing in a corner, his back pressed into the darkness, looking at this carnival of excess, is Oonga, as repulsed by it all as he is tempted. His stomach groans with hunger. He looks at all the food thrown in a heap. And wonders if he should wrestle the dogs and cats for some of it. But the food looks peculiar – in colours he has never seen before. He's not sure he wants to put any of that into his stomach. But he is so hungry he could eat the earth if he doesn't find anything soon. He dips his hand into his pocket and fishes out his handful of coins. He counts them. Then he peers at the nearest poster and reads the rates. The numbers are all in double digits. And he has but nine coins on him. Either he eats tonight or sees Rama tomorrow. With nine small coins he can't do both. So he buries the coins carefully back deep inside his pocket, despondent, turns away, and – GASPS!

A pile of bananas!

On a cart with large wheels.

He's unsure of what to do. In the forest he could pick a fruit off a tree whenever he was hungry. But city people seem to want money in exchange for everything. He stands there, gawking from a distance, wondering what to do when a little urchin girl quietly melts out of the shadows, tiptoes to the far corner of the cart, gingerly picks up a banana, and dissolves back into the shadows.

What?! Hooray! Oonga is relieved. Thank the forest gods! Fruits are free everywhere!

He floats out of the darkness with abandon, walks up to the cart, and starts to circle it, surveying the bananas for the juiciest one, when he bumps into a pair of stout tree-trunk legs in a lungi. He looks up to see a slit-eyed man – his head tied with a gamchha, a bidi hanging out of one corner of his drooping, bored mouth – looking down at him suspiciously. Oonga raises his hand in a tribal greeting, sidesteps those tree-trunk legs, and carries on with his survey.

He finds it – the juiciest, most luscious yellow banana – ripened just right – nestled amidst its siblings in the most inviting bunch of bananas Oonga might have ever seen. Either that, or Oonga must be hungrier than he has ever been.

Little bombs of saliva exploding inside his mouth, Oonga reaches out for the banana, and in one quick, continuous movement he plucks it, peels it, takes one bite, two, three, and gulps the entire banana down in four. He tosses the peel over his shoulder, and then eyes the next one. He's about to reach out to pluck this one from the bunch too, when the slit-eyed man taps his shoulder and snorts, "That's two rupees, pup."

Two rupees?! For a free banana?! Oonga is horrified. "But that girl took it for free!" He points to the darkness where the little girl had disappeared. The vendor follows Oonga's finger, sees nothing, turns back to him, now very, very suspicious.

Oonga has plucked the second banana, when the vendor grabs his arm. "Are you that little thief I've been losing my bananas to? You have some nerve, walking up like this and eating my bananas in front of my eyes?!"

And without warning he lands Oonga a hard THWACK! on his head.

"Ow!" yelps Oonga. "Okay, okay, I won't eat any more, let me go!"

And he tries to free himself. But the more he wriggles, the tighter the vendor's grasp gets. And THWACK! he lands Oonga another one.

"Wait, tonight I'll hand you to the police only."

His large hand is about to land on Oonga's nut once more when another hand grabs it. These long fingers are strong. "Let him be, I'll pay," the wiry man with ropes for hair says. "Give me five more."

The vendor glowers at the tramp, and then at Oonga. And then backs away from the tramp's stench, barks, "Don't touch them. I'll pluck them for you. That'll be twelve rupees."

Tramp turns to Oonga, and speaks in Kuvi, "You choose the bananas you like. Five of them. Okay?"

Hot tears have sprung into Oonga's eyes now. But Tramp's voice seems to soothe the tears away. Oonga feels them retreat into his eyes, slide down past his mouth and quench his throat. He walks around the cart one more time, his eyes darting back and forth between his foe the vendor, and his friends the bananas. He picks five, hands them to Tramp, who is ready with twelve one-rupee coins that he drops in a tumble onto the cart, looks deep into the vendor's eyes, and says, "Count them."

The vendor takes a deep long drag of his bidi and lets the smoke trail out of his nostrils as he counts the coins, nods and pockets them. His eyes don't leave Oonga. Oonga's don't leave the vendor.

Tramp walks away quietly. Oonga lingers for a moment, confused about what he should do. But Tramp has the bananas, and so Oonga trails after him, keeping safe distance, skeptical of what this new city fellow might have up his sleeve.

But…

Wait…

He spoke in Kuvi!

Oonga scurries up to Tramp, grabs his hand, and forces him to turn. Tramp's face looks familiar. "How do you know Kuvi?" asks Oonga.

Tramp looks at Oonga mysteriously.

That look!

Oonga has seen it before.

But he's never met Tramp before. Then how?!

"He is safe now," says Kunja, his eyes still immersed in the fire.

"When will he return?" asks Oongamma, wondering if she should've asked that, since her last question didn't really get her a reply.

Kunja wants to say so much to this woman now. About how her son coming back to her won't be the end of her worries. About how some of the spirit of the city will now return with him. About how the entire village will pay the price for her boy's strange destiny. About how much he would like to help them through the oncoming storm, but cannot. He wants to say all this now. To her. To someone. Anyone. But the only words that escape his lips are – "When the sun goes down again."

Oongamma gasps in relief. She wants to kiss this holy man's feet now. But she refrains. Kunja does not like any unnecessary show of emotion. He is of the rock. And the rock is steadfast. Oongamma thanks Kunja, hurriedly pushes herself up off the ground, steadies herself, and dives into the darkness to make it back home before the wild dogs take over the jungle night.

|||<·V·>|||

Oonga's finger points up at his blue archer Rama, and then at the map on his arm, ending at the small white tribal drawing of an archer. Having finally found someone who understands him, Oonga is taking no chances. "I travelled from Pottacheru to see Rama. You know how far that is?" he asks Tramp. Tramp nods. He wants to smile, but it's been very very long since he did, and he's not sure which muscles in his face can help him do that.

"And that grumpy man just didn't let me in," Oonga continues.

"He looks just like that –" and Oonga points at Ravana. "But he has only one head, not –" and Oonga peers at the poster closely, counts, re-counts, turns, "ten heads." Oonga gets straight to the point. "I need to go in. I need to see Rama right now. Can you speak to him? Please!"

Tramp gets it. Once, many hungry, filthy years ago, he too had come to this city on a reckless whim, chasing an impossible, bizarre dream. Cities these days show little tribal boys all kinds of dreams. Dreams that start to crumble to little obscure pieces as soon as they start chasing them. The harder they chase, the more the pieces. But what's life without a dream or two, no matter how unreasonable. And this boy's dream seems somewhat reasonable. This boy who has an army of jungle spirits hanging about him. This boy whose soul seems to be as ancient as the mountain this city was carved out of. This boy who shows a jaded tramp cosmic possibilities he had deserted decades ago. This boy who almost made him smile for the first time in a hundred full moons.

Tramp points at the timings written on the poster. "There's a show every afternoon. You'll have to come back tomorrow. They've closed for the night."

Oonga is reluctant to leave. He wonders if he should plant himself right here so that he'd be the first to get in when that grumpy monster opens the gate tomorrow. But then Oonga looks around, and notes that the lights and the noises of the mela seem to be swelling. No! He won't survive the night if he stays here!

He turns to the tramp, but the tramp has disappeared. Oonga panics. He scampers in the direction they came from, and spots the tramp trying to cross the road outside.

Tramp is about to dive into the traffic when a small hand slips into his. He looks down to see Oonga grimacing in the blinding criss-cross of a hundred hurrying headlights. Tramp closes his long strong wiry fingers tight around Oonga's little hand, and gently pulls him – through a sea of honking and blaring and rumbling and screeching – safe to the other side.

|||<•V•>|||

"Dhichhkyaaonw!" Pradip mimics the firing of a gun. "Didn't die? Here... eat some more iron... Dhichhkyaaonw!!"

Pradip staggers through the dimly lit lane, dead drunk, bouncing off the walls in slow motion as he makes yet another point to Sushil. "Everyone... every – one – who does not like national development... note, digging the ground for iron is development, okay?... everyone who does not agree... will have to eat – some – iron!"

And then he mumbles, "It's good for health."

Sushil walks a few paces behind Pradip, pulling their bike along, looking around at this place, uncertain. He's made some bad decisions today. This one might just be the worst of the lot.

"And do you know where all this iron comes from? Hayn?" Pradip asks, building up to some punchline that he alone is going to laugh at, like always. "Do you know? Suseel?"

And he mumbles to himself again, "Suseel. What a name. The – good – boy. He's so fucking good. Good – boy. In the bad – lands."

And he whips around, to face Sushil, "Do you know?"

Sushil shakes his head, again, ever so slightly. But he needn't have. Pradip isn't looking for permission to continue.

"From the farmer's land," Pradip sneers. "They pull the iron out from the farmer's asshole, turn it into bullets, and then blow the farmer's asshole to smithereens with it! Fair trade. Iron goes back to where it comes from." And Pradip starts to guffaw. "Fair – fucking – trade!" He laughs and laughs and laughs, his laughter bouncing off the walls with him, filling up the empty belly of this lane with a creepy sadness that slithers through the gutter, circles Sushil, slinks up his legs, and darts into his heart, giving it a squeeze that makes his head spin.

It's going to be another sleepless night tonight.

FIFTEEN

In the early morning when you look out over the city and the sun is shining across it, the elbows between buildings fill up with both shadow and light. The world looks so full. Like a bowl filling up by bleeding into itself.

If you watch it with rapt attention the light shifts very slowly, being nudged out of its nooks by the shadows, but sliding into those crannies the shadows slid out of. This happens so slowly, it's almost imperceptible – a sleepy, sluggish, cosmic hand slowly painting and repainting the cityscape. If you keep watching it without looking away, in those long minutes, life feels like an eternity.

But if your mind is on something else while you're watching this, the picture changes before you know it. The light slices meaty shadows out of the elbows of buildings. And shadows fall like guillotine blades on the heads of light.

Everything is sharp-edged in the city. And brutal. Even mornings. Tramp has seen thousands of them. He doesn't sleep. And when you don't sleep, you don't wake. Tramp slides from one day through its night into the next day.

He has learnt, then, to stare.

He could tell you things about the light and the shadow and how they both miss the gentle curves of the forest. But you wouldn't have the patience to listen. To listen to that is to stare with your ears. And staring requires a deep, meaningful ignorance of Time.

The adivasis used to have that.

Dreams of the city rob you of that first. The city needs you to be a dedicated slave to Time.

Tramp had turned Slave too.

But then, over the years, he turned into Garbage – the human waste of the city, the debris of unfulfilled dreams. And when he finally recognised himself as Trash, he learnt to stare again. It was when he found himself sleeping on the streets that he finally started to really 'see' the city, 'listen' to it, and found his ragged thoughts falling in sync with the million jagged noises of the city, like the coloured glass shrapnel inside a kaleidoscope.

|||<•V•>|||

Tramp watches Oonga sleep, his little head rising and falling gently pillowed on a stray dog's stomach. Oonga had asked Tramp the dog's name. Tramp had told him, "Dogs don't give themselves names." That's when Oonga had asked Tramp what his name was. And Tramp had finally managed a trace of a smile, and shrugged.

Any other person in Oonga's place would have found that curious, and asked further questions. But Oonga had gone quiet. Perhaps he understood. Perhaps he was just very tired. But he had looked at the dog then, put his head on the dog's stomach and dropped off the edge of sleep. The dog had not moved a muscle.

|||<•V•>|||

Ever since the door with gaudy gold and pink curtains gulped Pradip in late last night, Sushil has been watching... This street, soaked with the smells of all kinds of bodily fluids... The men, all kinds of them, being spat out of their respective gaudy doorways, staggering to work, stumbling home, their souls chewed to the bone... The sun, that has risen as if to admonish all these lurid lights to shut their shameful blinking and go off.

Sushil is waiting for Pradip's doorway to vomit him out. If it doesn't soon Sushil might vomit himself. The now baking morning sun seems incapable of sanitising this street of its decades-old smell of loveless sex and reused rubber. Exposed to the light now, Sushil is being inspected by several pairs of eyes, from behind suspiciously parted curtains, through warily opened windows, from around mossy corners. Sushil's back is aching from the precarious position he's been lying in atop the bike. He had the option of stretching out on the stairs. But the minute he had sat down on the lowest one, two pairs of red rat-eyes popped out of the dark gutters on either side and announced their eagerness to have Sushil surrender to them. Sushil had shot out of the stairway like a pea out of a catapult. And had spent the last few hours precariously perched on the trembling old bike, his feet and hands bundled into him, many inches off the ground where no gutter rat could hopefully reach him.

Pradip calls out just then, "Oi! Suseel!"

Sushil stiffens, swings his legs off the bike, eager to leave.

But – "Go find some chai, no? I'll be down after another quick round. God knows when I'll get any again!" And Pradip's head dissolves back into the window it had suddenly melted out from.

Sushil marvels at his own tolerance. So many times last night he was ready to up and leave, and not look back. Yet here he is this morning, still ready to up and leave, and not look back, and still completely incapable of doing it. He clenches his teeth till his eyes hurt, starts the bike, and goes looking for the chai that his senior officer will need now to fuel up the tank he must have spent all night (and morning) emptying.

The thirsty lizard slurps his chai noisily from the cheap plastic cup. “You had some?” he asks. Sushil shakes his head in the non-committal manner he has come to master over the last twenty-four hours. “Arrey? Why? How can you hit the road without greasing your machine with some chai?” asks Pradip, particularly perplexed.

“I haven’t been able to take a dump yet,” mumbles Sushil, unwilling to have this conversation, but unable to dodge it either.

Pradip sniggers. “Should’ve got your pipes cleaned like I did. You would’ve shat like a king. Don’t stress, you’ll clog your exhaust further. We’ll stop at a dhaba on the way back.”

This startles Sushil. “Back?! What about that Sitaharan?”

“I’m done with mine brother,” Pradip chuckles. “I’ll tell Manoranjan what I did last night. It’ll sound just like what Ravana did, don’t worry.” And Pradip crushes his cup and tosses it recklessly in the middle of the road, waiting for Sushil to straddle the bike and start it.

“Sir,” Sushil protests, his reluctance rapidly growing roots into the ground beneath his feet. “I’m sorry. I’m not going back without watching the play. I would like to give sahib a full report,” and he flinches, expecting – at the very least – a slap right now.

Pradip studies Sushil's face for a long moment, before a most uncharacteristic smile crackles across his scaly face. "Which part of my story last night did this to you boy – turn you into a man?" and he thumps Sushil's back like a proud parent. "Let's go. You allowed me my Sitaharan. I'll let you have yours."

Sushil gapes, bewildered. Pradip did it again – caught him by surprise.

"There's an abandoned mill behind the mela," Pradip adds. "Let's go mark our territory there first."

"Sir?!" Sushil didn't understand.

"You need to shit or no?"

Sushil nods.

He's never encountered someone like Pradip before. There are people you meet in life you learn things from. Well, Pradip is the exact opposite. Sushil can't remember the last time he *unlearned* so many things in the span of a day.

He kicks the bike awake, lets Pradip settle in snugly, and twists the bike's wrist into making it whinny and bolt out of the street.

|||<•V•>|||

Tramp has had to steal after years today.

He has trained his stomach to accept the most uninviting of discarded foods from the garbage heaps he scavenges every day. There is a stoic confidence that it brings. Deep in the recesses of his soul Tramp knows that if the city ever has a meltdown, and supplies start to dwindle, the only beings that can survive the catastrophe will be scavengers like him.

He has the constitution of a dog, the survival instinct of a rat, the careless courage of a crow, and the resolute patience of a cockroach.

The dog, the rat, the crow, the cockroach and the tramp can survive anything. Unlike the citizens of this city. Who sometimes fall to helpless pieces after a few hours of loadshedding. Or an incessant night of rainfall. Or simply a missed meal.

This village boy, though, his blood is clean. To put some stale bread from the trash cans into him first thing on waking might unpleasantly surprise his intestine. This boy's words are the kind spoken by a tongue that has never tasted a drop of preservative. And Tramp would like it to stay that way. So this morning he washes his misgivings down with some of that rusty municipal water and pisses it out in the gutter. Lightened thus, he sneaks behind the coconut truck, and pretends to scavenge through the discarded coconut shells. He slinks two full coconuts into his sack, pausing to knock on them to ensure one is only water, and the other cream. This is to sort the boy out for the day.

But when he reaches his little crumbling cove beneath the eternally shuddering flyover, he realises he doesn't have a knife to slice these coconuts open with. That would entail more thievery for one morning than he likes. So Tramp sits down to think of a way to do this, when Oonga – rattled awake by a speeding truck overhead – scrambles to his feet in mild panic. "It's daylight! Rama! I can't miss him again!"

"You won't," Tramp assures him. "You still have some time."

He places the coconuts before Oonga, asks, "Want?" hoping the little jungle monkey will know how to unlock them.

Sure enough, Oonga – his eyes turning into excited little marbles at the sight of the coconuts – picks one up, shakes it to his ear, puts it down, and looks around, searching for something. He gets up, his pillow – the dog – trailing him, and disappears round the flyover pillar.

Oonga returns a while later with a stone. Tramp watches as Oonga hits the coconut with the stone, repeatedly, hard enough to make it crack little by little, but not too hard, so it won't burst and spill its precious insides onto the tarred road.

Give this boy a few years and he could learn to survive this city too, thinks Tramp.

But is that the best all of us can do?

Survive?

Are we not allowed to become something that's greater than the sum of our surviving parts?

Now, that thought is unwelcome. Tramp does not like such thoughts. He has spent years draining them out of his mind and heart, so he can focus on getting through this life with minimum damage to his soul. So he does now what he often does when plagued by such heartache – he slowly sinks to his haunches, fishes out his matchbox, slips out a few matches, lays them out in a row before himself, picks one up, and strikes it against the side of the box. He holds the miniature roaring flame before his staring eyes, and watches it burn down to his fingertips, which are permanently charcoal-black, from doing this quite often.

He drops the dying match now, picks up the second, repeats the ritual. As long as he keeps gazing into fire, no matter how small or how sulphuric, his soul does not sink into complete darkness. For now, this seems enough.

If the despair becomes too much some day (Tramp hopes it won't) he might set the city ablaze. And himself with it – a sulphuric end to a sulphurous destiny.

Kunja, unslept, seated before his fire still, has been watching Oonga.

The boy has slept.

The boy is unhungry.

The boy will be fine.

But this wood and this sap that he used to light this fire with one day ago – neither contains any – then how, Kunja wonders, can he smell sulphur now?

Oonga drinks his coconut dry, licking the last few drops thirstily. Tramp strikes his fifth match, watches the boy over the flame.

He wishes this boy would stay, but he knows he won't.

The boy's quest has only just begun.

SIXTEEN

The gate is wide open, frozen in a welcoming laugh. The blue glow deep inside its throat has returned. Oonga stares into the tent's mouth, eager to be gobbled up by it. From deep inside its belly float out faint hoots, whistles, claps and an indecipherable excited murmur. Oonga's heart starts doing the dhimsa! He turns to thank Tramp but he's disappeared. Oonga looks this way and that, spins around full circle, even looks up to see if Tramp might have floated up off the ground. But no. Nothing. There isn't a trace of him. He's disappeared as mysteriously as he had appeared.

Some way off, the familiar wiry figure watches Oonga from the shadows where he has now returned. In his hand he holds a ragtag pinwheel made out of bits of old plastic milk packets. Tramp blows on it, and it spins silently. Tramp bunches the ropes of hair atop his head into a tangled bun, and pierces it with the pinwheel – Oonga's parting gift. As he walks away the pinwheel spins like a magical halo – a little wheel of destiny that whirls forest whispers through Tramp's jungle hair.

181] No matter how loud the traffic in this city gets, Tramp can hear those whispers that tell of all the things Tramp could have been but might never be, and all the things little Oonga will now become.

Oonga finds himself floating in through the gate, the magnetic blue of Rama pulling him in. This is the moment he has waited for. He is so close. Another few seconds and he will behold his Rama. All that trouble, all that heartache, all that travel, and he's finally here! Oonga can't control his feet, they're about to start running now, when he finds that he's running in mid-air! He's supposed to be going in, but finds himself being sucked back out! And the back of his neck hurts. It's like a tiger's jaw has grabbed it. And is pulling him… urgently… back… out… of… the… gate… to –

Grouchy.

Red eyes.

Redder mouth.

Reddest fury.

"You? Again?! Trotting in like it's your father's house?" and Grouchy drops Oonga on the ground like an inconvenience.

"Rama costs money," he scowls, spits some paan spittle near Oonga's feet, and points to a board near the entrance that reads –

ENTRY: Rs 10/-

His eyes now fixed firmly on Oonga, Grouchy goes back to his little table and chair outside the gate, where a couple waits to buy their tickets.

As soon as the couple collects, turns to leave, Grouchy beholds – Oonga!

Oonga steps up to the ticket counter, decisively brings up his fist, holds it an inch above the table and unfurls his fingers, letting the coins inside tumble out onto the table. Grouchy waits for the last coin to spin, spiral and clatter to a dead halt, before sweeping them all into his cupped hand, and counting them out, back onto the table, lining them up neatly, before Oonga's triumphant face.

One…

Two, three…

Four…

Four-fifty…

Five…

Six…

Six-fifty…

Seven-fifty…

Eight.

And then he waves Oonga away dismissively, saying, "Read the board again. Ten rupees to enter. You're two short." But seeing Oonga's confused face, he sighs, points at the coins, raises eight fingers – "Eight" – and then points at the board behind him, raises all ten fingers – "Ten."

Oonga doesn't look like he wants to understand any of this. He reaches for the box before Grouchy and plucks a ticket out. That flicks a switch inside the man. He grabs Oonga's hand, whacks him a hard one over the head, plucks his ticket right back, scoops up all the coins, pockets them, and then shoves Oonga, hard.

Oonga staggers back and stumbles in a heap of tangled limbs.

 His eyes sting with hot angry tears. He holds them back in, collects his broken pieces off the ground, picking up his broken heart last, and backs away, watching Grouchy go back to his chair, fish out a cheap magazine and bury his face in it, as if nothing happened right now.

The blue glow seems to have grown since Oonga saw it last. It looks desperate to have Oonga inside! Oonga decides he will have to do this the sly way. If he could steal away from the village, steal onto the top of a jeep, steal across the countryside to get here, he can surely steal into a measly little tent.

But for that he'll need a plan.

And he'll need it fast.

He pretends to walk away, shoulders slouched, as if he has accepted his defeat. He knows Grouchy is watching him over the rim of his magazine. He also knows Grouchy kept his eight rupees. And if Oonga steals in late he will only get to see eight rupees worth of a ten-rupee play. Fair trade! This won't be stealing after all. He's already paid up!

So he turns the corner and disappears from Grouchy's view. He decides to count till ten, giving Grouchy enough time to forget about him. As Oonga crouches behind a large water drum now, obscured from sight, counting, unseen by him Pradip and Sushil walk up to the ticket counter. Grouchy darts out of his chair and salutes Pradip, stepping aside to allow them in. Sushil is fishing out some coins from his pocket to pay for their tickets, when Pradip stops him. "It's the least he can do for us. No?" And he looks sternly at Grouchy, whose spine suddenly finds it can bend over wonderfully well when faced with dire consequences.

Pradip and Sushil walk in through the gate, Grouchy straightens, sighs deeply, and then pulls the gate firmly shut.

No more entries today, he thinks. *I'll let these cops watch this play in peace.*

He starts to rummage his many pockets for a bidi, when Oonga finishes counting "...ten," and pokes his head back out. *Oh no! The gate's shut!* Oonga surveys the battlefield. His determined eyes settle on the little opening above the gate, the one he was trying to climb in through when Grouchy had whacked him yesterday.

|||<•V•>|||

Grouchy tries to light his bidi, but a naughty wind suddenly picks up just then and blows his match out. Grouchy looks at the dead match, surprised, then looks around. The wind died with the match. Puzzled, he strikes another match, and with it – whooo! – a gust of wind blows across the field, puts out the fire, and kicks some dust in Grouchy's eyes. Grouchy grimaces, drops his bidi, starts rubbing his eyes.

Oonga can't believe his luck. His friend the wind has returned just when he needs it the most. Oonga darts across to the gate, is about to rocket in, when Grouchy straightens, blinking frantically. Oonga vanishes into the folds of the large red curtains on either side of the gate.

Grouchy is a little spooked now. He picks up his bidi again, fishes out another match, is about to strike it, when he looks about – up, down, left, right – no trace of wind.

His magazine sits on the table, still, not even the slightest flutter in its pages.

He looks at the curtains behind him.

So motionless, one could think they'd been carved out of rock.

Still, Grouchy is taking no chances. He strikes the match, holds the flame aloft, as if testing the air.

A few seconds pass.

His eyes dart this way and that.

Nothing. Except –

"Sssszzztch!" he squeals. The match burnt down to his fingers.

Oonga, frozen, his breath held, is getting restless. He wants to ask the wind to "Figure this out, fast, come on!" but he knows better now than to order it around. The last time he lost patience with it, it had simply left. Oonga stays quiet, peeking out of the stinky curtain warily, to see Grouchy relax now, pick out another match, strike it, bring it up to the tip of his bidi when – WHOOOOSHHH!! – the wind blows the match out, and rocks Grouchy right off his chair!

Grouchy scrambles to his feet, and scampers in panic to the far corner behind the tent, tripping over ropes, unable to see clearly with all that dust in his eyes. He tries to rub his eyes but yelps in pain. He will have to wash them. But how does he get to any water with his eyes shut?!

Just then a strange unseen shape starts to slither up the insides of the curtains, to the top of the gate, where Oonga reveals himself, leaps down into the passage, and scurries in at top speed… just as the wind outside silences itself to a dead hush.

Grouchy, blinking desperately, peeks from around the corner of the tent. His face is white. What is going on? Who could it be? The only faces he sees now are the ten angry ones looking straight down at him from the poster. From deep inside the tent, a voice floats out, "His name was Ravana. And he too had wanted to marry Sita at her swayamvara. But who wouldn't get alarmed at the thought of having to kiss ten faces each morning and having ten voices say 'Good morning' in chorus!"

Another voice sniggers uncontrollably at that, and adds, "So she chose Rama?"

SEVENTEEN

"Yes," the first voice continues, "the son of the king of the forest."

Oonga feels his way into the tent in the dark. Over the tops of dozens of heads he sees a stage, and on it – two monkeys, one old and grey, and the other younger and green, talking. The young monkey moves about the stage, friskily, impatient to get the story started. The older one has much to say yet, and watches his ward disapprovingly. "Chhotu, the Ramayana is so long, if we keep going like this, I'll grow much older by the time this show even begins."

"Kaka, you're already so old, it'll be hard to tell," Chhotu jibes, sniggering, and encourages the audience to laugh too. "Somebody tell him that monkeys that grow too old turn into humans, isn't that right?"

"Let's stick with the story, Chhotu. You have the attention span of a fish." And Kaka turns to the audience. "Please ignore this fellow. His tongue is longer than his tail. If you let him lash it about too much, we'll all forget why we're here!"

Oonga has been gaping, his lower jaw come loose from his face. He has never seen anything like this – the colours, the dazzle, the shining baubles, the pretty paper trees, the paper clouds, exactly like the ones Hemla didi draws on the blackboard when she tells the class a story. All those stories he has heard until now look like they've come alive all at once on this stage before him today.

He quickly drops down on all fours and sneakily scurries along the aisle like a mouse, brushing past dozens of legs, ducking under some, until he reaches the stage, right beneath the monkeys' snouts!

Three rows behind Oonga, on the cornermost bench, sit Pradip and Sushil. But neither can see the other in the rapt darkness that has engulfed the audience. While Sushil hangs onto every word being said on stage, Pradip's eyes have started to droop, and he sinks into the wall, ready to put his lights out any moment now.

"So see, basically, Rama and Sita got married, and Ravana was upset – but naturally. Rama took his Sita to her new life in his forest kingdom," Kaka continues.

"So see," Chhotu apes his Kaka. "Bay-sick-ull-lee, why are you so booorr-ring?" And Chhotu shakes himself all over in exasperation. "This is the theatre, Kaka! Where are your theaatttriccckkssss?!"

He leaps to the side of the stage, announces, "Now watch this!" And he wails dramatically, "Raaaavannnnaa was fyooorrriussss!"

The lights dim.

A towering man clad in shiny black metal from head to feet stomps slowly onto the centre of the stage. He snorts in anger, and smoke rises from his body. One by one by one, more heads slide out from behind the one, until there are ten heads and twenty arms flailing in rage now.

An ominous red light starts to slowly reveal him from the front.

His ten faces... are featureless! Save for ten pairs of blazing, wrathful ember eyes.

And even as Oonga watches, his heart gripped with dread, from Ravana's ten pairs of unfurling hands emerge not fingers, but – snikt! snikt! snikt! snikt! snikt! snikt! snikt! snikt! snikt! snikt! – a hundred knives!

This industrial Ravana is a war machine!

"Rrrraaaavannaa rrroaaarrred in anggerrrr... He warrrrnned the world that he would have his Siiitaaaa one way orrr anotherrrr!" announces Chhotu, dramatically, overcompensating just a wee bit for his oh-so-matter-of-fact Kaka.

"Annndd heeerrrre is where we begin this terrrrrrrific tale... the story of SIIITAAAAHARRRRRRAANNNN!"

And the audience explodes in excited clapping. Oonga looks around at the people in wonder. *This is how stories are told in the city? Look how excited they all are*, he thinks. *I'm going to go back home and do exactly this! And they will all clap like this for me!*

|||<·∵·>|||

The lights switch suddenly.

Ravana disappears.

Chhotu bounds to the centre of the stage, grabs Kaka's long tail, gives it a patronising shake, and says, "See, old monkey? Now that's how it's done."

Kaka frees his tail from Chhotu's hand, turns to the audience. "But Rama doesn't like drama. The prince of the forest people carries the ancient wisdom of the blue skies mapped on his skin. He sees through frivolity." And Kaka darts Chhotu a disapproving scowl. "He seeks patience, and understanding, and peace. And if you're telling his story, he would like it to be straight-up, no frills, you know?"

Chhotu raises his eyebrows, yawns, and pretends to nod off, as Kaka ignores him and continues, "Rama returned to his kingdom now with his new bride."

Once again the stage goes dark.

The sounds of a forest bleed out of the darkness.

A round golden sun rises at the back of the stage. And with it, paper birds chirp, cardboard trees sway, a white fabric stream murmurs, and magically from out of the blue of the backdrop sky emerges a graceful, lithe figure, as if sculpted out from the sky itself. He is wrapped in only a langot, a bow slung on one shoulder, and a quiver of wooden arrows across the other.

Oonga forgets to breathe.

Rama is a blue... adivasi!

This must be why Hemla didi brought them to this play.

Oonga wants to grow up to be Rama. Actually, no! He wants to be Rama right now! Back in the village, he too wears the same langot. And he has the same bow and arrows. He wants to turn blue... right away!

Unable to contain himself, Oonga squeals, "RAMA!"

"Shh, oi!" someone scolds him.

Oonga reins in his eagerness and sinks to his haunches again. He can't have himself thrown out, not now. He's only just met his Rama.

Rama reaches a hut, as Kaka continues, "The forest welcomed Sita as one of its own. She was the daughter of Bhoomi. Her skin was earth. Her hair, a river."

Magically, Sita emerges from the brown of the thatched hut,

as if moulded from the same mud, wrapped in a stream of flowing white.

Rama and she start to dance in cosmic union to the tak-a-dham-mridangam-tabla-tabla-tabla-taal of love, drenching the forest with the pitter-patter of their prancing feet.

Oonga's eyes are growing wider and wider. Rama and Sita… are dancing… the dhimsa!

His heart is filling to the brim. This – right here before him – is *his* story! This forest is *his* home! And Sita looks so much like Hemla didi! He is so happy right now that he forgives Hemla didi for everything.

Rama is forgiving, he tells Hemla didi inside his head, *and Rama likes you a lot. He's going to be returning soon, to dance the dhimsa with you. Okay?*

|||<•V•>|||

The drums climb to a crescendo, as Rama and Sita and the forest and the earth and the sky and the river and the deer and the birds all dance with one another, becoming one euphoric, joyous tangle of love.

Chhotu pipes in, "But does happiness like this ever last?"

Kaka glares at him. "The only drama you ever have is bad news, you black-tongued monkey?"

Chhotu grins a wide, fake grin. "Humans pay good money to hear bad news these days, Kaka. Ask these people." And he turns to the audience. "When was the last time any of you read any good news in the newspaper headlines? Or heard any on TV?"

Pin. Drop. Silence.

Oonga, though, can't get a word of what Chhotu says.

191] Chhotu is starting to irritate Oonga. Either he brings Ravana each time he opens his mouth or he brings darkness upon Rama. *Shoo! You stupid monkey!*

Chhotu looks at Kaka triumphant, "See? They can't even remember. Now would a monkey ever pay money to have his mind shat on for him?"

Kaka snaps, "Aye! Filthy monkey. Go wash your potty mouth."

Titters run through the audience.

Sushil has been affected by what Chhotu just said, though. The joke is on us, he thinks, but no one here seems to be worried by it. That monkey has a point. Monkeys always have a point. Chhotu reminds Sushil of the little one to whom they gave a ride to this city yesterday. He too leapt and scampered and muttered like a monkey. That memory brings a hint of a smile to Sushil's face.

Kaka though, continues. "One day Rama had to go hunt for food. As he left, he told Sita –"

Rama takes Sita in his arms, and urges, "Be careful Sita. The forest will watch over you. But the forest has a weakness. She is too benevolent. And her benevolence is misused by those who don't know her intimately enough. We too take from her. But we do not take more than we need. And we give back as well. There are those who pass through, and take much more than they need. They leave our forest wounded. Be careful of them, Sita. You are of this forest now. And you too are benevolent. I fear for you."

Sita cradles her Rama's face and assures him, "As long as my feet can feel the earth I will be fine. Rama, my king, go."

"As soon as Rama left, a small spark ignited between two rocks at the rim of the forest," recounts Kaka, solemnly. "It started a small forest fire... "

"Which hissed and snaked and zig-zagged through the dry grass," continued Chhotu, "raising a smoke trail that climbed into the sky like a serpent so high... "

"That in his distant empire across an oily sea of fire, Ravana saw it, and hissed back... "

"Sssssssiiiiitaaaaaaaah! I offered you a shining bright future. And luxury. And pleasure. And speed. And power. But you sssssspurrrrrned it all for a life of leaves and wood and seed and mud?!" Ravana's metallic voice echoed off the distant mountain tops and rang like harsh bells through the descending night.

"I will have you," Ravana announces, as he enters. "I am Might. I am a blinding light even in the darkest night." And beacons of light spring out of Ravana's body every which way, like ramrod tentacles, slicing through the darkness of the entire tent, blinding Oonga, who frowns, and clenches his teeth. He doesn't like these lights in the city. He most definitely doesn't like this Ravana!

Sita sleeps now in the quiet dark womb of her hut.

Slowly the hut is lifted off the ground from around her, exposing her to the darkness that engulfs the forest now.

A ten-headed, twenty-armed shadow falls across her.

That single figure splits into ten ghost-like looming human figures that circle her in a hideous, demonic, lustful dance.

The music now is metallic, raspy, with industrial clanging and the whirring of engines.

Sita sleeps through it all, drugged by dreams of love.

The ten pairs of arms lift Sita off the ground, waking her, and she screams, "RAMA!" Her feet disconnected from the earth now, Sita thrashes helplessly. Ravana ties Sita in a tentacled embrace, fires up his engines, and storms away with her.

Oonga springs to his feet. His heart throbs inside his mouth. It feels like Sita called out to him to save her. Should he do something? Should he go after this Ravana? But thapakk! – an invisible hand whacks him on his butt, and a low voice growls, "Sit down, kid, we can't see!" Oonga's heart leaps out of his mouth, and he sits down again, confused.

The music builds like a ravaging storm.

As Ravana carries their beloved Sita away, the forest tries to stop him. Trees reach out for his stampeding feet with their branches. His blade-fingers slash them to bits. Birds flap frantically in his face hoping to make him drop Sita to the earth which lies ready to carpet her daughter safely into its womb in a trice. Hot red embers bullet out of Ravana's eyes, turning each bird into a heap of helpless ash. Flowers sprout from the ground in Ravana's path, entreating him to leave the daughter of the earth be. Ravana stamps them out, sending clanking tremors through the forest floor. Oonga claps his hands over his vibrating ears.

All this is too much for his forest ears.

Too much.

"Ravana sizzles, and blasts off like a rocket into the pitch-black sky…"

"…Leaving the forest a wasteland of craters," finishes Kaka sadly. "High up in a quivering tree a shocked monkey gasped at all this destruction."

"Were you that monkey, Kaka?!" Chhotu is incredulous. "Is that how you know all this?"

"Does it matter, Chhotu?" Kaka looks at him admonishingly.

"Look around you. The forest is burning. The land is ravaged. The colour has been crushed out of the flowers. The trees tremble. The birds are feathers and bones. In an instant our world has gone from the brightest spring to the darkest apocalypse. How does it matter who saw this? The only thing that matters is... that this monkey... saw something else as well... "

|||<•V•>|||

Rama, a bundle beneath his arm, is returning on a trot, eager to get home to his love. His gait slows when he sees the devastation. The music now is the sound of a hundred sinking hearts. The trail of ruin leads in the direction Rama feared it would. He drops his bundle, races into the jungle, calling out, "Sita! Sita!"

His hut is in smithereens.

A blot of shame has eclipsed the sun.

Rama drops down on his hands and knees, puts his ear to the ground and asks, "Bhoomi, O Bhoomi, tell me what happened!"

But the earth is still. Her heart has seized.

Rama scrambles from one limbless tree to another, imploring, "Trees, O trees, tell me what did this!"

But the trees choke. Their voices are a low hum of mourning.

Chhotu pipes in, "But Kaka, where did that monkey go?"

Kaka rolls his beady old eyes, "This new generation has no patience. You wanted drama. You're getting some now. Do you have to ruin it?"

And shaking his head, Kaka turns to the wings of the stage – and disappears.

"Hayn?!" Chhotu, puzzled, follows him. "Kaka? Where did you go?"

Where Rama stands now, forlorn, his head hung, a monkey-sound rolls down from the broken tree-tops.

"Ulululululululu…"

Rama stiffens, looks up, to see a monkey, pointing to the south. Wait!

This is no ordinary monkey.

This indeed is Kaka! Many years younger, green of skin, and bristling with grit.

Rama nods, follows the monkey's pointing finger. Young Kaka leaps from treetop to treetop, as Rama follows him on foot below, until they reach the rim of the forest where the fire had begun. Beyond this is a rocky wasteland. Rama looks up into the treetops but Young Kaka has disappeared. When suddenly –

THWUPP! Young Kaka drops down before Rama, says something urgently in monkey sounds and gestures, takes Rama's hand and pulls him gently into the rocky wasteland, where –

On the barren grey ground lies one solitary wilted white flower.

"Sita!" exclaims Rama, drops down on his knees, lifts the flower with revering hands and puts it to his forehead. This flower was in Sita's hair.

Young Kaka is quiet. He watches, allowing Rama his moment of grief. And then he says something urgently again, takes Rama's hand, and gently pulls him to the next bauble – a large maroon bead.

Tears spring into Rama's eyes. This too was Sita's. On her

wrist. And when Rama looks up to where Young Kaka is pointing next he sees an endless trail of bits and pieces of Sita's adornments, dropped like milestones for Rama to follow.

Even at her most terrified, Sita had the presence of mind to leave Rama traces to herself.

Oonga can't quite sit still any longer. "Go go go, Rama, go. Get Sita back. If you won't then I will. Don't take so long. Go!"

Oonga hasn't realised it but he's been muttering loudly enough to earn him another "Shut up, oi! Or I'll break your mouth".

Oonga shuts up, but turns to the dark faces behind him, gnashes his teeth and SNARLS!

Silence.

Then he turns back to the stage where Rama and his monkey lieutenant have started to collect Sita's jewellery one by one as they chart their trail towards her… and Ravana.

EIGHTEEN

Two cautious feet stop near a bicycle lying in a ditch. On these feet are dusty sandals so worn out that they have been held together with coarse string and tape. The ditch runs by the side of a tarred road. The road is familiar. It has seen violence. This ink black ribbon that unfurls into the horizon is a permanent testament to a history of violence. All roads must be. If some life-giving green is not beheaded, if some bountiful brown is not wounded, if some of the blue that we breathe is not infected by fuming black, it's impossible to birth a road.

The two cautious feet know that. They belong to Linga, who scans the horizon before crawling into the ditch and heaving the cycle out. He's dressed like a villager. From a distance it's impossible to detect the history of violence he too carries within him. But if you look closely, into his eyes, you can tell that he carries not just his own wounds, but those of the green, the brown and the blue. He speaks for them, since they don't speak in tongues that most humans can follow. But Linga gave up on words a long time ago. Instead, he taught himself to speak in fire. *Fire,* feels Linga, *gets a lot of things done.*

Linga sees jeep tracks in the dirt. The dirt from its tyres has traced the jeep's tracks on the road as well. Linga knows the kind of jeep this must have been. And he knows where these tracks will lead him. He checks the cycle's tyres. They're taut. They must have been filled just yesterday. The teacher must have planned a long trip on them – a trip she never got to take.

Linga climbs on, and starts to pedal along the jeep's tracks. *It wasn't enough that the teacher didn't listen to Amma,* Linga thinks. *If she's gone and said a word about them to the soldiers he will kill her before they do, Amma be damned.*

|||<•V•>|||

A farmer with a large upturned empty cane basket dangling off his forehead onto his back limps tiredly past the Birsa Munda Ashram School. The basket hung thus hoods his face. It isn't too often that someone without uniform walks past these gates. Anxious eyes from the watchtower glue themselves to this figure. A soldier peels himself from behind the wall of sandbags, climbs over onto the dirt path, and calls out, "Aye! You! Why you here?" He gesticulates as much of his query as he can, aware that locals in these parts don't quite understand Hindi.

The farmer turns, the basket's shadows making his face indecipherable. "Going to the river, sir," he calls out, and then mimes 'water'.

"Go by the road. This is off limits."

"It's a short cut, sir. And I got bitten by a snake. Can't walk on the road," the farmer points at a messily tied bandage on his shin. Unwilling to engage in further conversation, he keeps walking.

The soldier's not sure what he should do. He calls out to the watchtower, "He's going to the river. Keep an eye on him."

The farmer's shadowed eyes dart from the sentry to the walls. Linga has mastered the art of subterfuge. It's what keeps him alive. He learnt very early in life that all truth and all deceit sit firmly by the windows of our eyes. If you teach yourself to look into eyes and read them, no enemy can outmanoeuvre you, ever. But it's imperative you not allow them access to your own.

In war, your eyes must be your biggest secret.

Linga keeps his pace slow as his shadowed eyes scan the barricades.

He knows the CRPF in these parts don't get as many supplies as they would like. All the barbed wire and sandbags and corrugated sheet fencing they received in rations must be up here in the front. They cannot have got enough to cover their behinds with it too.

As Linga passes the last of the sandbags and turns down another dirt path around a massive pile of cruelly chopped trees, he smirks. He was right. The System is so predictable. The same things that make you want to cry make you want to laugh your head off as well.

When he is out of sight of the two watchtowers in the front, Linga melts into a patch of leafy darkness, ditches the basket, slips a camouflage print CRPF cap out of his pocket, and puts it on. It fits perfectly. If Laxmi hadn't stopped him he would've stolen the dead jawaan's shoes and shirt as well. He was the same size as him.

Linga takes a deep breath, and plunges into the undergrowth to crawl closer to the school's back gate. A gap between the steel sheets is all he needs to be able to scan the compound.

He settles himself into the shrubbery near a small opening, peeks in, sees food being cooked, uniforms being washed, rifles being oiled. If he didn't despise the soldiers so much he would've admitted that all this makes it appear exactly like a naxalite camp.

The soldiers on both sides of a war get hungry, need to wash their clothes and oil their rifles.

Bullets make the same kind of holes in both.

The colour of the blood spilt is the same.

But these bastards do it for a salary, thinks Linga, trying to shake off that feeling of pointlessness that creeps up on him sometimes.

The pointlessness of this anger.

Of this fear.

Of this constant need to make someone pay for what he lost.

The pointlessness of this desperate need for justice. A justice that he is not even sure they might ever get.

Linga averts his eyes for a moment. He tries to breathe, slowly. To shake off these feelings. So he can focus on the job he has come here to do. He has seen too many of his Comrades lose their lives in a crossfire because they had that one fleeting moment where pointlessness gripped their hearts.

Linga hates pointlessness. If there isn't a point to the battle it becomes impossible to fight it.

And fight it he must.

He takes a deep breath, and creeps closer.

But this deep breath brings with it a dull smell. Of shit. He looks down. His feet are suddenly starting to sink… in not mud, but shit. Human shit. No wonder this stretch is unmanned. It's their sewage canal!

 He was so focused on what he was looking for that he didn't notice what was right before him. The stench suddenly grows, becomes unbearable.

And the anger returns.

Linga's eyes flash fury. The stink is fuming up his brain. If he had a gun right now he would have charged in and killed all of them. And smeared each of them in their own excrement, impaled their bowels with their bayonets, and created an artwork of human corpses and shit that the System would never forget.

But thankfully, just then Linga spies a classroom door open into the courtyard. And a jawaan steps in with a plate of food. He seems to say something to someone inside and drops the plate of food on the floor. Linga strains his eyes to see who is inside. The classroom is dark. And all this sun out here makes it impossible for the eye to adjust to darkness this suddenly. The jawaan steps out now, and in the brief moment when he turns to shut the door again Linga spots her – Hemla – lying face down on the floor, her body almost bare, bits of her saree having been torn off her, her wrists and ankles tied. The plate of food has been placed before her mouth. The door shuts. And is locked again.

Linga has never liked the teacher. He has wished all sorts of vile things upon her. But this – what he just saw – is too much. *They expect her to eat that food like a dog lapping it off the floor with her tongue.* As much as he disagrees with her, no adivasi should ever be treated this way.

He will kill them all.

But he cannot do it alone.

Neither can their ragtag group of women and kids.

They will need help.

Laxmi sits on her tired haunches by the edge of the river, trying to catch some wireless frequency with a walkie-talkie. This came off the belt of the soldier they killed. Every shred that comes off a dead soldier is ammunition in this war. If she manages to catch the right channel on this walkie she might be able to listen in on some or the other official conversation. And who knows what that conversation might reveal about the CRPF troops in this jungle. The CRPF, unlike the army, aren't very well trained. No one ever teaches them to speak in code so cryptic that the rebels cannot decode. And Laxmi has spent the better part of her naxalite years decoding.

Communication is key.

Communication can prevent war. And it can provoke it too.

Laxmi was taught to decode the elements by her father who was the medicine man in their village three hundred kilometres south of here.

It is said that a man cannot bequeath such secrets to a girl. But her father was a special man. He had renounced his masculinity when she was born. And spent the rest of his life genderless.

In general, humankind has trouble accepting such thought. But her tribe didn't question it. Gender is elemental. And like all elements, it too can shift shapes with alchemy. Her father became her mother some days. And on some new moon nights he was both. That taught her to wear her own womanhood lightly. She can be a sister to an equal, a brother too if necessary, and a father to this family she has cobbled together for this war.

What she can never be, though, is a mother.

For that her womb would have had to be nourished to nurture.

And her breasts are incapable of feeding.

Laxmi has forgotten she even has breasts.

Her father taught her so well that she had managed to decode the algorithm of procreation. When that alchemy first revealed itself to her, she remembers feeling repulsed by it. What use bringing another soul into this world when we are so incapable of cherishing what we have?

Decoding is now second nature to Laxmi. She hopes this walkie will catch something soon. But her thoughts are interrupted by Linga. One look at him and she knows what he may have seen.

His legs are covered in shit up till the knees. She can smell it from here.

His hands are clasped around the handlebar of Hemla's bruised cycle.

He is bathed in sweat from frantic speeding.

And his eyes are conflicted.

This is new.

In the few months she has known her young, decisively cold-blooded lieutenant, if there's one thing he has never been, it is 'conflicted'.

Laxmi rises to her feet as Linga gasps, "Amma, the CRPF have Hemla."

Laxmi's eyes are brimming with questions about the teacher. Linga doesn't know how to answer them. He lowers his eyes. Laxmi doesn't want to, but she feels the stirrings of emotion. The teacher is a special woman. She was conceived of some alchemy of grace. And grace is this war's foremost collateral.

Of all the things Laxmi dreads, the news Linga carries she has dreaded the most.

Laxmi switches off the walkie, and in a voice drained of emotion she tells Linga, "Clean up, then round up the others. We're going to Pottacheru."

NINETEEN

"The land is parched for a single drop of rain," Kaka sings mournfully.

"The trees may never sprout flowers again," Chhotu joins in.

"The forehead of the sky misses her bindi – the sun… "

"The river runs riot, her tresses undone… "

"The elements mourn Sita's sorrow. Ravana has ensured her feet come nowhere close to her mother, Bhoomi, so Sita will stay in an eternal state of powerlessness… "

"Unless she gives herself to Ravana."

Many feet above the ground, buoyed by a cloud of dark smoke, is a cage whose bars are hot fingers of red light. Sita sits hostage inside, wilting, small black holes where her eyes ought to be. The walls and floor of this metal chamber vibrate louder and louder now as Ravana's stomping feet approach.

Ravana stops before Sita. His ten heads and twenty arms disengage. And ten Ravanas start to circle Sita's cage, growling. Ten pairs of sweltering red eyes glower at her now from all sides.

Ten Ravanas growl in succession:

"Rama's.

"Skin.

"Has.

"Singed.

"To black.

"Making.

"His way.

"Across.

"My sea.

"Of fire!"

The voices echo off the metal walls all around her, till those frightful words clang back and forth and back and forth and fill up the chamber with a deafeningly manic metallic wailing.

As the wailing starts to drop, Ravana 1 growls, "He approaches because I…"

"Have allowed him to," roars Ravana 4.

Ravana 6 bellows, "Be mine."

"Now," snarls Ravana 9.

"Or I will bring you his head…"

"And his arms…"

"And his legs…"

"And all his other pieces…"

"Ssseparately."

All the ten Ravanas keep speaking by turn, their words banging about the room and piercing Sita's gentle forest ears like hot arrows.

"And I will burn them…"

"One by one... "

"Before your hollow eyes."

The Ravanas wait for Sita to understand this, and make the safe choice.

Their words pain Sita, but her demeanour stays tranquil.

"I was born of the earth's womb, O Ravana," says Sita, her voice calming the deafening roar of all that metal into a murmuring hum. "You cannot own the earth. It is the earth that owns you."

The circling Ravanas go still.

Their angry clanking stops.

"I cannot be yours," Sita says. "I am not Rama's either. But he is mine. And I cannot have more than him. He satiates me. He is the roots of the sapling in my womb. There is no room within me for more than that. But the earth, my mother – her heart is infinite. When you die, Ravana, she will have you as well. She accommodates us all. I am sorry. You seek what you cannot have. And you have torn and plundered for it. You have wounded my mother. Her wounds can now only be filled by the ash from your bones. And the congealed blood from your veins."

Ravana's pieces start to converge once again into the singular ten-headed, twenty-armed monster, angry smoke rising from where their joints clang back into place.

Sita finishes with a small but infinitely gentle sorrow, "O Ravana, I already mourn you."

This seems to singe Sushil's eyes. And little streams push out of them. Caught unawares by this, he looks around to see if anyone has seen him weep. But Pradip is softly snoring.

Even if the tent caught fire now he might only wake after turning into ash.

Oonga, though, just cannot understand why Rama is taking this long to arrive. Oonga thinks that when he narrates this story back in the village, he will reach his Sita even before Ravana can put her in that awful cage.

|||<·∨·>|||

"Blackened and bruised, Rama finally arrived before Ravana," says Chhotu, excitedly, "with our very own Kaka right behind him! Now this is my favourite part of the story – the fight sequence! Come on Kaka! Show us some of your Kung Fu!"

Young Kaka ducks behind a pillar, shushes Chhotu, "Aye! Watch your tongue. This is no cheap action film hero here, okay? This is Rama. And Rama doesn't like to kill. Go climb a tree, and be quiet."

|||<·∨·>|||

Rama drops his bow and arrows on the floor. "I have not come to fight you, Lord Ravana, I have come to escort my wife back to her rightful home. Please allow her to leave. She is the green of the trees in our forest. With her gone, all green is grey."

"As it should be," rumbles Ravana. "Win this war and take your trophy."

And the ten Ravanas disengage once again, their blade-fingers flashing, and start to encircle Rama like bloodthirsty vultures.

Rama drops his head and shakes it, disheartened. "Ravana, you have done much for your land. I see shine. I see power. I see big things. And lusty things. And enticing things. Everywhere.

It's blinding for a pair of jungle eyes like mine. But I am sure it serves a purpose that I cannot see."

The Ravanas are getting impatient. They growl and snarl and hiss by turns.

"You are powerful, Ravana," Rama says, almost in entreaty. "You must easily get most of what you ever wish to have. But I cannot understand why you would wish this. Force is pain. Please don't do this. I do not wish to cause pain. I do not want this forcing. Please let Sita return to the earth that trembles without her.

"We need her.

"You want her.

"The difference is immense. But still not deserving of war."

Ravana 1 leans into Rama's right ear, singeing it with his heat, and sneers, "Lift that bow… "

Ravana 2 steps up to Rama's left ear, hisses, "Draw that arrow… "

Ravana 3 charges at Rama, grabs him by the neck, lifts him clear off the ground, roars, "Fight me like a man!"

And he drops him like a rag. Rama tumbles.

Young Kaka leaps to Rama's side, snarling. Ravana 4 flicks him away, sending him soaring across the stage, crashing into the far wall.

Rama gasps, "Don't hurt him!"

"THEN HURT ME!" Ravana 5 shrieks, and stamps his foot, making the entire chamber quake.

From two ends of the stage Rama and Sita lock eyes.

They both do not want this. But they both do not want to be here either.

Stamping around Rama, the ten Ravanas begin a demonic chant – a call to arms, a call to war, a call to shed blood, hack limbs, break bones, to fight fight FIGHT! As they go round and round and round around Rama, the circle grows smaller and smaller, tightening like a noose, leaving Rama with less and less and less of a choice.

TWENTY

Gamchhas wrapped around their faces, Laxmi's dalam of naxalites slithers quickly and silently through the darkness of the foliage, steering clear of any pathways or roads. The forest is their ally, and keeps them shrouded, only their eyes visible to the stray glints of the obscured sun. These desperate faceless women and children have been trekking through thick shrubbery and creepers and streams as fast as their bruised, aching feet can carry them, for almost an hour now. Linga, the oldest male in the group, leads the convoy, his eyes darting about like a wolf's for any sign of peril. Laxmi walks behind him, her eyes lowered, trusting Linga to do the seeing for her today, as she plays and replays the words in her mind – the words that must win the villagers of Pottacheru over to them today.

In the distance, along the lower slopes of the hills, as if walking alongside them in solidarity, are their red flags, planted like saplings of protest many moons back. They hang limp and fearful today. Linga's eyes keep darting to their flags as they walk. He has been counting them. He always counts them, hoping the number wouldn't have dwindled. Each flag that goes missing is a little more of much-needed support lost from the scared, fatalistic tribes of these hills. And flags have been disappearing regularly recently. At first one or two would vanish, plucked out by some disheartened, drunk adivasi who would rather have a job in the city and is starting to get disillusioned by the angry, violent promises being made to them by the jungle Comrades. These one or two flags were swiftly replaced under cover of night by the ghosts in green. But recently they have been disappearing in droves. It can't be the villagers who do this.

Linga has a sense of what is coming. And that always brings some sticky bitter bile rising up the back of his throat… bile that he just can't seem to swallow back down, but has to spit.

Linga has been gathering this acidic spit in his mouth for the last few long minutes. He has been saving it up for that which he spots now, down the slope, away from them to the right, where the sun shines unobstructed on a vast stretch of open grassland… a two-legged metal signboard, whose sinister humming is audible even from way up here in the gnarled jungle shadows.

Linga stops, turns to Laxmi who stops too. *"Amma, you carry on. I will join back in under five minutes."* And before Laxmi can protest his unnecessary detour, Linga has hung his rifle on a nearby low branch and darted off down the incline, into the sunlight, homing in on the Company signboard as its humming grows louder as if warning Linga to not get too close.

The unblinking, unwelcoming Eye above the 'INDIA ALUMINIUM INC.' watches impassively as Linga walks up to it, looks around warily, grabs its right leg with both his hands, heaves, uproots it, and topples it with all his might on the ground. The grass ensures a noiseless fall, muffling the hum. Linga makes a low growl, gathers every last drop of venom onto his tongue, and spits it into the Eye.

And then he is gone.

Twenty-three uprooted red flags have been avenged. But, Linga notes with dismay, it doesn't make him feel any better about anything.

Idma is still ensconced in the belly of the tree. She's been here all day, having hurried home only for a quick-as-an-arrow lunch, so no one will think she has run away like Oonga. Her eyes are aching from peering into the distance without blinking for so long now. Above her head, atop the 'Pottacheru' sign on the bark of the tree, the pinwheel is dead. Its leaf-blades have not budged since last night. They miss the wind that Oonga's feet stir up when he flies past ten times a day... running towards the jungle... and running back home.

Worried she might fall asleep, Idma had raised her arms a while back. The cramps in them now ensure that she stays awake so that she will be the first to spot Oonga or Hemla when they return. With her arms held up like this Idma looks like she is in a permanent state of surrender to an unknown enemy.

With a gasp she drops her arms when she sees – one – then two – then three – then four – then an endless silent trail of green ghosts slide out of the forest and walk towards her, rifles on their shoulders, their faces concealed.

The dalam pours into the village like a wisp of smoke. The children with rifles circle the huts swiftly, looking for all the entry and exit points, parking themselves one by one around them, their eyes vigilant. The women with rifles slide silently into the clearing in the middle of the village, placing themselves at the four corners round the ashes of last night's bonfire, their backs to it, their eyes darting about the village, peering into its gullies, scanning its treetops. Danger, the naxalite learns early, is everywhere all the time. And death always comes from behind, either as a knife or a bullet. So every Comrade is taught to keep feet pointed forward but one eye towards the back, and the nozzle of the gun hinged loosely, ready to turn every which way in a heartbeat.

Linga goes from hut to hut, calling, "Come, quick, Amma wants to talk to you."

The villagers have already stopped whatever they were doing, their hands frozen at the sight of all those rifles. If Hemla were around, these guns wouldn't have dared to arrive uninvited. Something is wrong. Hemla must be in trouble.

Laxmi squats near the remains of the bonfire, fiddling absently with the cold ash, her face unmasked, her gamchha hanging loosely around her neck. Her mind is a jumble of emotion and thought. With her fingertips she is trying now to gingerly pick the pebbles of her thoughts free of the shifting dust of emotion, so that she can make the case she has come all this way to make. She cannot tell if Hemla's absence from this scheme of things is a good thing or a bad thing. *But in this fight,* thinks Laxmi, *one even takes poison and tries to make tea from it.*

What other choice is there?

She smiles at the villagers as they arrive – confused, scared, curious, unsure where they should sit. She waddles backward, making space, gesturing to them to sit in front of her, close to her. Her demeanour is warm, welcoming – not something the villagers expected of a leader of a naxalite dalam. They have heard legends of Laxmi, some from Hemla herself. Of Laxmi's ruthless ways. Of her raging wrath. Of the number of cops and soldiers she has killed. Of the humongous reward placed on her head by the state. It was said you could buy a car in the city with the money you'd get if you ratted her out to the police.

Although the last man who tried to was found nearly skinless with the whipping he had received. His face was unidentifiable.

Laxmi acknowledges the fear and bewilderment in all those dozens of eyes peering at her now. All that innocence makes her heart bleed. But she pushes her emotions aside, and clutches at her thoughts, tight.

Every last villager rounded up and presented before his leader, Linga arrives. He plants himself steadfast next to Laxmi, lets his furtive gaze run through the crowd one last time, and then warily unwraps the gamchha from his face.

"Where is our teacher, Hemla?" asks Laxmi, keeping her words straight and few, so that Linga can translate without trouble.

But the same words dropping off Linga's tongue simmer with an undisguised impatience, "Where is teacher Hemla?"

"She hasn't come for two days," says little Bela, peeking out from behind her mother's legs.

Linga translates that for Laxmi.

"Do you know why?" Laxmi asks, kickstarting her performance, aware of the impact each of her words is now going to have on these people. And hoping and praying that by the time she is done with them there will be enough dread in enough hearts here to pull them into the dalam's fold.

"Do you know why?" Linga translates.

Silence. Some eyes drop to the ground. Some eyes search others'. Some eyes look on, unwilling to learn any more, but unable to turn away from this either.

"You had all refused to sell your land to the Company. So the CRPF police have taken her."

All eyes turn to Linga as he translates that.

A scared murmur grips the crowd.

"Oonga is also missing, no?" old Timi asks Oongamma. But Oongamma – her gut going colder by the second – stays quiet.

Laxmi watches Oongamma. Could this be worse than she imagined?

"Before the Company appeared in these parts did our people ever go missing like this?"

As Linga translates that to Kuvi, Laxmi studies the villagers' faces with hawk eyes, looking for some small spark that she can grab and start a fire with.

Some heads shake fearfully. Everyone knows that all hideous things have started happening since the Company appeared. But everyone has been too scared to admit it. Laxmi doesn't waste time. "We have to go save her," she says, firmly, "before it gets too late."

When Linga is done, Dalmoni stutters nervously, "B-but if we go and fight them, they can throw us in jail!"

Linga wants to scold Dalmoni then but is reined in by Laxmi's gaze. He translates that for Laxmi. She turns to Dalmoni, nods, fighting the urge to say so many things right now.

"But Hemla never fought them either. Then why did they lock her up?"

Somaru's is the first flicker of doubt. "How do we know you speak the truth?"

Linga turns to Laxmi, unwilling to ask her that, but helpless in the face of his current duty.

Laxmi's and Linga's and the villagers' voices are playing out like a duel. Two languages saying the same things, the edges of their words sharpened by different histories, but their syntax drenched in the same coloured blood. Two languages that struggle now to align themselves into one mutual resolve.

Laxmi's voice becomes steely. "Go see for yourself in the CRPF camp in the school. We don't lie to our own." She points at her dalam. "Look at us carefully. Do you see a single grown up male in our midst?"

She stands up, walks up to one of her women turned away from the villagers, turns her around, takes the gamchha off to reveal her face. Some of the villagers gasp. Oongamma gapes. This is her dear friend.

"Recognise her, no? Sanmati. You met her every time you crossed Padua on the way to the market. She must have even made you some tea? She still does that. Only now she does it in different places in the jungle every week."

Sanmati doesn't know where to look. She shutters her eyes, to barricade any emotion that might want to spring out without warning. Laxmi allows her to veil her face again and turn away, back to her vigil, where allowing your vision to be obscured by tears is a sureshot way to get yourself killed.

Laxmi knows how helpful it can be to focus on duty. It helps keep unnecessary thoughts of a tragic past from taking hold of the mind. The less vacant the mind, the less the past can mess with it.

"Padua had also refused to sell their land to the Company. You all know that," Laxmi continues, coming and squatting again, even closer to the villagers now. "One day Sanmati's husband didn't come back home from the fields. She waited. He didn't return the next day either. Just like your Hemla. So she went to the police. Not once. Not twice. But many times. No one would speak with her. Then one day all of them went together," Laxmi indicates all the women standing around them, turned away, their faces invisible, their shoulders weighed down by rifles.

 "Fed up of being pestered, one of the officers finally told Sanmati that her husband had been thrown in jail. Not in a small jail, mind you. The big jail in the city. You know why?"

The villagers fall so silent that Laxmi can almost hear all their hearts thudding. She points at Sikoka, who stands far behind the rest, just returned from foraging in the forest, a bow slung across his shoulder. "Because he was wandering about with a bow and arrows."

Confusion ripples across all the faces there as Linga translates that.

"The adivasi walks around with bows and arrows all the time, no?"

Many heads nod, dreading whatever Laxmi might say next.

"But the cityfolk call your harmless bows and arrows 'weapons'. And so their system calls it 'illegal'. Sanmati had no choice. She went to the nearby town. Lohabad? To the court there. You know what a court is, right? Hemla Teacher must have told you."

Many heads nod again, but more timidly, as if not wanting any part of this conversation any more, afraid already of the high probability that someone from among them might soon feature in a story quite like this one, told by this woman, in this same forlorn voice, in some other tribal village on some other lush hill on a day as sunny as this one, but with a lot less likelihood that things may go back to how they once used to be.

"A court is where you're supposed to get justice. Where you can ask for your rights. Sanmati was asked to wait outside in a police van, where four officers raped her at gunpoint."

Laxmi watches the villagers intently as Linga translates. He takes a few extra seconds to explain to them what it means to be 'raped' by the police. It's too much for even Oongamma. She closes her eyes and sends silent prayers into her womb. When she opens her eyes again, she wishes she could delay the arrival of her little girl. But would any delay be enough any more?

"I tried so hard to convince these people of Padua to act in time, but no one listened to me," Laxmi says, and then points at another of the women standing vigil there. "That's Soni."

There is something odd about Soni. But it's hard to say what.

"You must know her too. Hers was the corner hut in Padua. The first to burn when they set fire to the village. You must have seen the burnt remains, no?"

The villagers exchange looks. Two nights back it was Hemla, seated at this very spot, speaking to them of this very thing. Where Hemla urged them to hope and believe, Laxmi now speaks to them of the inevitability of despair, and why it might be much too late for believing.

"Soni made the mistake of going alone to the Collector to ask what they should do," Laxmi continues. "The police caught her on her way there. They kept her in lock-up for a week. When she protested, they shoved stones, and then a big rock, inside her."

Linga pounces on that detail, burnishing it with some flourish as he relays it to the horrified villagers.

"Who knows, they might be doing the exact same thing to Hemla right now."

Ducked behind a hut, Idma has been watching all the little naxalite kids wide-eyed all this while. She has been studying their ill-fitting green shirts and pants, their beady, watchful eyes, and those long heavy things in their hands. She has learnt about those long heavy things by weaving together bits and pieces she has overheard from hushed adult conversations. They spit out small iron pebbles that make holes in people. She always meant to ask Hemla didi about them. Why they even exist. And if one can destroy all of them in the world once and for all so no one can make holes in people ever again. But for that Hemla didi will have to return.

"Till this day blood leaks out of Soni without warning sometimes. Every other day she sits down for hours by some stream or pond trying to wash the bloodstains off her pants."

And suddenly Soni's oddness reveals itself. While all the other naxalites have their loose shirts tucked tight into their pants, Soni's shirt hangs loose, trying to cover her behind. This makes her look particularly dishevelled. If one looks closely, the untucked shirt seeks to conceal the ghosts of many bloodstains – her own personal history of violence mapped intricately on the seat of her pants.

"When she finally came to me, she brought with her a fistful of ashes. She opened her fist and said, 'Didi, this is all that's left of my house.' "

Soni has been resisting the urge to turn and watch her leader speak about her. Until she met Amma no one had ever cared for her story. Every time she shared it with someone, she was either raped, or jailed, or brutalised, or ignored. She had begun to dig a grave for her story when Amma took it from her. A story destined for burial was being rebirthed in this village now. Soni wants to see the faces of all those who just heard her story. But she's too ashamed to reveal herself to them. Some of them know her from Padua. And they must have already seen traces of her blood on her behind by now. So Soni stays turned away, her eyes filling with tears.

They could be tears of gratitude.

Or mourning.

Or fury.

Soni cannot tell.

"So what do we want to do? Keep sitting here like this? God knows how many times they must have raped Hemla by now. The longer we do nothing the worse it's going to get for her."

Waves of confusion lash the shores of each heart there. Laxmi can hear those waves. She has heard so many thousands of them over the years that she can pick up those sounds from a mile away.

She will need to calm this storm.

"Don't worry. We're here for you. If we join hands we can save her. And your village too. But we cannot do it without one another."

Tulsa has been hanging onto every word Linga relays. Troubled, she protests, "But Hemla didi would never want us to join you."

Laxmi's face betrays her disappointment for a fleeting second before she shutters it again. "I understand that. I do. Hemla and I have spoken many times about this. Our ways are different from hers, yes. But think about it – when you're out on a hunt and faced with a tiger would you try to talk to it into not eating you? Or would you turn into an animal yourself to survive? Hemla's been captured. We don't have any other option right now. Without our help Hemla could die."

Laxmi instructs Linga this time, "Make sure they get this loud and clear... She – could – die."

Laxmi watches Linga's words slide like an unwelcome dagger into each mind and heart gathered there. When they have all muttered and mumbled and nodded and shaken their heads to one another, she continues, "Think about this. Think hard. But think fast. Every minute you spend sitting here and talking, it's getting more and more dangerous for her out there. Let us know. There's no time."

And Laxmi springs to her feet, her demeanour switched. She lets Linga finish speaking, and then tells him, "Show them how to reach us."

Laxmi wraps her face up in the gamchha again while Linga pries open a bullet, taps out some gunpowder, strikes a quick match, and shows the villagers how to send a quickly made smoke signal high up into the skies where their guardians of the forest will be able to see it.

|||<•V•>|||

A long minute after the dalam has disappeared, Dalmoni gathers the scattered bits of her frightened heart, asks, "Hemla didi was going to the Collector, no? Could the police have caught her on the way?"

No one knows what to say to that. Everyone feels too heavy right now to even get up off the ground.

Madvi speaks for everyone. "If they could arrest her they can arrest any of us."

"What if I get picked up tomorrow and never return?" asks Damboru, and his fingers start to tremble. He tries hard to imagine what he would do when grabbed by three policemen, but cannot. If he is already so anxious at merely the thought of it, he might turn to stone when it happens.

Ghosa concurs, "Perhaps these people are right."

"How do we know anything for sure?" asks Timi, her wise old quivering voice fanning the flames of confusion further. "Hemla has always said we must not trust anyone blindly."

"Where could Oonga have gone then?" asks Somaru.

Oongamma's tongue is heavy with questions, but she doesn't ask them. She knows no one here will be able to answer them. And there have been more than enough questions asked here today, none of which might find any easy answers soon. She swallows them all with a heavy gulp and feels them sink into her already heavy heart.

It doesn't help that Dalmoni asks, "Didn't Kunja say Oonga will return?"

Oongamma stays quiet. Kunja. Hemla. The wind. The earth. The sun. The trees. This Laxmi. All of them keep saying a whole lot of things. But Oonga is still not here. And nothing that rolls off any of their tongues seems to be changing that.

I will have to deal with this myself, Oongamma thinks. *If Oonga does not return by sunset today I will set out with my unborn little one and go looking for him. I will go to the police if need be. It will be very difficult for them to rape a pregnant woman.*

That last thought whips a tear out of Oongamma's eye. Dalmoni spots it. But before she can reach for her hand, Oongamma turns and stumbles towards her hut. She carries too many terrifying thoughts within her. She needs to find a corner where she can sit by herself and pluck these thoughts out and toss them into the wind. She can't have her little one enter this world diseased by thoughts such as this one.

Idma creeps back to her lookout point, praying to the spirit of the banyan tree to send at least one of them back by evening – either Hemla didi or Oonga – or she herself might have to run away now to go find him.

TWENTY-ONE

Young Kaka's bruised and bleeding body tremors, convulses, and goes limp in Rama's arms. Ravana 7 takes his heavy foot off Young Kaka's bloodied tail, and snarls, "He died because of you, Rama."

Rama is silent. He mutters a prayer to Sita's mother. The earth yawns open beneath him, swallows Young Kaka in, and closes up again. A moment later a small white flower springs up where the brave monkey returned into the earth. Rama cups it gently, as a tear drops on it from his eye. Watered thus, the flower shimmers, but for a moment only, before –

STOMP!

Ravana 4 crushes it!

Leaving Rama no choice.

Rama rises to his feet slowly, raising his bow, drawing an arrow. All ten Ravanas throw their heads back and howl in glee. Their howling fills up the tent, making Sushil's hair stand on end.

Rama fires one arrow… then two… then three… then dozens… Shhwoopp! Shhwoopp! Shhwoopp! Shhwoopp! Shhwoopp! Missing again and again and again. Blink as hard as he might he just can't see clearly. His tears refuse to stop flowing.

The Ravanas' howling gives way to laughter – nasty, mocking

laughter. Ravana cannot believe what he is seeing. The prince of the jungle has the aim of a blind old hermit. "This is why, you fool... This is why your jungle is no match for my lustre," laughs Ravana. "You do not know how to protect it!"

And just then one arrow finds Ravana 3's neck, taking his head flying with it!

As the head clatters into a corner, one by one his parts start to fall off his body.

Until all of him crashes to the floor.

Oonga leaps up in the air! He pumps the darkness with his fists! Rama did it! Rama has won! Rama has saved Sita! Ravana has been felled!

Nine Ravanas now start to run around the stage pell-mell as Rama – his bow strung, his arrow taut, his eye aimed – waits for a Ravana to pause so he may fire. But the Ravanas are picking up speed, bouncing off the walls, springing off the ground, skidding around turns, screeching, revving, tumbling, sliding... until Rama realises that this is not chaos...

But instead, a ritual... of regeneration!

A metallic clanging starts to rise to a sharp crescendo, as the nine surviving Ravanas, having collected the tenth's pieces off the ground, start to toss all those parts into the centre where they get magnetically pulled together – Clink! Clink! Clink! Clink! Clink! –collapsing back into one whole.

The last piece to slam back into place is the head.

And even as Rama gapes in horror, the Ravana he thought he had killed shakes and rattles and shivers back to his feet, and lets out a furious wail!

Oonga could cry. His hands are cold. His gut is cold. This tent has gone cold.

There seems to be no way now that Rama can win this fight.

Rama keeps firing his arrows, faster and furiouser. But every time a Ravana falls, the others kick and toss his pieces back together in no time, laughing, wailing, howling in glee, singing a thumping song about –

This being the fight
The show of might
The ballet depraved
That Ravana craved.
Once he is done tiring Rama out…
and exhausting his arrows…
he will tear him asunder.
And finally –
finally he will have won Sita fair and square…
to possess and plunder.

Sita's cage trembles.

A whirlpool of sorrow eddies within her now, sucking into its dark entrails every last shard of her shattering hope. She calls out to her mother for help. Rama hears his Sita shriek. He drops down to his hands and knees, digging his fingers and toes into the earth, burying his face in her folds, to tell her that her daughter needs her, more than ever, now.

The stage plunges into darkness.

Mother Earth sings to Rama… a heartrending lament of –

How she has been plundered
How deep her wounds now run
Wounds that may never heal
Wrought upon her by this greedy one
Ravana's ravaging
His ravenous savaging
Cannot be undone
Little by little
Or bit by bit.

227] It cannot be reversed
By upturning a single fallen tree
Or returning the hum to one silenced bee
By repairing one broken bird wing
Or hoping for a patch of sky to sing
Once more.
No.
An evil like his can only be undone
By taking it ALL down – ALL AT ONCE!

And just as the lights blaze again, the ten Ravanas charge Rama from all sides, bellowing a terrifying war cry! As suddenly, the earth opens up, gulps Rama in, and the ten Ravanas crash into one another, tumbling in a large heap of scraping, squealing, sparking, startled metal.

Rama has disappeared.

Ravana grrrrowls, his many pieces clanging back into one many-armed, many-headed beast, as Rama EXPLODES out from the earth behind Ravana!

Rama is caked in brown earth, only his eyes visible, his last arrow held taut, ready to fire, waiting for Ravana's convergence to complete.

And as the ten blazing heads turn together to face him, TWANNNGG! Rama fires. The arrow slices all ten heads off. They clatter chaotically to the ground, screaming and ranting in a cacophony of shocked hissing voices.

Nine pairs of red eyes sizzle and extinguish in puffs of black smoke. The giant many-armed body – now headless – topples slowly and crashes to the ground, raising a cloud of black dust that eclipses all the shine of Ravana's world.

Ravana's singular head remains on the ground, gasping for breath, his endless fury still burning in his eyes. Ravana coughs,

sputters, and snarls, "Rama, you are foolish. I am the future. You cannot fight what is eventual. Your time is gone. You may think I have been defeated. But this is a chimera. There will be another Ravana. He will have a hundred faces, not just ten. And the earth will be no match for him when he decides to take her as his own. Power, speed, shine are a juggernaut. All who stand in its way are fools. You will lose your home, your idyll, your forest, soon. The jungle will have to make way.

"Sita, you have spurned a life of greatness. You have made a terrible mistake. May you end in a miserable, unloved fire. A fire that Rama himself puts you into..."

Rama lifts Ravana's severed head off the ground, cradles it gently, and begins to weep. "Ravana, I have never met anyone like you. Thank you for teaching me the value of loss. I am sorry I had to terminate you. I did not wish to. I do not know where it is that we go to when we die, or if we go anywhere at all. But if I am to meet you somewhere after I die too, may we meet as brothers. I wish you a painless journey. Release yourself now. All this wrath can only cause you more pain."

The stage is plunged into utter silence as Ravana's eyes gaze into Rama's. Ravana looks at him bewildered. Yet again this was not a response he expected. The red rage starts to drain from his eyes.

"Hate has always beg-g-gotten hate. Anger has always earned anger," Ravana stutters, his life starting to ebb, smoke trailing out from his ears and mouth. "But the t-t-two of you... I-I..." **and Ravana's eyes extinguish... his thought unfinished... but his cycle complete.**

Sita's cage quickly crumbles, dropping her in a relieved tumble

to the earth. Sita fills her fists with mud as life returns to her eyes. A white stream bursts out of the ground and runs little white ribbons around her feet. Flowers bloom in her hair.

Rama, a brilliant blue once again, holds his hand out for Sita to take. As soon as Sita slides her hand into Rama's, trees spring out from the metal walls, the sky erupts in the flapping of a hundred birds, and the stream swells into a white river that wraps them in its flow as the two of them, reunited, begin to dance.

They dance and dance and dance, filling up Ravana's world with the sweet sounds and colours and scents of the forest until the clouds above them burst and it starts to rain flowers!

Chhotu crawls back in frontstage, untouched by the revelry, looking sombre. "Why didn't Kaka ever tell me that he died for Rama?"

Just as he was about to break into a jig, Oonga freezes. What is this? Why is this monkey sad? We just won the war! Why is he not dancing?

Chhotu looks lost and bewildered. "If Kaka died so young, then who was that old monkey who told us this story?!"

Chhotu is lost in thought as the curtain starts to fall from above him. "I must get to the bottom of this mystery," he says, and bounds off as the curtain starts to obscure the celebration in Rama and Sita's world.

Oonga bends down lower and lower as the curtain drops, unwilling to miss even a second of the festivity behind it. Until all sounds die out and the stage goes pitch dark.

The moment the lights come on in the tent, Oonga looks around startled and scampers into a corner. If Grouchy spots him now he's not going to ever be able to say hello to Rama. As the crowd leaves, Oonga ducks beneath a bench.

Sushil and Pradip are the last to leave. Pradip totters, unhappy at being woken so suddenly from such a peaceful nap. "Even my grandma never told me a story that put me to sleep. These monkeys are damn good at this. They had barely started and my lights went out," he sniggers. "Hope you made notes for Manoranjan?"

Sushil doesn't know what to say. His mind is a whirl of emotions. What will he tell Manoranjan? That the teacher has been teaching her kids the value of love? That they care for their forest? That they don't want the CRPF there? That this troop should vacate the camp? Return all their rifles? What can he do to help the sinking feeling in his heart right now? Write the CM a letter? The PM? Resign from this job? Go back to his village to protect the tree behind his hut?

I've made notes, sahib, more notes than you would like, Sushil wants to say, but he stays quiet, like always, and continues to ensure wobbly Pradip doesn't topple any more chairs on his way out of here.

TWENTY-TWO

The big unblinking Eye on the side of the Commander jeep stares at the lush countryside. Its stare seems to be one of stoic certainty. As if it knows that all of this, and beyond it, will someday soon be vomiting out its bauxite for them. As if it believes that everything green is destined to turn red someday.

The dark-paned windows are rolled up on all sides of the jeep. It stands so still that it's hard to tell if anyone is inside. Until a figure, his face hooded by an empty cane basket hanging off his forehead, worms his way through the fields towards the jeep. The jeep lurches gently, as if someone inside might have spotted him and is shifting impatiently in his seat.

The figure arrives at the window behind. His langot might make him one of the adivasi farmers from any of the nearby villages. But it's hard to tell who is what any more. The windowpane rolls down. Rabbit, his glares obscuring his eyes, turns to the faceless farmer.

"The jungle Comrades came to the village today," the farmer says. Rabbit turns to Rat for a translation. "He's saying the naxalites came to the village today," says Rat, shifting uneasily in his seat. He doesn't like this one bit. *These city people finish their jobs and go back to their safe flats in their buildings in their gated communities in the city, leaving us permanently trapped in the crossfire here.*

Rabbit reconfirms, "Pottacheru village, right?"

The faceless farmer nods. Rabbit slips out a five-hundred-rupee note and holds it out of the window for the farmer to pluck from his fingers.

All three look around to check if anyone has seen this transaction. What you didn't see in these parts never happened. And if you did see something then it can always be made to unhappen for a price.

The windowpane rolls up as the jeep starts.

Rabbit scrolls through his cellphone for a number as Rat's eyes keep darting to the side mirror. The farmer hasn't left. He still stands where they left him, watching them recede, his reflection growing smaller and smaller in the mirror. This gives Rat a bad feeling. A common villager would have disappeared into the fields by now. Rat hopes that the farmer won't remember his face. But he could have noted this jeep's license plate number. *I'm going to quit this job and open a shop or something,* thinks Rat, as they hit a pukka road, and he swerves onto it suddenly to shake that tiny reflection out of his rear-view.

* * *

An old landline phone rings in the principal's office of the Birsa Munda Ashram School. It rings for a long minute before a nervously sweating jawaan comes into the room, waves his hand before Manoranjan's face, and points to the phone. Manoranjan looks up from his newspaper, startled, asks, "It's ringing?"

Sweaty jawaan nods.

"Then answer it, fuckface!" Manoranjan bellows.

Sweaty jawaan pounces on the phone, afraid now that if it stops ringing before it's answered, Manoranjan might land him a tight slap.

"He-hello?" he asks, and listens carefully, his eyes betraying his alarm. Manoranjan is on his feet in a flash. He peers into the jawaans face as he covers the mouthpiece, takes a deep breath and relays, "SAHIB! HE SAYS THE TEACHER IS LYING."

Manoranjan orders him, "Ask who he is – the same fellow who tipped us off about the teacher and her kids two nights ago?"

Sweaty jawaan uncovers the mouthpiece, corroborates, looks at Manoranjan, and nods. "What does he want?" asks Manoranjan.

Sweaty jawaan asks, then listens, thick beads of sweat appearing around his brows. He covers the mouthpiece again, turns to Manoranjan, dreading already what he is about to set in motion, and says, "SAHIB, NAXALITES WERE SEEN IN POTTACHERU TODAY!"

And he waits to be told what to do next.

Manoranjan's eyes take on a cruel, angry gleam. This piece of information vindicates him. All these years he has spent in the bleeding gut of this conflict. How dare anyone think his instinct is anything but right! He knew it all along. He felt it in his bones the second he laid eyes on that woman. All that innocence is a facade, used to hide an uncontrollable bloodlust. These tribals are born to kill. The younger they are the more fearlessly they kill. Unlike these stupid, fearful, sweating jawaans that the state keeps tossing into his lap. If he didn't hate these stinking adivasis so much he might have let them have a glimpse of how much he reveres them for the pluck they show. Hell, he might want to send half his squadron to them in the jungles for some training someday!

Manoranjan storms off, slipping his belt back into the loops on his pants, and buckling it tight. He can't tell what he is more of right now – furious, or in awe. *The teacher's been raped a dozen times since the day before,* he wonders, *by a dozen different men. And she still won't relent. Okay. I'll show her. These naxalites might have minds made of rock, but their bodies are flesh and bone, just like ours.*

And Manoranjan knows just how to make flesh and bone make the noise he wants to hear.

Sweaty jawaan doesn't know what to do now. Nervous, he uncovers the mouthpiece, wipes his sweating palm on his shirt, asks "Hello?" but is met with a creepy silence. He senses the informer is still on the line. So "Hello?" he asks again.

Inside the slowly moving jeep, Rabbit cuts the call, leans in to Rat, taps him on his shoulder and gestures that he can pick up speed now.

Oonga has scoured every inch of the stage, peeking behind every cardboard tree, walking around all the paper clouds. He tugs at the long white fabric stream lying limp on the floor now, to see if anyone drowned in its waters. But there is no trace of Rama. *Where could he have disappeared?* he wonders, when he spies in the far corner – a secret exit.

The makeshift door is like a portal to a secret world. Oonga walks into a room with large mirrors all around, their peripheries lined by dozens of dull yellow bulbs. In one corner, like a silent ghost, sits Ravana's metal armour. High up on the wall, hung in a neat line, are his ten heads. They seem to watch Oonga with dead, hollow eyes. Oonga scowls, sticks his tongue out, hoping to annoy him and pick a fight right here right now. But Ravana doesn't react.

Rama really did kill him after all.

Then why are his pieces still hanging about here like this?

They were play-acting, you fool, that's why, Oonga reminds himself, and chuckles. He wants to be Rama so badly that he's starting to believe all this to be true.

But it is!

Okay. But then where is Rama?!

Oonga catches his reflection in the mirror.

Oonga has never seen himself this clearly before.

He goes closer, studying his face. The water always makes his face wavy. He never knew his nose looked like that. Or his ears.

He puffs his cheeks. *Look, I'm a monkey!*

He notices that he has buttoned his shirt all wrong. The buttons and the holes are askew. That's probably why his right collar had been tickling his ear all this time. He starts to unbutton his shirt to realign it, when a magical blue glow catches the corner of his eye.

Oonga finds himself pulled towards it like a nail to a magnet. In a large tray below the mirror sits blue paint… Rama's blue. Two empty cans sit next to it. Oonga doesn't know why but he finds himself slipping his shirt off, dropping it to the floor… and finds his hands sinking into the tray. When he takes them out, they are blue. From his wrist to the tips of his fingers, his hands have turned into Rama's hands.

Rama left this for me here, thinks Oonga. *He wants me to be Rama now, otherwise he wouldn't have disappeared.*

And before Oonga knows it his hands are smearing Rama's blue all over his face. He smears himself thick and full… around his eyes… his nose… above and below his mouth… behind his ears… his neck… and then over his shoulders… his arms… and his chest.

As his skin changes colour, Oonga's demeanour starts to change too. His back straightens. His face upturns. His shoulders stiffen. He imagines a large bow on one shoulder, and a quiver of arrows slung across his chest. His arms swell from his sides like a warrior's, ready for battle.

Oonga covers every inch of his skin with blue. Well, at least every inch his puny arms can reach. A mirror behind reveals a small patch on his back still the colour of Oonga. But what Oonga can't see, isn't true. And now 'Oonga' is history. The little man who stands before that enormous mirror now has the regal bearing of the guardian prince of the jungle, and is as blue as him too.

Oonga studies his image in the mirror, trying to memorise the arch of his back, the raise of his chin, the square of his shoulders, the flex of his arms. And even as he marvels at all of this, his image proclaims, "I – am – Rama!"

Grouchy shoves the benches into corners, grumbling at the empty packets of chips and biscuits littering the floor, when he hears a voice from the stage. The lights are out. The curtains are down. Everyone has left. Is his mind playing tricks with him again? Grouchy has had enough spooking for one day. All that blowing in the wind has ensured he couldn't smoke a single bidi since the show began. Grouchy ignores it, gets his jhadoo out and starts sweeping the floor, when he hears it

237] again, clearer now – a small voice, proclaiming bigly – "I AM RAMA!"

Grouchy drops down on all fours, crawls to the stage, reluctantly lifts a corner of the curtain, peeks underneath it, and sees – a miniature blue Rama, imperially draped astride a cardboard tree. Mini Rama spots Grouchy, raises his hand and blesses him, "Be good, you naughty monkey."

Grouchy cannot believe his eyes. He might have to consider giving up alcohol if such be the games that cheap desi spirit intends to play with his mind. Wielding his jhadoo like a sword, Grouchy slides in under the curtain and approaches this bizarre little illusion, expecting it to disappear as soon as he reaches it. But Oonga is unaffected by the advancing catastrophe. He smiles indulgently at Grouchy as the scowling man stops before him and waves his broom about as if to dispel the ghost. Failing which, dumbstruck, Grouchy gestures, unnaturally politely, "Who are you?"

Oonga points at the heavens above, then at himself, then unfurls his arms like an eagle's wings, tilts his head back in awesomeness, and proclaims, "Ra-ma!"

Grouchy leans to one side, inspects Oonga's face from the left. Then leans to inspect it from the right. And then leans in real close to peer into Oonga's eyes, and snarls, "You?! Again?! You filthy little twat!" and he tries to whack Oonga with the jhadoo, when Oonga springs out of the tree, and rockets off the stage. Grouchy tumbles to the ground, his limbs tangled up in the tree.

Grouchy chases Oonga all the way out, lashing out at him with his jhadoo, missing him once… twice… thrice… "Come here, you cockroach!" he barks. "I'll skin you and feed you to the dogs. Steal my paint, will you?!"

But Mini Rama springs about like a warrior, leaping over benches, skidding around tent poles, bouncing off the cloth walls, until he cannons out of the gate, leaving Grouchy panting and heaving.

Oonga races past a chai shop where two familiar monkeys stand sipping tea, their tails sticking out of plastic bags in their hands. Kaka gapes as Mini Rama whizzes past, then looks at Chhotu, asks, "Did you see that?"

Chhotu nods, dumbstruck.

Oonga has been running so fast for so long that he forgets which way he needs to go. He screeches to a stop now, nearly toppling over, heaving for breath. He looks around him and notices several pairs of eyes peering at him curiously. *This is not how Rama would behave,* he reminds himself, and straightens, puffs his chest up, sticks his bum out, tilts his head back ever so slightly, and starts to walk with that regal demeanour. Some people point at him and giggle. Oonga acknowledges them with an ever-so-slight nod of his godly head.

But as he walks, he wonders, where is he supposed to walk to?!

Is home this way?

Or that way?

Straight?

Or back around?

So many cars and bikes and buses are zipping this way and that, that it sends his blue head into a tizzy.

"O Mother Earth, send your Rama a sign," Oonga mutters. And just then, as if in divine response, Pradip and Sushil speed past on their bike.

"Aye!" Oonga yelps. He knows them! They can give him a ride again! But where are they headed? If Mother Earth sent them as a sign, then chances are they're headed where he should be headed too.

So Oonga looks in the direction the bike went, and then scans his surroundings for the next cosmic sign.

TWENTY-THREE

Hemla's eyes are glazed now. With the first stone that Manoranjan pushed into her, she had screamed. She had never felt pain like this before. She had instantly thought of Soni. Laxmi had made Soni tell Hemla about those stones. Soni never spoke much. But she had told Hemla about her pain. The tearing, burning, shooting kind of pain. Pain that set the brain on fire. Hemla had tried to imagine it. But it hadn't seemed like enough to justify picking up a gun. She had grudged Soni her decision that day. And left in a huff.

The second stone had set Hemla's brain on fire. Her legs went numb. Her face began to swell.

The third stone makes the pain so sharp and so big and so heavy it makes Hemla dizzy. Even if she wanted to she couldn't have answered the questions Manoranjan is spitting into her face now. About naxalites… in Pottacheru… and children… with rifles… *her* children. Her brain struggles to wade through all that pain and put these pieces together. But it can't.

Hemla teeters on the brink of blacking out, but something keeps her from falling off the edge. It could be the stone-cold floor against her naked brutalised skin. Or the throbbing warmth of all the blood oozing out of her. Or the mention of her children. She tries hard to draw a definite shape round what Manoranjan has been saying all this while. But can't.

Manoranjan heaves with the exertion. He could kill this lying piece of shit right now. But death wouldn't be enough. He'll bring those children here, lay them all down naked, face to face, and have himself a classroom conversation. Teacher. And students. It's only fair. They are in a school after all.

Manoranjan leans into Hemla's face and sneers, "Keep your lies. I'll bring your kids here now. A little fatherly whipping with my belt and they're sure to tell me a thing or two."

Kids?! Here??!! And it all suddenly falls into place inside Hemla's aching mind – Manoranjan is going to go to the village!

As Manoranjan pulls away, staggering to the door, Hemla, despite the pieces her body has been broken into, starts to struggle against her ropes. "Sahib!" she pleads, "Please. Not the kids. They have done nothing wrong." But her voice is a starved whimper. And the near-deaf Manoranjan cannot hear her.

"Sahib! I'll tell you what you want," Hemla implores, ready to lie, to concoct whatever false truth Manoranjan might need her to, so he'd leave her children alone. Those children are her hope. The adivasis' hope. They are the future Hemla has dreamt of. A future of justice. And education. And healthcare. And fundamental rights. A future where the village and the city won't mistrust each other. A future where everyone speaks in tongues that the other understands. Her children are that future. And she needs to save them from Manoranjan.

From the floor, sprawled face down in a pool of her own urine and blood, Hemla now offers Manoranjan everything he sought of her all this while. But Manoranjan cannot hear one word. His back to her, he steps out of the door, and locks it once again, wiping Hemla's blood off his hands with a torn piece of her saree, determined to make those children pay for this unwelcome endless silence in his lifeless ears.

|||<•∨•>|||

A rickety taxi leaves a bustling parking lot, nearly tipping over with the many suitcases and boxes and trunks strapped in a heap atop it. As it hits the highway and starts to pick up speed, a familiar blue face emerges surreptitiously from amidst all that luggage. At first Oonga is taken in by the breeze. He closes his eyes and lets it attack his face. But suddenly it strikes him that he is not Oonga any more. So he straightens his back, places his forearms on the two cartons on either side of him, throws his head back like a king, and gives the wind permission to whip through his hair.

Every time a vehicle approaches from the opposite direction, Mini Rama raises his hand, nods, gives it permission to roar past. Mini Rama blesses every passer-by, motorist, bullock cart driver, stray dog, bus passenger, pedestrian, face-in-window, waving-arm, leaving a trail of startled, curious people wondering if they really saw a little blue god atop his modern-day chariot, or imagined him!

|||<•∨•>|||

Far behind Oonga, on the same road, Pradip, his tank full with the big, oily city lunch they made a pit stop for, makes their bike fly. Sushil's knuckles have turned white from gripping the edge of the seat tight so he won't fly off. He wants to tell Pradip to slow down. But Pradip is trying to make up for lost time.

"At least one of us enjoyed that piece-of-shit naatak," he shouts so he'll be heard over the dull roar of the wind. "By sitting through it and not falling asleep you've won yourself the rare privilege of narrating the story to Manoranjan sahib!" Pradip guffaws, full-throated and gleeful. "Imagine," he shouts, "you yelling all of it out for him to hear. Don't keep it short, okay? Give him the details. Each little nuance. Screamed out in his ears." And Pradip laughs so hard his pot belly starts shaking. Sushil lets him, hoping that his laughter will make the bike wobble, and he will be compelled to slow down.

"Oh, and Suseel…?" Pradip leans back, beckons Sushil closer. "Just don't start sobbing while narrating it." He chortles again. "Suseel, Suseel, emosunal Suseel! I didn't know they even made them like you any more."

Sushil's heart is crammed so full with Sita and Rama and their jungle and their love and their reluctance to kill, that there's no room in there for anything Pradip says now. So Sushil stays quiet, letting all that he saw and all that he felt continue to tumble about in his mind, even as Pradip continues to jabber.

Sushil's eyes wander into the landscape, watching it change from brown and grey to rusty red. They are passing through the red mining land once more. All the iron pipes and excavator trucks and shiny signboards of the Company remind Sushil of Ravana. He remembers Pradip warning him to not think too much. All kinds of trouble begin inside our heads and hearts when we think too much. But how can Sushil control it?

His heart is still flip-flopping when suddenly it freezes!

He spots –

Walking through the red vista –

A miniature blue Rama!

Sushil wants to tap Pradip's shoulder, tell him to look, but refrains. What if it's just his mind playing tricks? Unable to tear his eyes from the vision, Sushil keeps gaping at it, as his neck twists to snapping point. Just as he's about to look away, he does a double take –

Wait!

No!

It cannot be!

This little Rama's face resembles the tribal boy's – the one they gave a lift to!

Sushil quickly pulls his eyes away. And clenches them shut. All that emotional churn is causing him hallucinations. If Pradip finds out what Sushil just saw he might have the CO report him and have him sacked right away.

But, thinks Sushil, his mind a stormy whirl, *isn't that what I want?*

|||<·∨·>|||

The last few minutes have felt like an eternity to Hemla. The pain is so crushing it has slowed down time itself. She cannot tell if it's many minutes that she has been struggling to free her hands, or hours, or days. She hasn't feared for her own life all this time as much as she now fears for her children. The longer she takes to get out of here and get help, the higher the odds against her getting any. But get out of here she must. All this blood. All this dread. All this nakedness. All this dishonour. All the things that were keeping her from pushing herself up off this floor and finding a way out – all these things have ceased to matter now.

Desperation is a sharp knife through helplessness. And Hemla uses the heavy stones of her pain now to sharpen her faculties on. She pushes air into her lungs, forcing herself to awaken fully. With every rasping breath she feels her pain numb a little bit, and the gears of her mind start to click back into place bit by bit. Until it hits her that she doesn't need to struggle to pull her hands free this way. She could loop her arms round herself to bring them to the front. But to be able to bring her knees up to her stomach she will have to empty her insides of these stones.

So Hemla thinks of little Oonga and Idma and Bela and Hurre and Drika and Dasru and Laichan, clenches her eyes shut tight, reaches down behind her with her knotted hands, and grits her teeth to pull out the first stone.

|||<•V•>|||

The back of the tractor is heaped with people of all sizes, shapes, girths and ages. Farmers returning from the market. Anxious young men returning from lowly job interviews in the town. Worried villagers with files and papers returning from the city court. Unhappy looking men and women returning from the hospital. Couples. Families. The aged. The young. All crammed together in a single tray-on-wheels bumping and grinding across the rocky countryside. In one corner of this pile of people is a familiar small blue figure, strategically situated so that he can catch the occasional reflection in the quaking rear-view mirror up front.

Oonga retains his kingly demeanour. If one didn't know better one wouldn't have been able to tell that this was the same little anxious boy who was headed in the opposite direction just the day before. And is now returning to his kingdom a victorious king. But then, where are the drums? And the trumpets? And the chants? And the rainfall of flowers?

 It's okay, thinks Oonga, *I forgive you all.* And he raises his hand and carelessly tosses everyone gathered there a blessing, whether they want it or not.

A young woman, who has been endlessly curious about this oddity, fishes her small cellphone out, and clicks a photo of Mini Rama. The flash blinds Oonga, and he scowls at her. But then she turns the phone to him and shows him his picture. Oonga's eyes go rounder than coins! He has never seen anything like this. She just made an instantaneous miniature painting of him. Like the ones he makes in white on his skin. Only this one is blue! Just the way he wants it. He grins, and points at her dramatically, as if silently proclaiming, "You're the one!" The woman giggles.

The tractor stops at a crossroads, and a few people tumble out. An old woman with a broad tilak on her forehead, endless beads round her neck, and all kinds of bangles on her arms, jangles onto the tractor. Just as it lurches and starts to move again, her devout eyes fall on everyone's favourite distraction. She chokes a gasp, pushes some people aside to waddle towards him, bends over and touches Mini Rama's feet.

Oonga is confused, but holds still. If anyone, he knows the devotion Rama inspires. Rama pulled him all the way out of his dusty little village, across river and forest and road and mountain and valley and redstinkyland, to the big city, where he had never been. If Rama could do that to him, he could do that to anyone.

And even as Oonga watches in amazement, his new devotee starts to untie a small bundle at the corner of the pallu of her saree. Oonga's eyes light up. He knows what women keep hidden there. She fishes out a heavy coin, reverentially clasps Oonga's little blue hand, and fills his palm with it. Unsure what he ought to do now, Oonga repeats his superhit procedure, raises his other hand and blesses her. She seems to be very moved by that, and bows again. Oonga quickly pockets the coin, and turns to the landscape again. A god must play it cool.

|||<·V·>|||

Out in the landscape, under a particularly leafy tree, a soft rumbling is interrupted as the tractor trundles past. Pradip grunts and snorts and turns over to his side and resumes his snoring. Sushil has been standing worriedly by the bike for about ten minutes now, wondering if he should shake Pradip awake. What was meant to be a fifteen-minute nap has already clocked over an hour. He shakes Pradip, gently at first. And then with a little more agitation, until he hears his snoring disrupt. "Please wake up, sahib, we're already very late."

Pradip snorts, poots, wheezes and peels himself up off the ground. He looks at the sky, panics, glowers at Sushil. "Why didn't you wake me earlier? You have any idea how late it is?!"

Sushil doesn't know what to say. This man is incorrigible. He steps aside and lets Pradip's panic take charge. Pradip kicks and kicks and kicks the bike till it finally thrums to life. Sushil quietly takes the back seat, unwilling to drive anything any more.

|||<·V·>|||

Nagamma is right where Oonga saw her last. If yesterday her left arm pointed him to the west, today her right arm points him to the east, back home. But Oonga doesn't need to be told that. He's the lord who turned blue making his way across half the world. He knows where he's headed.

As he strides past the scarecrow, acknowledging her with that signature tilt of his Rama head, her gamchha-scarf slips off in astonishment. Her wide pumpkin mouth gawps. She looks like she wants to call every last crow in the neighbourhood to come behold this apparition with her. But that's easier said than done, given how many summers she has spent scaring them away!

Oonga knows the effect he has on everyone, scarecrows included. He slows down, letting the birds and the trees and the honeybees watch him glide past. So they can announce to the forest that their prince is here. The tall green grass is the first to hear the rumour, and leans to either side now to let Oonga through, brushing his new skin gently as he passes, collecting small flecks of blue off it onto its awestruck green fingertips, wondering what it must feel like to be here on the ground yet turn into a piece of sky.

|||<·∨·>|||

Pradip drives into a nervous flurry of activity in the camp. The dank smell of dread in the air tells him that something unwelcome has been announced. Sushil, though, is confused. It's evening. The sun hasn't even begun its final descent yet. This is usually the time things start to go still around here. Hearts start to sink. Spirits start to sag. The jawaans start to think about their homes. And families. And fields. Evenings are when someone or the other starts to talk about something mundane that they miss – like taking goats for grazing, or milking a cow, or sprinkling fertiliser, or the taste of the last rajma crop – normal things, that take their nerve-wracked minds off the omnipresent prospect of death.

Pradip parks the bike slowly, as if unwilling to proceed with protocol, cursing himself for arriving at such an inauspicious hour. If this over-eager, ignorant fool hadn't woken him they might have returned late enough to miss this funeral procession.

Sushil can't understand that look in Pradip's eyes. He scampers towards the CO's office, eager to report his findings and discover what he missed. Pradip lets him take the lead, dragging his feet behind him, his stomach lurching with the thought of what they will all be subject to tonight.

|||<•V•>|||

Manoranjan has an unnaturally large map spread across the office floor. Sushil notices that it's been put together like a jigsaw puzzle from several separate maps of each of the talukas around here. Strips of cellotape glisten where they have been joined, already tearing away again in some places, as if unwilling to reveal to Manoranjan the path to where he's determined to go tonight.

Manoranjan is squatted atop this map, on the shore of a river that crawls like a light blue snake round his feet. With a red sketch-pen he traces a route. In the jaundiced yellow light of the only bulb in the room this trail of red looks like that of the blood that Manoranjan intends to spill. Manoranjan's brows are knit, his mind racing.

Sushil can't figure how to reach Manoranjan's ear to shout his salutations. To get any closer he will have to step on this map, and run the risk of crushing a patch of pristine forest. He looks to Pradip for help. Pradip's eyes are shuttered. He wants no part of this conversation. He's switching a thousand gears inside his heart right now, one by one, to get into following-orders-blindly mode – the only mode that ensures survival on such expeditions.

So Sushil sucks in an unwelcome breath, and shouts, "SAHIB!"

Manoranjan barely hears him. As if having sensed a presence behind himself, he turns, looks at them without the slightest change in expression, then turns back to the map beneath him, and grumbles, "Go empty yourselves of piss and shit, and get ready. We leave in thirty."

Sushil is flummoxed. "Le-leave? Wh-where for?! Do-don't you want to know about the naa-naatak?" He looks to Pradip for answers, unsure of shouting out his question to the CO, who just slammed the door shut on any and all dialogue.

Pradip turns and is out of there in a flash. On nights like tonight, piss, shit and death – all come without warning. One has to get the first two out of the way early, so one can focus on dealing with the third.

Sushil is bursting with things to say. But the back of Manoranjan's head is a particularly ominous sight. The back of any head is featureless. Just like Ravana's face was. It doesn't want to listen. It doesn't want to engage. It wants you to follow, or retreat, or rebel. None of which Sushil wants to do right now. But the thought of having to load his rifle makes his stomach squeeze. So he reminds himself of the piss and the shit still inside him. And he too turns and is out of there in a flash.

Behind him, Manoranjan seems to have found what he was looking for all this while. He draws a thick red circle around a spot deep inside the jungle, and leans in to peer at it closely, like a giant demon god looking down at the village he intends to descend upon tonight.

TWENTY-FOUR

Over a small fire by the edge of the river, a large fish, neatly skewered on a porcupine quill, turns slowly, its flesh roasting to a crisp. The boatman is trying hard to be patient with the roasting, his stomach making frighteningly hungry sounds. He has had to wait one whole day to eat his fish because he forgot to bring turmeric and coriander and chilli from the village when that troublesome boy made him row over to the other side. *This meal will be such a satisfying one,* he thinks. *I can't believe I let that boy make my life so difficult. There ought to be a law against boys like him!*

That thought brings him some glee, and he smirks, but for only a moment, because just then two small blue feet stop before him. The boatman's startled eyes follow the blueness up from the feet, past blue knees, a blue belly, blue arms, up to a bizarre blue face. He blinks once, twice, thrice, trying to place this face. Until Oonga smiles that dazzlingly deceptive smile. And the boatman stutters, "Sc-scoundrel boy?! Is that you?!"

Oonga closes his eyes with an air of meditative importance, and nods, as if affirming some life-altering cosmic rumour.

"Wh-what happened to you?!"

But Mini Rama doesn't speak to lowly menials any more. He gestures to the boatman to get up off his bum, and points businesslike to the other shore.

The boatman is in a fix. This boy's so blue, this might be important. But his fish?! The fire will go out by the time he returns. What to do?!

The boatman kicks sand onto the fire, dousing it, muttering to himself about some karmic debt he must owe the boy from a past life.

Or perhaps it's a sign to not eat fish any more.

That thought causes a small cranky rumble in his tummy. So he extinguishes his thoughts, undoes the boat's leash, and pushes it into the water. Oonga is already in the boat, unwilling to risk the water washing his blue away. He stands as tall as his scrawny self allows, looking at the far shore like a conqueror would, gesturing to the boatman to *hurry-hurry*!

The boatman does as told, too puzzled by all this to protest.

When they are almost upon the shore, the old man steps out into the shallow water and pushes the boat to dry land so His Highness can disembark without bother. The boatman has resigned himself to his sorry fate with this boy. Oonga turns to him, and raises a closed fist, like he had done before. "It's okay, boy," the boatman sighs. "Go now. Don't try this drama with me again."

But Oonga clasps the old man's hand, turns his palm upwards, and plants on it the heaviest coin he has ever seen! The boatman cannot believe this is happening. He watches the small blue apparition leap out of the boat, steady himself, and stride like a village chieftain into the forest, raising his hand to greet the trees as if they have stood here all these many decades with the sole grand purpose of receiving him today.

|||<•V•>|||

The school camp is buzzing with stamping boots, clicking rifles, hushed murmurs, and orders being barked, along with the rustle of leaves and the snapping of twigs as the jawaans fix bits of shrubbery onto their selves. Sushil's not sure how two branches hitched to his back like this can camouflage him from the naxalites' jungle-eyes. But he doesn't know whom to voice his doubts to any more. All of this feels a little ridiculous now. The arrest of the teacher. The trip into town. Ravana's haran of Sita. This combing operation. Sushil is starting to feel that he was never hired as a soldier, but as a two-bit actor in an inconsequential side part in a play in which the performers themselves are its only audience.

Don't think so much! Sushil warns himself. *Don't think. This isn't the time for it.*

He slips his rifle onto his shoulder, switches off all the lights inside his head, and with measured steps he goes and takes his position in the single file into which Pradip has been arranging everyone.

Pradip notices the change in Sushil's demeanour, but keeps away. He is in no mood to engage in any conversation for the rest of tonight. His ears have room only for orders.

Manoranjan waits for the troop to settle, and then he speaks, in a low, clear drawl, never too loud, lest the trees around the camp hear him and tattle to those he now speaks of.

|||<•V•>|||

Hemla can hear Manoranjan's distant droning voice. She strains her ears to pick up a word or two. But her blood has caked inside them, making her almost as deaf as the man whose slaps did this to her.

She had passed out from pain when she pulled out the last stone. She doesn't know how long she lay unconscious, but she knows that time is running out fast now. The floor tremors slightly with the distant crunching of many boots. Hemla inhales as deep as her aching ribs allow, painfully pulls her knees up to her chin, and loops her arms around her bloodied body, to the front. The effort makes her dizzy again. But she keeps her mind firmly shut to all other thoughts save one – to get to her kids before the CRPF does.

She brings her trembling hands up to her mouth, clenches the rope with her teeth, and starts to pull at the knot. Sharp needles of pain shoot through her brain. But her face is numb. She had felt her cheeks start to swell after the fifth hard slap. But it was the smashing of her face into the ground that finally took all sensation away. She's grateful for that now because she feels a tooth dislodge with the exertion. *It's just a tooth,* she tells herself, *just a tooth.* And she tugs harder, until she feels the rope starting to give.

The big Eye still lies on the ground where it had been flung. It has been staring haplessly at the sky ever since, as if wondering what it might take to stake claim to it. A small blue face eclipses the sky, looking down into the Eye curiously. Oonga remembers this Eye upright, humming creepily, when he had passed it yesterday. *What angry wind could have done this?* Not that Oonga minds, though. The eerie humming has been muffled. And Oonga doesn't feel his skin crawl. Which is good, because he is in no mood to run today. Rama never runs. He walks like he owns the land he walks upon.

Oonga walks with a swagger now, staking claim with every decisive step. The earth feels this. The soles of Oonga's feet carry the plod of arrogance from the city. The boy that left was *of* this earth. The boy that returns believes the earth to be his. That blue is taint, thinks the earth, and goes cold with disappointment. The grass starts to droop. The roots of the trees start to curl.

If the Eye had a mouth it would have smirked now.

|||<•V•>|||

Ghosa has brought some wood for the bonfire. He notes with dismay that this wood is damp.

"There was some dew last night," says Somaru, watching Ghosa.

"That's surprising," says Damboru. "This isn't the season for dew."

All this tension in the air, thinks Ghosa. *The trees and the grass – they feel for us, and soak it all in*. And last night was particularly saturated with anxiety.

Ghosa is about to light the wood, when old Timi stops him, "The wood is wet. It will raise a tall smoke. It shouldn't be mistaken for a signal."

Ghosa goes quiet. "We light a small fire tonight. Go get some twigs," Timi says. Ghosa leaves, as everyone goes quiet.

Oongamma, though, is restless. The sun is about to go down. Kunja said Oonga would be back by now. She's not taking a chance on anyone's words any more. Oongamma collects her heavy self off the ground, announces, "I'm going to go look for Oonga."

Madvi panics. "Should I go speak with Kunja once more?"

"Go. But I'm not waiting. Forgot what Hemla told us? Sitting here scared like this is not going to solve our problems," says Oongamma, her mind made up. "Who knows where that boy might be now? If he can go so far despite being so little, I can too."

Oongamma walks to their hut, hurriedly making a mental list of what all she ought to carry with her, given that she isn't going to be travelling alone. "Think about the little one that hasn't arrived yet," pleads Madvi, trotting after her.

"What use bringing her into this world, Madvi? If we cannot guarantee the safety of the one already here?"

Many scared words have hurried up into Madvi's throat yet again. But he swallows hard, pushes them back down, and just stands there, paralysed by his dilemma. He doesn't like being forced to think about such things. Now is when he needs his salfi most of all. If he can get a few gourdfuls down his throat right away, his mind might just about start to work again. But he sees Oongamma gathering her things into a basket, and tying it into a cloth to sling across her back. She means business.

What should he do?

|||<·V·>|||

In Kunja's hands the bracelet is finally finding shape. He scrapes it on a stone now. There is an urgency in his actions that makes the top of this hill vibrate nervously. Kunja chants in a low whisper as he scrapes the trinket, trying to exorcise it of all its primeval memories. He speaks in ancient guttural sounds to the atoms of the metal itself, telling it that although it is the child of rock, with the next sunrise it will also become the pride of man. Of one man in particular. A little man.

A man whom the world of men cannot consider to have become a man yet. But by sunrise his expanding spirit will have outgrown the smallness of his body. And he will be more man than most in his tribe. And this bracelet will welcome him to that which cannot be reversed – growing up.

|||<•V•>|||

The jawaans creep cautiously through the darkening forest – a single long snake of men, their rifles raised, their ears alert to every chirp, their muscles taut, their heavy booted steps wary to not land on anything that shouldn't be in a jungle. So far Manoranjan has avoided leading them along any of the regular jungle trails. But here his map informs him that they have no choice but to walk along a particular path for a couple of hundred metres before they can slither into the undergrowth again.

This is one stretch Manoranjan would have liked to avoid. For the rest of his life, if possible. In fact, he would like very much to set fire to this stretch right now. And wipe it off the map. But he knows his limits. And so he stops, turns, leans to gesture to Pradip who is bringing up the rear. No one else understands that gesture except for the two of them.

They emerge onto a dirt track, wide enough for a jeep to drive on. Sushil notices jeep tracks too. *This deep in the jungle?* thinks Sushil. Who would drive their jeep this deep in the jungle? It's a known fact that the naxalites only move on foot.

And that's when it reveals itself… *the* jeep… or whatever is left of it. Burnt to a cinder. Its metal underbelly exposed. Its chassis gnarled outwards, as if it had exploded from within.

Exploded?!

This is THAT jeep! thinks Sushil, a terrified chill running down his spine. *The one that was blown up by the bomb that also took the sahib's ears!*

He turns to look at Pradip, who looks away, his face and skin starting to turn really oily now with the thick sweat of apprehension.

Manoranjan walks past the ghost of the jeep without acknowledging it. The other jawaans though cannot tear their eyes away from it. It's almost as if the jungle guardians have allowed it to lie there untouched since, as a memorial to the day they made their point to those who refuse to pay heed.

|||<·V·>|||

Sweaty jawaan has passed by the classroom door half a dozen times now. The camp is empty tonight save for the four sentries in the watchtowers, and him. Manoranjan has never considered Sweaty man enough to trust him with *real* officer duty. So he has him answering the telephone and bringing him his meals. Nothing more.

Sweaty has wanted to prove that he can do what the others do as well. But whenever the opportunity arises he breaks into a sweat – the kind that soaks as big patches under his arms and on his back. And he sees Manoranjan note that and throw him *that* look. The one that makes the sahib's lips curl up slightly in disgust. That look makes Sweaty feel pathetic. On most days he feels like he cannot rise above this. That he is destined to be wretched. And hapless. And not worthy of being taken on a combing operation.

He watched yesterday through the crack of the partly open door as all those jawaans took their turns to rape Hemla. He wanted to have a go too. To prove to Manoranjan that he too is capable, and can be trusted to cause pain when called upon. But Manoranjan never called upon him. And Sweaty was too nervous to volunteer.

He is alone here now. And only a lock separates him from her. She has been beaten to within an inch of her life. *She'll barely have any fight left in her*, he thinks. But those stones! He had watched slyly as Manoranjan shoved those stones into her. Everyone braced themselves for the endless howls of pain that always follow. But she let out only one solitary scream. Perhaps she passed out? That would make this easy.

Pacified by that thought, Sweaty darts a look to the watchtowers. The sentries are all looking away, their eyes pasted to the jungles, alert to the point of nervous breakdown, aware that there is no one here to bring up the rear should they be attacked. It's all up to them tonight.

And so Sweaty will never have a chance better than this one. He fishes out the key, turns it in the lock, bracing himself for the unsavoury task of pulling out the stones from inside Hemla before he lets himself in. He had stolen a used, washed condom from Manoranjan's clothesline a month back. He can't let any of her filthy jungle blood onto himself. *These tribals let their pet pigs roam loose inside their homes. Who knows what diseases they carry?*

He steps into the dark classroom, unhooks his belt, rolls it neatly and keeps it by the door, slips out a torch, flicks it on, places it on the floor, turning its beam to light –

The teacher?!

Where the bloody hell is the teacher?!

Sweaty feels his socks slowly drench in a cold sweat. Dreading going any closer he picks up the torch, and slowly scans the floor with its beam.

Undone rope.

Big smears of blood.

Two bloodied stones.

And what is that?

Sweaty leans in to look closely…

A bloodied tooth.

The torch runs its fat long finger of light along the wall, checking the windows. The far window is open, creaking on its hinges. A small blood-soaked stone lies on the sill where a latch hangs, its wooden neck broken. A cool gentle draft of wind leaks in through this window, ripples over the angry stained floor and runs its unwelcoming fingers over Sweaty's soaked uniform. His hair stands on end.

His is the only breathing in this classroom.

He knows now that he ought to leap out that window too, and give Hemla chase. But night is approaching. And Sweaty is forced to admit that he is scared. Too scared to risk going after her in those jungles, alone. The thought makes him feel the urge to piss urgently. And as he turns, steps out of the door, and starts to turn the key the other way in the lock now, he realises Manoranjan is right about him.

As Sweaty rushes away, a shuddering rises inside him. His face starts to quiver. His chest grows heavy. Till his legs can't hold his weight any more.

When the sobs come he rushes into a dark corner, drops down to his haunches, and curls into the cold wall, a pathetic, weeping mess.

TWENTY-FIVE

Dusk falls thick today. It threatens to turn all green into grainy, smoky white. Hemla cannot see it too well though. Her eyes are blurry. All that beating has damaged most of her senses. She bullets through the foliage in near-blindness, trusting the forest to get her to where she needs to be. Her saree is ripped and shredded and clotted with her blood. It was harder to manage to cover herself with it than it was to break that window open. She's grateful it will soon be night. She cannot let her children see her like this by daylight. Some things the eyes cannot unsee. They will remember this vision of her if they see her too clearly. And visions like this can turn a child's heart permanently. She cannot risk that.

Every step she takes sends jolts of pain darting through her battered body. But she keeps running, letting the forest tell her where to turn and where to climb. She knows the troop will have to circle this hill. All the well-trod trails run round the base of this hill. And the base is wide. They would never risk climbing it to get to the other side. This is – as they call it – naxalite country. For a brief moment Hemla is almost thankful for that, but then she checks herself. Her faculties are sharp enough to keep her prerogatives in sight. It is the naxalites that caused this misfortune that will befall her village today. If she'd had more time she would have come up with something to convince the CRPF commander. They might be a bit too brutal. But they're human too. And scared. Most brutality rears its spiteful head from the depths of fear. Hemla could smell fear all over the school.

School.

Its crazy, thinks Hemla, *how I still call it a school.*

She starts to climb, her feet bruised and cut in a hundred places by now. For a moment she slows down to speak to her feet. Every part of her body has had to overcome dizzying pain today. *Now it's your turn,* she tells her feet. *I need you to not give in. Not now.* And she places one foot on a jutting rock and heaves herself up, ignoring another stab of searing pain.

The deathly silence of the trees is suddenly broken by a CRACK!

Half a dozen rifles cock simultaneously. Pradip gestures "Sh!"

Everyone freezes.

Fourteen pairs of eyes fearfully scan the shadows all around. One of the jawaans spots something, waves his hand silently, catches everyone's attention, and then points at Sushil's feet.

Sushil had stepped on a dry twig.

Pradip glares Sushil down, waving his hand to the convoy to start moving again. Sushil silently curses himself. His mind had wandered again, to all those things he was trying to shut out. Ironically, it's only when he starts to think about why he's here, that his departure from *here* is total. Not only had he not realised he had stepped on a twig, he hadn't even heard the 'Crack!' that froze everyone's blood.

The troop tries to hurry now, as much as they can without making a noise. They need to catch up with Manoranjan, whose dead ears ensured that he kept moving when the others paused.

Sushil wonders how Manoranjan must keep his thoughts from flying the coop every now and then, given that he can't rely on his hearing to keep him in the present. *There, I'm thinking again,* Sushil checks himself, and jiggles his head to shake the thoughts out. That action startles the jawaan behind him, and Sushil hears his rifle click.

But then they look at one another, take a deep breath, and stay in line.

|||<•V•>|||

The kuchcha trail from the village turns sharply into the forest to the right. Oongamma approaches this turning now, not quite sure how she will get across the river tonight. The boatman will refuse. He doesn't like wrestling with the rapids in the darkness. Oongamma could have offered him extra money to take her across if that incorrigible son of hers hadn't stolen every last coin she had saved. Such irony. She now needs the money he stole so she can go find *him*! She mutters a curse, imagining the thrashing she will give him when he appears before her, when –

A blue boy melts out of the forest, turns the corner in style, and strides up the path in a beeline for Oongamma. Oongamma gawks. That figure looks familiar. It's colour, though, anything but. Oonga spots Oongamma. His eyes light up, and he forgets who he's pretending to be. He dashes to his mother, grinning, and squeals, "Amma! Look!" Then he suddenly remembers, tips his head back, drops his voice to a drawl, and finishes with a mini flourish, "I'm Rama."

Oongamma doesn't quite care. She grabs him tight by his shoulders. So tight that they might have turned blue if they weren't already that colour. "Where did you go off to, you scamp?!" and she suddenly registers why her boy seems so odd. "Who did this to you?!" She lets go of his shoulders to check the rest of his body, afraid she might find bruises or scars.

Oonga recoils, afraid his colour might come off if she cuddles him all of a sudden. "Tch! Amma! Don't touch me. I'm Rama now. Show some respect!"

"Respect?! I'll show you respect! You troublesome goat!" and she whacks his bum, hard! Mini Rama leaps away, snarling. Oongama doesn't know whether to laugh or to cry. She wants to grab him now in a tight embrace. But Mini Rama has other plans. "Can I go to my kingdom now? My subjects await me."

Unable to decide what she would like to do to this little monstrosity, Oongamma steps aside, and lets him take the lead. Oonga nods his approval, raises his hand, blesses her, and swaggers past her, allowing her to follow. Oongamma's eyes are glued to her boy. She's going to stay right behind him, to ensure he doesn't dart off anywhere without warning again.

|||<·V·>|||

The hot bracelet sizzles as Kunja dunks it in a wooden bowl of water. He holds it up against the fading daylight to let the cooling silver metal absorb some red from the dying sun.

As the bracelet starts to change colour slowly, Kunja tips his head into the wind. It brings him a sound and a scent that he has been waiting for.

The boy is back.

|||<•V•>|||

Mother and son turn to head back to their village when Madvi, swaying on his feet, teeters in their direction. He spots his wife, throws his hands up in the air in relief, announces, "Come on, woman! Let's go find our son!"

It's not hard to see where Oonga must have got his penchant for dramatics from. Madvi reaches out to hold Oongamma's hand and lead her into the jungle. But Oongamma rolls her eyes, shakes her head, and walks past him in the other direction. Madvi totters to a stop, turns, puzzled, and scrunches his eyes to see – a small blue creature leading his wife back to where she just came from.

"What's that?" he asks, befuddled, pointing.

Oonga ignores him completely, continues his march, murmuring a note to self, "Subjects need to find their new king a new father."

Oongamma suppresses the urge to giggle. She's starting to enjoy this. How this day has flipped and flopped.

|||<•V•>|||

Idma springs to her feet, her eyes nearly popping out of her head when Oonga stops before her, puts his hands on his hips, and tips his nose up to the sky, seeking to dazzle her with his regal splendour.

There is so much Idma wants to say to him – Donkey. Idiot. Fool. Rascal. *So* much. But she cannot even begin since Oongamma is standing right behind him, unwilling to leave Oonga's back unguarded for even a moment.

But Idma, unlike Oongamma, is truly dumbstruck. She lifts a finger and touches Oonga's blue skin. She rubs it, then checks her fingertip. The blue hasn't come off. Oonga tosses her a smug smile. "Idma, I'm no fake, unlike all of you. I am the true Rama."

Idma starts to circle Oonga to study him from all sides. He lets her. She finds a patch on his back that's still the colour of Oonga. "Aye! You painted yourself!"

Oonga is unaffected. He clasps her hand like he had seen Rama clasp Sita's, and whispers, "I will allow you to be my Sita, if you bring me gur every day." And before she can agree, he reaches down to the ground, gathers two fistfuls of mud and smears her cheeks brown!

Madvi is dizzy with confusion. He looks from the boy to his wife and back to the boy, trying to piece this puzzle together. Oongamma pushes Oonga's bum now, "Get a move on, O king. Your subjects await you!"

And Oonga gestures, "Ya ya, okay, going, going." He turns and swaggers into the village, followed by his entourage of three.

Waist deep in gushing rapids, Hemla struggles to wade across the river. The river gets narrow and shallow down here where the valley dips sharply. And so the water is forceful. No one uses this stretch to get across. But when she was little, Hemla had won many childhood bets here. Her feet recognise each and every rock underneath this rushing water, although in the years since, these rocks have become smoother and more slippery. Hemla's bleeding feet have trouble gripping them.

But Hemla trusts the speeding water, just like she trusts the forest. She tries to empty her mind completely, and tackle this one rock at a time. If she slips even once this river will carry her at top speed at least ten kilometres out before it lets up to allow her to swim across. That is if it doesn't slam her head against one of these rocks before that.

Hemla uses the water spraying into her lungs to burn her brain into numbness so she can shut out these thoughts. The river doesn't wish to delay her. It's in its nature to be this way. The more Hemla submits to that truth, the surer her foothold gets. And the other shore finally seems reachable.

Far upstream, the jawaans try to wade across the river too. The river is far less agitated here. But its shores are further apart. Some of the soldiers have stopped in waist deep water, worried that they will get too drenched this way to survive the cold unpredictable night ahead. Against better judgement, though, Sushil advances. He has been trying to cease all the thoughts tumbling about inside his mind. And for that he needs to keep moving.

Being shorter than most in the squad, Sushil is quickly chest deep. To keep his rifle dry, he has been holding it aloft with both arms raised above his head. This means he doesn't have his arms handy to paddle against the flow of the water. Without warning, his foot slips on a loose rock on the riverbed, but Sushil stamps his other foot down in time, and just about manages to stay upright.

Soon he is neck deep, and starting to get unsure of proceeding this way. He turns to check if he should keep moving, but a sudden eddy swirls him off his feet. Thrown off balance, and with no foothold, Sushil starts to drift away, confused if he should bring his arms down and risk flooding his rifle, when the jawaan in front of him grabs his belt, and tugs him back into line. Sushil gasps for breath, trying to find some foothold to steady himself. The others get nervous.

Bringing up the rear now, Pradip has stopped. He notes with dismay that this might not be the best idea for this lot of louts. If he lets Manoranjan push them now there could be a mutiny. He scans the river this way and that, turns to Manoranjan, and shouts, "SAHIB, LET ME QUICKLY RUN A RECCE UPSTREAM. THERE'S BOUND TO BE A BRIDGE. THIS RIVER COULD GET TOO DEEP IN THE MIDDLE."

Manoranjan isn't happy with the suggestion, but a second look at his squad confirms that this river indeed isn't something they're capable of crossing this way. Manoranjan nods.

Meanwhile, Sushil has noted something with dismay too. His cap toppled off his head when he slipped. The river fled with it. Of all the heads in this troop now his is the only one without the safety of camouflage. Sushil wonders if that could get him a bullet through his temple.

Given their current circumstances, that almost sounds like a welcome idea.

Pradip has scampered out of the water and is slithering fast, lizard-like, along the shore, his eyes darting about the oncoming darkness, looking for anything that could connect this bank to the other. When he's out of Manoranjan's sight, Pradip slows down, licks his drying lips, spits, and drops down on the gravel – CRUNCH!

A few extra minutes never killed anybody, he thinks, and lies down, savouring each heaving breath as if it were a drag of a bidi.

Two kilometres downstream, something whips into Hemla's leg. She reaches down into the water, and fishes out – a CRPF cap! She turns to look upstream, startled. How did they get here this quickly? Is someone guiding them?!

Worried now, Hemla lets the rapids pluck the cap from her fingers, and watches it gush away into the thickening darkness. She's about ten treacherous steps from the shore now. But her legs are starting to quiver with pain and fatigue.

TWENTY-SIX

Tulsa's worry hasn't abated at the sight of Oonga. "Hemla didi wasn't with you?" she asks Oonga.

"Rama doesn't need anyone."

"The police didn't catch you?" Sikoka asks, unable to process this blue vision.

"No one can catch Rama."

"How did you go to the city alone?" Timi is awestruck. In all her years she's never heard of a child do that.

"Rama can go anywhere he wants."

High-as-a-kite Madvi has been peering inquiringly into Oonga's painted face all this time. Suddenly, realisation flutters across his face like a startled bird! "OONGA!" he squawks. "You're back!" And he dives for his boy with outstretched arms. Oonga ducks. Rama doesn't like to be hugged. Madvi misses him completely, grabs thin air instead, and tumbles in a drunken tangle of limbs.

But Madvi is undeterred. To celebrate his prodigal son's magical return, he announces, "Tonight we celebrate the return of Oonga, son of Madvi! Salfi for everyone, from my tree!" And he trundles off to bring his precious pot from behind their hut.

No one seems to share his enthusiasm though. Hemla might still be in trouble. This plays on every mind huddled there. But no one seems to be able to find the right words to wonder about it aloud.

|||<•V•>|||

It has taken the boatman a long time to relight the fire he had doused. The wood had got surprisingly damp in the time it took him to drop Oonga and return. His stomach is now twisting with hunger. He can't remember the last time he ate a hearty meal. Yesterday? The day before?

Anyway, it doesn't matter now. By the time night falls he will have a delicious piping hot mosla fish, ready to devour.

He's kept his small pot of salfi ready beside him as well. Tonight's meal is well earned. That boy surprised him with this coin. It's a five-rupee coin! That's worth two-and-a-half boat rides. The boatman has never before seen five rupees in a single coin, that too this heavy. He'll surprise the boy right back next time he comes screaming about an emergency! He'll give him a free ride!

That thought brings the boatman's heart much gladness. And he twists the fish over the fire, checking to see if its flesh is starting to smoke. The flickering flames make happy shadows dance across his famished face.

In a moment these shadows go still, as two heavy boots crunch towards him from the dark, and stop near the fire.

The boatman looks up to see a harrowed soldier, pointing to his circular little boat, "That's yours?"

The boatman nods.

"How many can it take?"

The boatman stutters, "I do-don't ferry at ni-night –"

Pradip forgot. He'll have to gesticulate the query. These jungle dimwits always make communication so difficult.

"How – many – passengers – can – your – boat – carry?" Pradip gestures, hoping he won't have to repeat himself.

The boatman gets it. He's been asked such questions by people in uniform before. Only those uniforms were a deep bottle green, and belonged to the jungle. This is not. He raises four fingers in reply.

"Including you?" Pradip gestures.

The boatman shakes his head, acutely aware of what the soldier might be planning to do now.

Pradip turns, walks ten paces in the direction he came from, cups his mouth and hoots, like an owl. The downstream wind carries his hoot to the rest of the flock.

A jawaan waves his arm at Manoranjan, points upstream and gestures they got *the* signal. Manoranjan nods back. The jawaan cups his mouth, clears his throat, and tries to hoot. What comes out of his throat is a squeal! Ten pairs of startled eyes glare him down. He can get them killed like this. He looks away, embarrassed. He had told Pradip that he could screech like a bat but not hoot like an owl. But Pradip insisted on owl, since a bat's screech is high pitched, and might carry far, to jungle ears.

The jawaans hurriedly gather themselves and start to scamper towards Pradip.

|||<•V•>|||

Oongamma hasn't taken her eyes off her boy ever since she laid eyes on him. She sits before a large leaf stacked with curry and rice, the next morsel held in her fingers, ready to plough it into Oonga's busy mouth when he turns towards her. Oongamma doesn't want to get in the way of his story. There are a hundred things she would like to scold him for. But all of that can wait until tomorrow. Tonight she'd rather just watch him and feed him and when he tires of this endless charade, put him to sleep, and then sit and watch him sleep.

Oonga is leaping about, replaying Rama's fight with Ravana.

He had gone and plucked a long stiff blade of grass, tucked it into the back of Drika's shorts, and turned him into Rama's whip-tailed monkey warrior friend.

Oonga had sat Idma down – her cheeks still freshly brown – next to Oongamma, instructing her to not move, and not worry, since her Rama is now here to save Sita.

All the other kids are being herded around as the many beings that make up the many-armed, many-headed Ravana.

Hurre has become bored of doing the same things as the others – marching in a circle around Oonga as Oonga makes them utter smoky demon sounds. She reaches out and scratches Oonga's skin, scraping some blue paint off. Oonga turns in a flash, raises his hand high. "Stop! O horrible Ravana! You will pay for this!" He glowers at Hurre, raises his bow and aims his arrow at her. She squeals and runs, with Mini Rama in hot pursuit. All the other Ravanas squeal and shout and utter demonic wails, thoroughly enjoying all this drama.

Oongamma, anxious, calls after him, "Stay in the village, Oonga, don't run out, or I'll beat you this time, I swear!"

Oonga screeches to a halt, swivels around to point his tautly drawn arrow at Oongamma, and bellows, "Try it!"

The boy is uncontrollable, giggles Oongamma, pops the morsel into her own mouth, and chewing, she pushes herself up, and waddles over to Madvi. She plucks the gourd from his hand, and knocks back some much needed salfi!

Tulsa watches all of this sombrely. It doesn't feel right to be sitting around here like this when they still don't know where Hemla might be. All this warmth and cheer feels like the misleading calm before a terrifying storm. She wonders if Kunja knows something he isn't telling them.

|||<•∨•>|||

More than any other night in his entire life, it is tonight that old Kunja will most regret being born with the 'gift'. He sits crouched at the edge of the cliff, watching the distant glow of the freshly lit bonfire joust with the descending darkness. That village down there has been the reason he looks forward to waking each day. He clenches his eyes shut tight now. And presses his palms over his ears to shut out the murmurations of the wind. He starts to stamp his feet to shut out the quaking whispers of the earth. He doesn't want to know any more, he tells them. He already knows enough.

The wind goes cold and slices his skin. And the earth starts to heat beneath his feet. He is their captive. They will not let him be. So he gets up tiredly and decides to do the only thing he can.

Prepare.

He'll spend the night gathering herbs, and preparing the ointments that the villagers will need when dawn breaks. If he cannot protect them from being wounded he can at least help heal their wounds when this night is over.

|||<•∨•>|||

The boat has sunk till its rim. Standing waist deep in the water, the boatman knows it's futile to protest. So he struggles to push the boat out, as the jawaan with the oar starts to paddle. Some water splashes into the boat. Manoranjan is forced to admit now that packing six men in was a bad idea. "One of you get out," he tells the five soldiers in the boat with him. Not sure which of them he means, three of them start to clamber out nervously, and the boat tilts this way and that, letting in a lot more water. "One of you!" growls Manoranjan. "Not all of you, dumbfucks!" All three freeze. Manoranjan clenches his jaw in frustration, points at one, and watches him leap out eagerly, making a loud splash.

Pradip waits on the shore with the ten remaining soldiers. Exasperated, he shakes his head, and mumbles, "This is going to take all fucking night." Without warning, he burps, then looks around slyly to see if anyone heard it, coughing to cover up the sound. The ten minutes that the troop took to get here were enough for Pradip to demolish the boatman's roasted fish. But before that, Pradip had to douse the boatman's fire. It's almost night now. Any fire – even a solitary match – could be enough to expose them to the ghosts of the forest.

Sushil watches Pradip keenly. Pradip's skin is thick with oil. His face has a threatening gleam. And, Sushil notes, the reptile hasn't blinked for a whole minute now. If he needs to survive this night he'll have to stick closer to Pradip than his own shadow.

|||<•V•>|||

Soni sits crouched up in a jackfruit tree. They were to move camp today. But something made Laxmi decide to stay at this spot one more day. It could be her female instinct, thinks

Soni, the kind of silent voice from an abyss deep inside a woman that she cannot explain to a man. Linga was unhappy with the decision. "The dalam is still alive," he had said to Laxmi, "because we keep moving every three days."

But Laxmi had been adamant. She knew the village would need them soon. And in the absence of Hemla, to move further away from them would be unwise. Linga had thrown a fit then, and refused his 'lookout' duty tonight. Without wasting a moment, Soni had volunteered. She felt like she could take a bullet for Laxmi today. For the first time in months her insides have stopped twisting in pain. The village hearing her story was the balm her soul needed.

She even made jackfruit curry for everyone this evening. It was her husband's favourite. He craved it each time they made love in the river. The river nearby reminds her sharply of him. He may not be alive any more. But she's still here, up in a jackfruit tree, looking out for danger. Some day she will make the men who killed him, pay. But what if no one had killed him? What if he was alive somewhere, thinking of her at this very moment? And her jackfruit curry? And the love that they made in the river?

Doesn't matter, thinks Soni, afraid that if she succumbs to such thoughts, that unbearable pain inside her might return. *Doesn't matter if they killed him or not. Keeping him alive in their jail is worse than death. And I will make them pay regardless. For the pain in my insides. And for all the jackfruit curry that he will now never eat.*

So lost in her thoughts is Soni that she doesn't notice the figure running pell-mell towards her tree, until it's nearly upon her. Soni gasps, sticks two fingers into her mouth and whistles.

In a flash three women pounce from the shadows, surround the running figure, cock their rifles at her, and freeze!

Hemla, caked in blood from her head down to her feet, stands shivering before them, her whitening arms clutching her drenched rag saree tight against her bruised skin. She looks ashamed, frightened, broken, but not yet dispossessed of her soul. It is that last thing – shining determinedly in her eyes – that the three naxalites acknowledge, and rush to gather her before she drops exhausted to her knees.

|||<•V•>|||

"You have to help me save my village," Hemla implores. Linga translates for Laxmi, unable to take his eyes off Hemla. He cannot believe this woman made it out of there in one piece. "The CRPF is on their way there. They will brutalise them. They might even rape the women. Please help me get them out."

Laxmi nods, her eyes suffused with admiration for this woman. "I knew you'd finally see sense," she says. "There was no other way."

As Linga translates that for Hemla, Laxmi ducks into a tent, and emerges with a green uniform. "Change, quickly," she says. "We'll ambush the CRPF before they get to the village."

Laxmi holds the uniform out for Hemla, as Linga translates, the speed of his words betraying the triumph he now feels in his heart.

Hemla looks at the uniform, and then at Laxmi, and then at the others gathered around her, perplexed. "I – I didn't come here to join you," she says, her gut going cold, afraid she's now going to lose precious time. "I came for your help."

Laxmi smiles warmly. "Yes, and help is what you will get." She gestures for a rifle, holds it out for Hemla. "You can carry this tonight. You don't need to fire it. You'll learn eventually. But it will give you strength."

Hemla pulls back, starts to stand up, her legs trembling. She came to ask for help. It's a human thing to ask for. All she wanted was for these people to help her evacuate her villagers tonight. So that those simple folk would get a fair chance to sit together, discuss the situation, and find a peaceful way out of this mess.

"I could've died today," Hemla says, placing each word like a mud brick, one atop the other, to rebuild the wall between them. "And it would've been okay."

Linga glares Hemla down now, unwilling to translate. But Hemla waits till he does. Laxmi, her warmth draining out of her, gestures for Linga to continue.

"You went to my village without my permission. And because of you they are in danger now."

As the words pour out of Hemla, her legs start to steady themselves. Their trembling ceases. These legs are all she can depend on tonight. If she's made it this far against such odds, chances are she'll make it to the village before the police do.

"If any of them die tonight," Hemla says, "that blood will be on your hands."

Linga has had enough. He cocks his rifle in Hemla's face, fuming.

Laxmi's face has shuttered itself.

Hemla looks down the barrel of Linga's gun. The only thing this makes her feel is a deep, inescapable sorrow. She turns to Laxmi. "I know you care, Didi," she says. "But by doing things this way you are no different from them. I had a gun pointed at me there. I have a gun pointed at me now."

Laxmi doesn't need that translated. She understands it.

"Don't come to the village again. Without you we may still have a chance. With you, we have none." Hemla lowers her eyes and turns to leave, knotting her torn saree tight around herself, preparing for the tough, lonely task ahead.

Linga strains at the trigger, every sinew in his being wanting to put a bullet in Hemla right now. But Laxmi's deathly silence works like a leash. He watches Hemla leave, and spits a curse at her.

Soni's insides have started twisting again. She was wrong about this night. It just might be her most painful yet. The others may have missed it but Soni didn't – the blood caked around the insides of Hemla's legs – that kind of blood is not the blood of a mere rape. Soni would know. It had taken her two days to be able to stand up straight again. And Hemla ran across half the taluka to get here. The rifle in Soni's hands suddenly feels too heavy to carry any more.

But her dilemma is shortlived.

"The teacher is foolish," announces Laxmi, watching Linga translate for her. "If those cops didn't spare Padua, they're certainly not going to spare Pottacheru."

Laxmi struggles to keep her steely facade from slipping. In all her years in this turmoil she has never ever seen someone be able to refuse the Gun after going through what this teacher did. Could the teacher be right? Is the way of the Gun doomed for failure? But then what is the alternative? How does one continue to try to hold dialogue when stones have been shoved mercilessly into one's vagina? Is dialogue possible with the man who does that?

Laxmi wasn't prepared for this. Everything had been playing out just like it always did. She had predicted all of it. The next step was clear. And inevitable. And she was ready to go through the motions like all the many times before this. Hand a gun. Turn a mind. Swell the ranks. Keep fighting. But this woman – this teacher – she had to go and change the narrative.

Laxmi deals with this too the way she has dealt with everything all along. "We leave in five minutes," she announces. "Carry all the ammunition we have. That village is going to need us. They just don't know it yet."

Her look to Linga unleashes him. He quickly translates that order for the group, and darts into the tent. Where the soft deadly sound of metal clanking against metal starts to fill up the tightening darkness.

TWENTY-SEVEN

Oongamma had instructed Idma to stick to Oonga like his shadow. "And if he tries to run away again, you have to come and tell me!" Oongamma had warned, with a stern wagging of her finger. Idma had promised. With those brown swathes on either cheek, she had been officially anointed Mini Rama's Mini Sita. Either she would have to run away with him, or set the entire kingdom on his tail, were he to take off without warning again.

Idma follows Oonga all over the village now, as Oonga pretends to fire arrow after arrow at the ten Ravanas scattering this way and that, hissing and yowling.

The ten Mini Ravanas dive behind the school banyan and scurry into the foliage. Mini Rama sends his monkey lieutenant to the left, his newly deputed commander Mini Sita to the right, and plunges straight into the foliage, to hunt down the ten troublesome little monsters he needs to terminate before morning!

Oongamma is tipsy. One half of her regrets emptying that

 gourd of salfi. What if she passes out? There's no telling what mischief Oonga might wreak. But the other half of her wants to go whack another gourdful from Madvi. It's been a trying day. She could do with passing out! But suddenly, she hears a voice –

SCREAM!

Oongamma rushes out of her hut to see many policemen with rifles charge into the village. The villagers run for their huts. The policemen smash pots, toss aside upturned baskets, kick down doors. Oongamma panics, pounces on Madvi, tries to pull him into their hut. But Madvi's body has gone limp with fright. Oongamma struggles but cannot pull him alone. She screams, "OONGA! OONGA!" but her little one is nowhere in sight.

Manoranjan strides to the bonfire, pulls a long flaming branch out, and sets the large community haystack alight. Many startled voices gasp. Cows start to moo. Goats start to bleat. Chickens start to squawk. The entire village erupts in a cacophony of terror.

The jawaans are tearing the villagers out from behind their flimsy cane doors to gather them in the open, when Manoranjan finally fires a gunshot into the air, "FUCK THE ADULTS. ROUND UP THE KIDS!"

|||<·V·>|||

In the underbrush, Oonga has heard the chaos. He cannot believe that his mind can conjure up all these sounds so well! He wishes Oongamma could see him now. All these sounds. All this action. Her little Rama out on the hunt for the demon king. He will bring her the monster's head when he's beheaded Ravana. He will need a coconut for that. He'll draw eyes and a snarling mouth on it with chalk. And he'll stick hay on top to make it look like hair. But Oonga's plan is interrupted by a large fire rising up into the sky from the centre of the village. "Wow! This story is really coming alive now!" he squeals.

|||<•V•>|||

Pradip drags Somaru to the bonfire and drops him grovelling before Manoranjan. Most of the men and women have been gathered there by now. Oongamma is trembling. She's not sure what she wants. That Oonga appear right now? Or that he stay out of sight?

"THERE ISN'T A SINGLE KID AROUND, SAHIB!" Pradip reports anxiously.

This is unnatural. What if Manoranjan was right all along?

Manoranjan spits into the fire, raises his rifle butt high, and smashes Somaru's face in, snarling, "Fucking naxalites! Using your kids to kill?"

The pleading and screaming of the villagers is so loud now that Manoranjan can actually hear it! And this makes his fury grow. He turns his rifle to Somaru's head, cocks it, and is about to make his point, when –

A bunch of children appear from behind the banyan tree, gaping dumbstruck at the scene before them.

The jawaans gawp at the kids, not quite sure what they should do now. They look perfectly harmless. One of them has a long tail of grass swaying about behind him.

Manoranjan sees that his troop's brains have jammed. He's used to this happening in a moment of crisis. The men jump to action. The boys freeze up.

"GET THEM!" Pradip barks, and rushes to round up the children.

Manoranjan's rifle is pointed at the kids as they are dragged into the clearing. Oongamma can't help herself. "Where is Oonga?!" she asks Drika, panicked. But the kids are so full up with fear that their mouths have swollen shut.

Manoranjan doesn't like the panic in Oongamma's voice. It reeks of things he cannot comprehend. He cocks his rifle, advances at her, when –

"SAHIB!" a voice hurtles into the village and collapses in a heap at his feet.

"SAHIB, PLEASE! PLEASE DON'T HURT THEM!" Hemla begs, holding onto Manoranjan's boots with both desperate hands. "NOBODY HERE IS A NAXALITE, SAHIB!"

Manoranjan's brain jams. How did she get here?! His eyes dart about the darkness beyond the periphery of the bonfire light. He squints into the foliage in the distance, wondering if someone out there got her here. But Hemla is unrelenting –

"SAHIB, SAHIB, YOU HAVE TO BELIEVE ME. THIS IS A BIG MISUNDERSTANDING. PLEASE!"

Sushil stands immobile near the burning haystack. This is not how this was supposed to play out. He knew it would all be wrong. But not this wrong. The fire leaps through the dry hay hungrily, zig-zagging this way and that, licking everything that comes in its way. Sushil's skin is turning red with the heat but he cannot register it. His mind is see-sawing wildly. Should he repeat Hemla's pleas into Manoranjan's ear? What if Manoranjan cannot hear her? What if she's speaking the truth? What if all this is a terrible terrible mistake?

Without warning, Hemla leaps up and tears towards the banyan. Pradip is so startled he fires! His bullet misses Hemla but gets Madvi! Oongamma screams, and drops down next to Madvi, a bloom of red spreading outward from his stomach.

 All the villagers huddle around him, their heads dropped, their hearts thudding.

Hemla rips the blackboard off the tree, rushes back and drops to her knees before Manoranjan with it. She points at it, her face streaked with desperate tears now, "LOOK, SAHIB, LOOK. I TEACH THEM HINDI."

The board still bears the last thing Hemla had written on it two days ago –

Ma se Maa.

Manoranjan is deaf to what Hemla says. His mind is a storm. *Those who helped her get here must be around us now. This smells like a trap.* He curses himself for not being able to pre-empt this. So cocksure he was of having locked this woman up in the camp. But he left only five jawaans behind. Five jawaans are no match for a naxalite attack. But what else could he do? The State hardly cared if they had enough recruits, or guns, or ammunition, or rations, or if their soldiers even got enough sleep at night. It didn't even train these fools well enough when it sent them here. *It doesn't give a little rat's fuck whether we live or die. We are simply a show of strength.* The State hopes that seeing these CRPF camps in these schools in their jungles will scare the naxalites into surrendering. But what if the naxalite doesn't get scared? What then? Who is guaranteeing the safe return of the CRPF jawaans back to the villages and little towns they come from? How is one solitary commander in this hellhole supposed to manage all this? WHAT ELSE COULD HE DO?!

Manoranjan is suddenly so furious he could burn this entire village down. And then shoot each and every one of his own jawaans dead as well.

But Hemla isn't done yet. As long as Manoranjan is being

 pummelled by Hemla's desperate entreaties, his forefinger is unable to pull the trigger, let alone point angry accusations at anyone.

"I TEACH THEM HINDI ONLY SO THEY CAN SPEAK WITH YOU, SAHIB. SO THAT THEY UNDERSTAND YOU. SO THAT WE UNDERSTAND EACH OTHER. WE NEED TO UNDERSTAND EACH OTHER. NO, SAHIB? OR WE WILL KEEP DOING THIS TO EACH OTHER, AND THIS FIGHTING WILL NEVER END," Hemla weeps now. "NO, SAHIB?

"REMEMBER THOSE BOOKS YOU FOUND ON ME? THEY WERE HINDI ALPHABET BOOKS. NO, SAHIB? YOU SAW THEM. YOU SAW THE SIGNBOARD ON THE TREE OUTSIDE. WE EVEN WRITE THE VILLAGE NAME 'POTTACHERU' IN HINDI, SAHIB. THAT'S THE ONLY THING I TEACH THEM," Hemla clasps her hands and drops down before Manoranjan again, hoping he will finally see what she has been trying to show him for two brutal days now. "WE DON'T DO ANY OTHER TRAINING HERE, SAHIB. YOU HAVE TO BELIEVE ME. YOU WON'T FIND ANYTHING IN THIS VILLAGE BUT CHALK AND THIS – THIS BLACKBOARD!"

Hemla sees Manoranjan's face still shuttered to her entreaties, his eyes still simmering with mistrust.

"THE NAXALITES TRIED AGAIN AND AGAIN TO MAKE US JOIN THEM, SAHIB. BUT WE HAVE ALWAYS REFUSED."

Manoranjan kicks Hemla in her chest. He's had enough of this. He hasn't been able to hear one word clearly. And her pathetic whimpering is starting to make him want to scream. All he needs to know is – "How the fuck did you get here?!"

He shoves the barrel of his gun into Hemla's mouth, and then pulls it out, to hear her answer. Another tooth tumbles out of Hemla's mouth, drawing out a small gush of blood. Hemla starts to finally grow dizzy. But no, she cannot stop trying. This man will have to understand her. What is the point of anything that came before, and anything that is to come, if he cannot understand the right thing to do? She struggles to her feet, swaying unsteadily now.

"We believe in the system, Sahib," she mumbles, unable to push the words out through all the blood in her mouth. "We do not want to –"

BANG!

A hole opens up in Hemla's chest.

She feels her faith – hot and burning – pour out of this hole and flood her skin.

All her hope starts to slowly drain out of her now.

She looks at the mouth of the rifle staring at her. Is that what she had been trying to talk to all this time?

Did she get it all wrong?

All sound, all possibility, all life drains out of Hemla then, and she sinks to her knees again, and crumples onto her face, right between Manoranjan's boots.

Manoranjan looks up, his face gnarled, his mouth about to explode in a barrage of orders, when his brain is brought to a hurtling stop. Falling, Hemla uneclipsed behind her… a small blue raging thing, furious little fires in his eyes. In his small trembling hands he holds a small bow – pulled taut – ready to let go a small arrow, aimed to make a hole in Manoranjan's chest.

Manoranjan's mouth hangs open, all orders forgotten. The other jawaans have gathered in a nervous cluster behind him by now, spooked by the way things are unfolding tonight.

Oonga is so angry that his eyes have blurred with tears. Through this blur Oonga sees not one, but ten Manoranjans

– his ten vicious heads clustered together – and ten spiteful guns pointed in Oonga's direction.

SPRONNGG!

Oonga lets his arrow fly. At the same split moment –

BANG!

A gunshot rings out from no one knows where.

Manoranjan watches bewildered as Oonga's little arrow bounces harmlessly off his chest. But as the arrow clatters to the ground a small pinprick of blood blooms like a red flower on his camouflage chest. Manoranjan recognises this flower. It's an exit wound. He feels the bullet burn his flesh in his back.

The jawaans scream and scatter. They are being fired upon from the trees behind. With no place to run for cover, they start to fire back blindly. But every bloom of gunfire from the trees is sharply aimed, and the jawaans start to drop one by one.

Manoranjan feels his knees buckle. His muscles start to spasm. His rifle drops from his hands. His brain starts to get obscured by dark clouds. Through the clouds he watches the small blue boy bring down his bow, tip his head back in triumph, and smile. He reminds Manoranjan of another little boy in another time in another jungle, who watched Manoranjan as he lay there, his eardrums bleeding. He was right all along. *Kids. Murderous fucking kids. They HAVE been training these kids to kill. I was right. I was fucking right. I knew it.*

Despite himself, Manoranjan almost grins in vindication, when –

BANG!

Another bullet stabs through his brain, and he drops, his face smashing into the ground like a rotten fruit.

The fire is swelling now, and slithering through the woodpiles, and climbing to the roof of the nearest hut.

Sushil stands beside it still, his rifle hanging limply from his hand. He doesn't know what he wants to do any more. He didn't want to be here. And now that he is here he doesn't want to run away. He has been staring at the blue boy, unsure if he is real or a vision. Unsure if the blue boy was a prophetic omen shown to him this afternoon. Unsure why he might have been picked by the universe to show an omen to. Unsure what to make of the omen if it is one at all. Unsure why he is thinking all these things. Sushil's brain finally starts to ache. And he's unsure if it is the fumes from this fire that's causing the ache, or the weight of all these painful thoughts piling high inside him like an unscalable mountain.

Pradip, firing blindly into the darkness, dodging gunfire, calls out, "Sushil!"

But Sushil cannot hear him. He just stands there – the last of the jawaans – watching the blue boy notice him, and start to scream and make for him.

Half the jawaans have fallen. Pradip needs to get the remaining ones out of here. He knows he's going to be made the 'in-charge' if some of them get back alive. This is what he's waited for all these years. And that teacher gifted him this on a platter tonight. He has to jolt Sushil into action or he'll get killed. So Pradip swings his rifle around and fires at the ground near Sushil's feet –

BANG!

This startles Sushil! Pradip screams, "SUSHIL! RUN!"

But what Pradip has done is shake Sushil back to coherence.

Sushil gapes as Oonga charges at him with a war cry, leaps onto his leg, scampers up his body to his shoulders, and starts pounding Sushil's face and chest with angry clenched fists. Sushil doesn't lift a finger. He just stands there, a fire raging around him, quietly taking the small blows raining down on him, until tears climb up his throat and into his eyes and explode from them. Blood springs from his mouth where Oonga has been pounding him with his furious little fists.

Sushil starts to sob, his shoulders shuddering. He wants to take this boy gently off his shoulders, plant him on the fuel tank of the bike, and take him away from here, wherever he asks to be taken to. He wants to sit in the shade of a tree and make pinwheels with him. And not stop until they've managed to make an entire forest of pinwheels. Sushil wants to tell the boy to hit him even harder now, when –

WHUMMP!

Oonga slides off Sushil's shoulder and crumples to the ground. Sushil turns, confused, when Pradip grabs his arm and starts pulling him away. Sushil cannot hear the things Pradip screams into his face. He turns to see the little blue boy's head start to bleed, where Pradip rammed it with his rifle butt.

Sushil finally snaps. He lifts his rifle, cocks it, and starts to fire! Blindly. Manically. Everywhere. All at once. Shocked, Pradip lets go of his arm. He screams into Sushil's ear. But. Sushil. Cannot. Hear. Him.

Sushil's rifle swings towards Pradip. Pradip ducks. The gunshot misses him by an inch! Pradip looks at Sushil in horror one last time before he turns and flees.

The gunfire from the trees blazes on either side of Sushil, the bullets whizzing past him. Sushil turns his hysterical rifle to the trees, and charges towards them, firing without aim or intent or anger. Just firing, hurtling into the flood of gunfire, hoping one of those bullets would be the one that would finally help him make sense of all this bloodshed.

Fallen on the ground, Oonga watches the soldiers run away. His head throbs like crazy and his vision starts to blur. He sees the last soldier fall near the trees. Oonga smiles to himself, mumbles, "Rama won!"

And then he blacks out.

TWENTY-EIGHT

The Dongria Kondhs believe that the earth knows things before they even happen. The jungle floor had trembled. It had spoken to the leaves through the hum in the roots of the trees. The hum had made the branches quiver. The quivering had made the leaves flap. The leaves had shivered as if caught in a restless breeze. But the air had been quiet. The air had gone still. The air had been trying to tell the villagers all that they needed to know. But the villagers' ears had been clogged with fear. A heart that carries dread cannot beat in time with the pulsing of the earth.

The first sound Oonga hears as he opens his aching eyes is the murmuring of a thousand distant leaves. He knows the leaves celebrate his victory. Rama's victory.

His eyes are blurry. He is on his back, looking up. He sees a dawn sky. And the insides of trees. And long trails of smoke rising up. And then he sees his Amma. She looks down at him from above, and smiles in relief. "Oonga," she whispers, and cradles his face in her bruised hands. In Oongamma's eyes is an abyss of sorrow. But Oonga cannot see it. His head has been bandaged with a torn piece of her saree.

"Amma?" Oonga grins. "Rama won."

Oongamma, unsure what she should say, nods, then pats his head, and pushes herself up from his side, tired of the tears that keep coming even though she's emptied her reservoir of pain many times over since last night. Her stomach is in terrific pain. For the first time ever the little one inside her kicks. Oongamma cannot tell if she kicks because she wants to be let out? Or because she's angry and wants no part of this world they are to bequeath her.

A wizened old hand appears on Oonga's shoulder. Oonga turns to see Kunja fix a bracelet on his little arm. Oonga's eyes sparkle! But he's suspicious, "You said I get this only when I become a man?"

Kunja nods, unable to say much else. Oonga beams as the bracelet sits tight on his faded blue arm.

Kunja stands up, steps aside, as two boys in green uniform appear and lift Oonga's makeshift stretcher off the ground. As Oonga floats away from Kunja, the bracelet gleams, sending a thrill rippling through Oonga's battered blue body.

He is a man. He is a king. He is a god. He is victorious. He avenged his Hemla didi. He saved his village. He killed Ravana. He is Rama. He is all the things no one else can ever be.

That glorious realisation is too much excitement for Oonga's tired little mind, and he passes out again, just as the boy carrying his stretcher trips on a small body in his path. He turns to go round the little corpse, not noticing the brown muddy swathes on either cheek of her slightly charred face.

Many makeshift stretchers leave one by one, carried by the dalam into the forest behind the village. Kunja has been tending to the wounded and the burnt with his ointments. *When they will all have left,* thinks Kunja, *I will still be here, and I will bury those who need not leave any more.*

It's what his kind has done for tens of centuries. The medicine man delivers the adivasi first into this world. And then into the next one.

But, thinks Kunja, *who delivers the medicine man?*

Kunja shakes off that thought and moves on to Timi, to tend to her burnt arm. She groans and mumbles about being allowed to die.

"You will die, Timi, don't worry, you will die. But only when the spirits allow it. I am here for you until then." And he calms her with his chanting.

Kunja's chanting murmurs through the burnt village… cooling all the ashes… clotting all the spilt blood… easing the gnarled souls out of their bodies… soothing down all the scared, anxious mumbling… making even Laxmi look away for a moment, afraid she might be seen shedding a tear for her loss.

She and Soni dig Hemla a quick grave below her classroom banyan.

The few unhurt villagers scrounge the huts for anything they can still use. The journey out of here maybe longer than it seems. And they must be prepared.

Linga is restless. He sniffs the air like a watchdog, certain that more trouble is on its way. "Hurry, hurry," he announces. "We need to get out of here soon. They'll be back with the sun. And they'll return in more numbers."

From beyond the dirt trail, and the forest, and the villagers' fields, down the slope, at the base of this hill, where the sun shines unobstructed on a vast stretch of open grassland, a two-legged metal signboard stands upright again, its large unblinking eye staring up the hill, as if preparing to climb it. Its sinister humming starts to grow louder, vibrating into the earth, through the rattling grains of its soil, up the recoiling roots of the trees, through the bark brittle with fright, to the nervously stuttering branches, from whose tips the coarse wind plucks it and scatters it through the mourning sky, through its pasts, its presents, and its inescapable futures, through green forest, yellow field, and blue river, over hill, and valley, and cliff, until it slithers through the shadows and tremors to a stop at the charred stump of the peepal tree. Where a crushed pinwheel lies charred.

The humming lingers here, swelling slowly into a metallic wail.

But no one leaving the village now can hear it.

AFTERWORD

There was a seventy-seven-year-old man in Kolkata who used to open his saree shop at the dot of 8:30 every morning. He would spend twelve hours at work. And then another six tending to his home, cooking his food, washing his clothes and dishes, thinking about his late wife and his children who now lived far away from him.

Some nights when he ran a fever, he was alone in the knowledge of it. And that filled him with such sympathy for himself that he was left with none to give the world the next morning when he opened the newspaper.

There was a thirteen-year-old adivasi tribal boy in Koraput jail. He was put there because his family refused to give up their ancestral land for a paltry sum to the 'Company' for bauxite mining. He was arrested for carrying a bow and arrow and sitting in the middle of the marketplace with his friends. He's confused because he's carried a bow and arrow ever since he was little. But now his warrant states his crime as 'armed unlawful assembly'.

There's no one to put the pieces together for him in this large puzzle. Worse, he's lodged in a jail for adults when he's quite obviously a minor. But, says the court, there's nothing to prove him otherwise.

There's nothing to prove his land belongs to him either, because he has no papers.

There's nothing to prove he is Indian because he has no ID card.

There's nothing to prove he deserves every bit of 'development' that the rest of us in cities are so used to because he doesn't live in one.

There's nothing to prove he is not a rebel naxalite because if he's angry about his land being taken away he must be a rebel, if not a naxalite sympathiser.

There's nothing to prove he even exists because his story is yet untold.

Stories that go against 'national development' go unreported in our country. And even if they do get reported the rest of us are so busy fighting to survive our own daily hell that we read and we move on. Quickly. Like the seventy-seven-year-old man.

It's nobody's fault really.

But with *Oonga* I thought I might be able to change this a little bit. Just a little. Perhaps it would be enough. Perhaps it wouldn't. But then stories have a way of making us think about things that we otherwise wouldn't think about.

That seventy-seven-year-old man was my father Raghunath Makhija. To have got him to not only think about a young adivasi boy but to actively question what caused the boy's misery would have needed a special kind of story. One that would have made my simple, hardworking, preoccupied father forget about his own life for a while. Perhaps *Oonga* is that story. Perhaps it isn't. But I know I tried. And that's always a start, I think.

Although that adivasi boy is still in jail.

He turns eighteen next week.

~ Devashish Makhija, December 2020

THANK YOU

Faiza Ahmed Khan, for taking me on that journey into the world of the adivasis, a journey I never returned from.

Sharanya Nayak, for all the selfless courage you show daily in your fight for justice for the adivasis, courage I borrowed for Hemla.

Amaresh Satapathy, for showing me the beauty and wonder that is the adivasi way of life, all the things that make little Oonga what he is.

Javed Iqbal, for the relentless questions you ask of the system through your images and words, questions that have found their way into this story.

Sarat Talluri Rao, for helping me find the seed of this story, and the soil in which to plant that seed.

Raju Singh, for being Oonga in a film that can never surpass your brilliance.

The Dongria Kondhs, and all the other tribes, for your grace, your courage, your patience, your love for nature, your reverence of trees, rivers and mountains, your resilience in the face of this never-ending onslaught on your identity. I hope we can all learn to live like you, in harmony with the earth.

Soni Sori, for giving me Hemla – determined, loving, fearless, unrelenting, beautiful – just like you have always been.

Tulika, for being the only publishers in the field who listen to their heart, because of which now a whole generation can hopefully listen to Oonga's.

Dr Rraajnath Chakravartty, for keeping me alive so this story could be told.

Bharati Makhija, who wasn't born an adivasi, but I suspect had an adivasi soul, one she left entrusted with me, and is the one that wrote this story, through me.

Raghunath Makhija, who will never read this book though he is whom I wrote it for. The blood in his veins has now returned to the sea. And the earth in his bones has now returned to the ground.